THE HISTORY OF THE UNITED ARAB EMIRATES

THE HISTORY OF THE UNITED ARAB EMIRATES

John A. Shoup

The Greenwood Histories of the Modern Nations
Frank W. Thackeray and John E. Findling, Series Editors

An Imprint of ABC-CLIO, LLC
Santa Barbara, California • Denver, Colorado

Copyright © 2022 by ABC-CLIO, LLC

All rights reserved. No part of this publication may be reproduced, stored in a retrieval system, or transmitted, in any form or by any means, electronic, mechanical, photocopying, recording, or otherwise, except for the inclusion of brief quotations in a review, without prior permission in writing from the publisher.

Library of Congress Cataloging-in-Publication Data

Names: Shoup, John A., author.
Title: The history of the United Arab Emirates / John A. Shoup.
Description: Santa Barbara, California : Greenwood, An Imprint of
  ABC-CLIO, LLC [2022] | Series: The Greenwood histories of the modern
  nations | Includes bibliographical references and index.
Identifiers: LCCN 2020058577 (print) | LCCN 2020058578 (ebook) | ISBN
9781440870439 (hardcover) | ISBN 9781440870446 (ebook)
Subjects: LCSH: United Arab Emirates—History.
Classification: LCC DS247.T85 S56 2021 (print) | LCC DS247.T85 (ebook) |
  DDC 953.57—dc23
LC record available at https://lccn.loc.gov/2020058577
LC ebook record available at https://lccn.loc.gov/2020058578

ISBN: 978-1-4408-7043-9 (print)
      978-1-4408-7044-6 (ebook)

26 25 24 23 22   1 2 3 4 5

This book is also available as an eBook.

Greenwood
An Imprint of ABC-CLIO, LLC

ABC-CLIO, LLC
147 Castilian Drive
Santa Barbara, California 93117
www.abc-clio.com

This book is printed on acid-free paper ∞

Manufactured in the United States of America

Contents

Series Foreword		vii
Preface		xi
Abbreviations		xv
Timeline of Important Events		xvii
1	The United Arab Emirates: The Land and the People	1
2	A Land Called Magan: Early Antiquity (5000–300 BCE)	23
3	Arrival of the Arab Tribes and Persian Rule: Later Antiquity (300 BCE–620 CE)	31
4	Rise of Islam and Khawarij Oman (620–1600)	37
5	Islam and the International Rivalry of Portugal, Iran, Ottoman Turkey, and Oman (1600–1700)	49
6	The Pirate Coast and the British Trade with India (1700–1820)	59

7	Trucial Oman and the Discovery of Oil (1820–1971)	73
8	Independence and the Birth of the United Arab Emirates to the Death of Shaykh Zayed (1971–2004)	103
9	The United Arab Emirates in the Modern International Arena (2004–2020)	123

Modern Shaykhs of the United Arab Emirates	143
Notable People in the History of the United Arab Emirates	147
Glossary	159
Bibliographic Essay	163
Index	171

Series Foreword

The Greenwood Histories of the Modern Nations series is intended to provide students and interested laypeople with up-to-date, concise, and analytical histories of many of the nations of the contemporary world. Not since the 1960s has there been a systematic attempt to publish a series of national histories, and, as series editors, we believe that this series will prove to be a valuable contribution to our understanding of other countries in our increasingly interdependent world.

At the end of the 1960s, the Cold War was an accepted reality of global politics. The process of decolonization was still in progress, the idea of a unified Europe with a single currency was unheard of, the United States was mired in a war in Vietnam, and the economic boom in Asia was still years in the future. Richard Nixon was president of the United States, Mao Tse-tung (not yet Mao Zedong) ruled China, Leonid Brezhnev guided the Soviet Union, and Harold Wilson was prime minister of the United Kingdom. Authoritarian dictators still controlled most of Latin America, the Middle East was reeling in the wake of the Six-Day War, and Shah Mohammad Reza Pahlavi was at the height of his power in Iran.

Since then, the Cold War has ended, the Soviet Union has vanished, leaving fifteen independent republics in its wake, the advent of the computer age has radically transformed global communications, the rising demand for oil makes the Middle East still a dangerous flashpoint, and the rise of new economic powers like the People's Republic of China and India threatens to bring about a new world order. All these developments have had a dramatic impact on the recent history of every nation of the world.

For this series, which was launched in 1998, we first selected nations whose political, economic, and sociocultural affairs marked them as among the most important of our time. For each nation, we found an author who was recognized as a specialist in the history of that nation. These authors worked cooperatively with us and with Greenwood Press to produce volumes that reflected current research on their nations and that are interesting and informative to their readers. In the first decade of the series, close to fifty volumes were published, and some have now moved into second editions.

The success of the series has encouraged us to broaden our scope to include additional nations, whose histories have had significant effects on their regions, if not on the entire world. In addition, geopolitical changes have elevated other nations into positions of greater importance in world affairs, and so, we have chosen to include them in this series as well. The importance of a series such as this cannot be underestimated. As a superpower whose influence is felt all over the world, the United States can claim a "special" relationship with almost every other nation. Yet many Americans know very little about the histories of nations with which the United States relates. How did they get to be the way they are? What kind of political systems evolved there? What kind of influence do they have on their own regions? What are the dominant political, religious, and cultural forces that move their leaders? These and many other questions are answered in the volumes of this series.

The authors who contribute to this series write comprehensive histories of their nations, dating back, in some instances, to prehistoric times. Each of them, however, has devoted a significant portion of their book to events of the past forty years because the modern era has contributed the most to contemporary issues that have an impact on U.S. policy. Authors make every effort to be as up-to-date as possible so that readers can benefit from discussion and analysis of recent events.

In addition to the historical narrative, each volume contains an introductory chapter giving an overview of that country's geography, political institutions, economic structure, and cultural attributes.

Series Foreword

This is meant to give readers a snapshot of the nation as it exists in the contemporary world. Each history also includes supplementary information following the narrative, which may include a timeline that represents a succinct chronology of the nation's historical evolution, biographical sketches of the nation's most important historical figures, and a glossary of important terms or concepts that are usually expressed in a foreign language. Finally, each author prepares a comprehensive bibliography for readers who wish to pursue the subject further.

Readers of these volumes will find them fascinating and well written. More importantly, they will come away with a better understanding of the contemporary world and the nations that comprise it. As series editors, we hope that this series will contribute to a heightened sense of global understanding as we move through the early years of the twenty-first century.

Frank W. Thackeray and John E. Findling
Indiana University Southeast

Preface

The United Arab Emirates (U.A.E.) emerged as an independent country on December 2, 1971, first as a union of six emirates, and then, on February 10, 1972, the union brought in the seventh emirate. Before that, two other gulf states were scheduled to join the union, but both opted out to form their own countries: Bahrain and Qatar. They became independent and recognized entities earlier in 1971.

The United Arab Emirates was formed from the sheikdoms that made up the very dry, infertile, underpopulated region of the Persian Gulf. Due to the lack of permanent water supply, before oil, the population was small and basically lived in huts made of palm wood and fronds called *barasti* or *'arish* in Arabic. The few permanent buildings were forts that also served as the homes of the ruling elite and mosques. When the United Arab Emirates began to export oil, things drastically changed, and a rush toward construction began. In 1971, there were few permanent buildings in most of the towns in the emirates, but in just ten years' time, these towns were transformed into important cities.

The United Arab Emirates grew in a region dominated by its more powerful neighbors, Iran and Oman. Both these countries played major roles in the development of the United Arab Emirates's history. As such, much of the past history reads like a history of Oman.

Iran occupied both Oman and the United Arab Emirates for long periods of history that was not broken until the Portuguese conquest of Oman and part of Iran in 1515. Subsequently, other gulf nations were drawn into the international conflict, as Bahrain was a vassal of the Iranian princedom of Hormuz. The Ottomans occupied the southern shore of the Arabian Peninsula to prevent the expansion of Iran into what is today Saudi Arabia. Saudi Arabia was declared as the name of the country in 1932, but the sultanate of the Najd (central Arabia) expanded its claims by conquest and by ideology before the establishment of the country. Thus, it is difficult to discuss the history of the United Arab Emirates without including discussions of events and places outside the area occupied by the modern country. Oman included the United Arab Emirates until the mid-twentieth century and, even officially on English-language maps, its older name was Trucial Oman.

Most people have no idea what happens in the United Arab Emirates, often seen as a super-rich oil power inhabited by rich Arabs who fund Islamic fundamentalists. Western ideas are born out of ignorance and the fact that it was established in December 1971, rather than on its long history. This is one of the ironies about the United Arab Emirates. It is located in the Arabian Peninsula, but its wealth was in pearls and dates until the 1930s, when Japan introduced cultured pearls as a substitute for natural pearls. The area of the lower gulf is an arid, parched desert with very little fresh water that acted as a natural barrier to human settlement. When Shaykh Shakhbut allowed drilling for oil after World War II, he made sure that foreign teams spent as much time exploring for water as they did for oil. Water was the main concern (not oil), and Abu Dhabi town had one well of brackish water to supply the town. Other settlements had similar concerns; even the oases that used an ancient Iranian system of irrigation called *aflaj* (in plural and *falaj* in singular). The oldest of these dates back to around 1000 BCE and the first Iranian occupation of Oman.

The United Arab Emirates was considered to be part of Oman and, as such, Oman played a major part in the history of the region. Oman still possesses the Musandam Peninsula and has several shared enclaves in the United Arab Emirates's Indian Ocean coast. The joint claim is with Sharjah and Fujairah, but Fujairah was recognized by Great Britain in 1952 as an independent emirate. Oman also still shares the oasis of al-Ain/Buraimi with the United Arab Emirates. Final control of the oasis was settled between Saudi Arabia and the United Arab Emirates in 1974, and Saudi forces evacuated from three villages claimed by

Preface

Oman. Separate recognition of the United Arab Emirates only came in 1971, as, before that, the country was called Trucial Oman.

Trucial Oman was the name of the small sheikdoms along the gulf coast in 1820, due to the British imposing a peace treaty between Great Britain and the numerous small states that also included Qatar and Bahrain. Before that time, these small states were under the Persians or the Portuguese, as both powers took control. The Iranian princedom of Hormuz (more properly *Hurumz*) emerged in the early thirteenth century under an Arab dynasty. The Prince of Hurmuz was a dependence of the Mongol Ilkhanids (1256–1353), Marco Polo visited Hormuz and, at that time, the southern shore of the gulf was also under their rule. The Portuguese conquered Hormuz in 1515 and occupied the town of Julfar, near the later town of Ras al-Khaimah, as well as other ports along the Omani Indian Ocean coast. Portugal remained for 150 years before being driven out by the Omanis.

Great Britain played an important role after helping the Iranian Safavid dynasty (1501–1702) push the Portuguese out of Hormuz in 1622. Iran's influence in the lower gulf and Oman was of long-term occupation. They were first able to take control of Oman during the Achaemenid period (550–330 BCE). They gained control over the region again in the Buyid (932–1062) and Seljuq (1040–1194) periods. Iran still exercises a good deal of power in the region, and the Gulf Cooperation Council was formed by the smaller Arab states, partially to counter the threat from Iran.

In the eighteenth century, Arab tribes moved into the region setting up the contemporary sheikdoms. The two most powerful of them were the Qawasim, who took the emirates of Ras al-Khaimah/Julfar and Sharjah, and the Bedouin Bani Yas that later established the ones around Abu Dhabi and Dubai. The United Arab Emirates actually began with their arrival and their conflicts with Omani and Saudi forces, but, more importantly, with the British East Indian Company. Conflict with the British grew in intensity in the nineteenth century, and as a result, the British called the region the "Pirate Coast."

The United Arab Emirates is a unique blend of traditional monarchy and republican government. Dubai has a reputation for being one of the most welcoming spots for foreign visitors, and today, it is the largest city in the lower gulf. People are a bit surprised to find that its laws are more conservative than their reputation. It is illegal for mixed couples on the beach to be seen embracing, and they have strict moral laws that are drawn from its strong Wahhabi (belonging to the Hanbali school of Islamic law) due to the influence from Saudi Arabia.

Nonetheless, the United Arab Emirates allows for recognized religions to build places of worship, and even Hindus are allowed their temples.

The United Arab Emirates remains one of the most interesting places, with an incredible mix of peoples and customs. It is a place with large shopping malls that even include an indoor ski resort. Its ruling elite have co-opted the people to believe in the state formed in the 1970s and is today only forty-nine years old. It includes the most-educated youth in the Arab world and an older generation that is mainly illiterate. It is a country where the "nationals" are a minority in their own country, and the majority are mainly Indian and Pakistani workers. This volume explores the history of the United Arab Emirates, as well as the history of the region before the country was officially formed.

Abbreviations

ARAMCO—The Arabian American Oil Company was founded in 1933, first as the California Arabian Standard Oil Company. It was later joined by Standard Oil Company of New Jersey (later Exxon) and Socony-Vacuum Oil Company (later Mobil) in the1940s. It was a major competitor for BP (British Petroleum) because of Harry St John Philby, who distrusted the British. In 1973, the company began turning over the administration to Saudis, and by 1980, it was fully Saudi.

BCCI—Bank of Credit and Commerce International was founded in 1972 by the Pakistani businessman Agha Hassan Abedi. It became the seventh-largest private bank in the world, with Abu Dhabi holding 77 percent of its shares. It became involved in a number of suspicious deals, such as laundering drug money; in 1991, the Bank of England forced it to close its doors, and BCCI was bankrupt. Abu Dhabi lost £2 billion, but Shaykh Zayed rescued the small holders and paid them £50 million to cover their lost accounts. Several bank officials were arrested, and in 1994, twelve were convicted of fraud and were imprisoned in the United Arab Emirates.

BP—British Petroleum was founded in 1909 to control the oil in Iran. Britain had begun to convert its navy from steam-powered ships to oil, and it was for Britain's continued naval superiority that the navy wanted easy supply of oil. Britain tried to make sure all of the gulf leaders signed treaties with a British company. Bahrain and Kuwait signed with British companies in the 1930s, but the Americans signed with Saudi Arabia and gave offers to the United Arab Emirates, then the Trucial Oman states. Eventually, Abu Dhabi signed with Britain, and all the other smaller British oil companies became part of BP.

The Company—This refers to the British East India Company, founded in 1600, with its charter granted by Queen Elizabeth I. It was to establish trade with India and compete with Portugal and Holland, also backed by their own state charters. It grew in power and wealth, and finally, the British crown took over its Indian properties in 1874 due to its overly corrupt practices that embroiled Britain in wars in China and India. As a result, the British monarch, Queen Victoria, was also made empress of India.

GCC—Gulf Cooperation Council, founded in 1981, for the Arab states in the gulf to serve as a security buffer and economic organization. The countries of Saudi Arabia, Kuwait, Bahrain, Qatar, the United Arab Emirates, and Oman met in Riyadh, Saudi Arabia, to agree on the purpose of the organization, which was set in another meeting that was also held in Riyadh. Many member countries were against the offer made by Saudi Arabia, the strongest member state. In 2011, two other moderate monarchies were invited to join, Jordan and Morocco. Yemen asked to join several times, but as of 2020, no decision has been made about these other three countries.

ISIS—Islamic State in Iraq and Sham (Syria) also called Da'ish in Arabic or al-Dawla al-Islamiyya fi al-'Iraq wa al-Sham or the Islamic State in Iraq and the Levant (ISIL). This fundamentalist Sunni organization was founded in 2004 in Iraq by Abu Musab al-Zarqawi as a branch of al-Qaida to fight U.S. troops occupying Iraq. It quickly took the back seat to the parent organization, but in 2014, Umar al-Baghdadi declared himself to be the modern caliph or the *Khilafat Rasul Allah* (Successor to the Prophet of God) in Mosul, Iraq. By 2014, the Syrian town al-Raqqah is declared the capital of the state. In 2016, ISIS began to lose territory to Iraq, Syrian, Kurdish, and American troops, and by 2018, the last battle was fought between U.S.-backed Kurdish troops and ISIS fighters. Many fighters were imprisoned, but events in the region, such as the COVID-19 pandemic, may cause them to be released to rise again.

Timeline of Important Events

PREHISTORY

125000 BCE   Earliest human occupation of the region.

75000 BCE   The Ice Age captures water on earth, and the Gulf Oasis period begins (the gulf is drained of much of its water, and an oasis is fed by the rivers Euphrates and Tigris).

8000 BCE   The Ice Age ends and releases the captured water. The gulf is flooded as the sea levels rise.

EARLY ANTIQUITY

5500 BCE–3200 BCE   Neolithic and early Bronze Age culture named for a place in Iraq, al-Ubaid, showing connections between the two. Perhaps early naval expeditions from Iraq made it to the area of the United Arab Emirates.

3200 BCE–2600 BCE	The Hafit or Jebel Hafit culture or early Bronze Age. Trade links with Sumerians in Mesopotamia have been confirmed by findings of Sumerian pottery in tombs.
2600 BCE–2000 BCE	The Umm al-Nar period begins. The region was known as Magan or Makan and is known from archeological discoveries in Mesopotamia. Magan serves as an important source of copper for the Mesopotamian peoples and shiploads of it are recorded not only in Mesopotamian cities but also on Dilmun (Bahrain). Hili Tomb Tower belongs to this period of history.
2000 BCE–1300 BCE	The Wadi Suq period. This was a development of the Umm al-Nar period, with the adjustment needed after the collapse of Indian, Mesopotamian, and Iranian cultures. Wadi Suq culture used a variety of other cultures for inspiration including Afghan and Central Asian. Swords made their first appearance, and tomb shapes changed to forms other than round.

MIDDLE ANTIQUITY

1300–300 BCE	Iron Age. Both the *aflaj* system of irrigation and the domestication of the camel change local life, allowing for greater use of the desert environment. The oldest of the *aflaj* was found in al-Ain and dates to 1000 BCE. Camels are domesticated around 1500 BCE, and they have a profound impact on the lifestyle in the Arabian Peninsula, giving life to the Bedouin people.

LATE ANTIQUITY

600 BCE–300 BCE	Persian kings conquer the region of the United Arab Emirates that was then part of Oman.
331 BCE	Alexander the Great defeats the Persian king Darius III (ruled 336–330 BCE), and the Persian Empire collapses, beginning the Hellenistic period in the Middle East. The region of the United Arab

Timeline of Important Events

	Emirates seems to have remained in the hands of local rulers who traded with Hellenistic cultures, such as Tylos (formerly called Dilmun in Bahrain), which lasted from 330 BCE to 622 CE.
140 BCE	The Parthian Empire is created out of the eastern provinces ruled by Alexander the Great's generals. They rule over both sides of the gulf, and Oman falls back under Persian control. The Parthians and the Romans fight over who controls eastern Syria and Anatolia.
200–300	Nestorian Christians begin missionary activities in the Arabian Gulf and establish monasteries from Bahrain to the United Arab Emirates.
224–651	The Sassanid period. The Sassanids fight a long war over control of the southern part of the Arabian Peninsula with the two Christian powers, Byzantium (or the Eastern Roman Empire) and Byzantium's ally, the kings of Ethiopia. The kings of Yemen become involved, supporting one side or the other.
226–640	The Arab Bani Azd tribe penetrates Oman from the northwest and begins the process of forcing the Sassanids out.
522	Ethiopia conquers Yemen.
531–578	The Sassanid shah Khosrow Anushirvan (ruled 531–578) withdraws from Oman except the city of Sohar, which remains under Persian control.
535	Ethiopia begins expansion into Central Arabia.
570	Battle of the Elephant, when the Ethiopian invasion of Makkah is repulsed by divine intervention (by birds that bombard the Ethiopians with stones—or a plague that broke out in the army), according to the Qur'an. The year is said to be the birth of the Prophet Muhammad.

EARLY ISLAMIC PERIOD

572	The Sassanids expel the Ethiopians from Yemen and briefly rule Oman and Yemen.

Timeline of Important Events

610	The first revelations occur to the Prophet Muhammad at al-Hirah Cave, outside of Makkah.
615	The Quraysh leaders of Makkah begin persecuting Muhammad's followers, and in a move to protect themselves, Muhammad sends a group of the most susceptible to persecution to the negus, or king of Ethiopia, for protection.
622	The Hijrah, or migration of Muhammad and his followers from Makkah to Yathrib, is now called al-Madinah al-Munawwarah or Madinah.
629	Al-Mundhir ibn Sawa al-Tamimi, leader of Bahrain, accepts Islam.
630	Muhammad takes the city of Makkah, and the Quraysh leadership submits to him. 'Amr ibn al-'As brings Islam to Oman.
632	Muhammad dies in Madinah, and the period called *Hurub al-Riddah*, or Wars of Apostasy begins. Muhammad's close friend Abu Bakr is voted in as the *khalifah*, or caliph, Muhammad's legal successor.
632–633	Victory of the Day of Dibba ends the Wars of Apostasy. The Muslim general Khalid ibn al-Walid fights the false prophet of the Azd tribe. Khalid and the two Julandah brothers and their followers remain loyal to Islam. At Dibba, Khalid and his allies are victorious. Oman and the region of the United Arab Emirates are solidly Muslim.
632–661	The rule of the *Khulafa' al-Rashidiyun*, or Rightly Guided Caliphs, Abu Bakr (632–634), Umar ibn al-Khattab (634–644), Uthman ibn Affan (644–656), and 'Ali ibn Abi Talib (656–661).
657	The Battle of Siffin between the forces of 'Ali ibn Abi Talib and Mu'awiyyah ibn Abi Sufiyan. The battle over who should have the right to rule as the caliph between the family of the prophet ('Ali) and the old ruling Quraysh of Makkah (Mu'awiyyah) causes a permanent spilt in the Muslim community between Shi'ite (partisans of 'Ali) and Sunni (followers of tradition) and the more radical Khawarij (followers of neither 'Ali or Mu'awiyyah).

Timeline of Important Events

UMMAYAD (661–750) AND ABBASID (750–1258) PERIODS

661	The Umayyads move the capital from Madinah to Damascus to be closer to their center of power in Syria.
684	Founding of the Ibadi Kharaji movement. Being similar to the Maliki Sunni legal school, the Ibadi are able to survive in Maliki communities.
750	The Abbasids take control of the Muslim world, moving the capital away from Syria and building a new capital near the old Persian/Sassanid capital in Iraq. Named at first Dar al-Salam, it nonetheless retained its Persian name Bagh-i Khoda, or Baghdad. Also, in the same year, the first of the Ibadi imams is elected, establishing a separate Islamic state. It lasted until 1435.
793	Nizwa's main mosque is used for the election of the Ibadi Imamate. Nizwa in Oman has been used ever since for the election of the imamate.
874	Rise of the Shi'ite Qaramitah movement.
886	The Qaramitah establish their own state in the region of Bahrain and the gulf coast.
892–902	Period of weakness of the Abbasids under Caliph al-Mu'atdid, who moved the capital to Samarra, up the river from Baghdad, due to problems between the local Arab residence and the Turkish palace troops. Distant provinces begin to break away from central control.
909–1171	The Shi'ite Fatimid dynasty established another caliphate, the Fatimid, spreading the 7er or Isma'ili form that soon becomes the dominant version of Islam. In 969, they take Egypt and finish building their new capital near in al-Fustat in 973 called al-Qahirah, or Cairo.
930	The Qaramitah attack Makkah and carry away the Black Stone from the Ka'abah.
932–1062	The Buyids or Buwahids, a Persian and 12er Shi'ite dynasty, take Baghdad, and the caliph gives their

	leader the title of sultan, or the "person with political authority." They control most of Iran and the gulf coast on both shores.
988	Most of the Qaramitah communities are absorbed into the Fatimid state as it expands out of Egypt, into Syria and the peninsula.
1055	The Sunni Seljuq Turks defeat the Buyids and conquer Baghdad. Buyid power declines, but in central Iran, they hold out until their final defeat by the Seljuqs in 1062. The Seljuqs take control of the gulf—both the northern and southern shores. In 1041, they establish the Great Seljuq State. with its capital in Isfahan, and the state lasts until 1194, when smaller states are founded by various princes and their atabegs.
1077	Sunni Seljuqs defeat the last of the Qaramitah in Bahrain, ending the 7er Shi'ite state. All of the gulf is once again ruled from Baghdad.
1081–1307	The Seljuqs of Rum (Anatolia), with their capital at Konya in central Anatolia, rule much of the eastern Arab lands.
1169–1260	The Ayyubid dynasty rules Egypt, Hijaz, Yemen, and Syria.

ILKHANID PERIOD 1256–1353

1256	The Mongol leader Hülegü establishes his own kingdom, based in Iran. Defeated by the mamluks of Egypt, the Mongols are unable to include Syria in their kingdom, but much of the Arabian Gulf is brought under Persian/Mongol control.
1258	The Mongol ruler Hülegü defeats and kills the Abbasid caliph, but a distant cousin seeks protection of the Mamluk rulers of Egypt who set him up as the new Caliph in Cairo.
1260	The Mamluks of Egypt defeat the Mongols at Ain Jalut in Palestine and continue to prevent Mongol rule west of Iran.
1260–1517	Mamluks rule Egypt, Hejaz, and Syria until the Ottoman conquest.

Timeline of Important Events

1262	The Arab kingdom of Hurmuz is founded, which rules both sides of the Straits of Hormuz. Unable or unwilling to exercise total independence, it remains under Persian/Mongol control.
1435	The Julandah family rules Oman as the imams of Nizwa, until they are challenged by other families.
1435–1624	The Imamate of Nizwa opens to election from different families.

PORTUGUESE PERIOD 1507–1654

1507	The city of Hormuz is captured by the Portuguese. The king is forced to pay tribute to the Portuguese based in India.
1515	Portuguese occupy Julfar (Ras al-Khaimah) on the Arabian side of the straits.
1515–1620	Portuguese return to occupy Hormuz.
1521	The Portuguese occupy Bahrain in the confused politics of the time, as allies of the king of Hormuz. Hormuz is a vassal state of the Portuguese in India.
1530	The Ottoman Turks occupy the oasis of al-Ahsa on the Saudi Arabian eastern coast of the gulf.
1550	The Ottoman fleet takes the Portuguese forts in Oman but does not occupy them.
1581	An Ottoman fleet returns and retakes the Portuguese forts in Oman.
1591	The Ottomans annex Bahrain to al-Ahsa.
1602	Bahrain comes under the shah of Iran. Portuguese economic power begins to be challenged by both Protestant Holland and England.
1621–1622	The Portuguese lose control of Hormuz to the Persian shah of Iran Abbas I (ruled 1587–1629), with the assistance of the English.
1624	The Ya'rubah dynasty is established in Oman and begins warfare against the Portuguese forts in Oman.
1633	The Portuguese loses control of Julfar and are forced to abandon the city to the local Arabs.

1650	The Omani sultan bin Saif al-Ya'rubi takes forts in Muscat from the Portuguese.
1654	In pursuit of the Portuguese, the Omani fleet forces them out of the Swahili cities along the East African coast and establish the Omani Empire.

OMANI, SAUDI, AND BRITISH POWER IN THE GULF 1700–1914

1700–1800	Arrival of the Qawasim in Ras al-Khaimah and Sharjah. Arrival of the Bani Yas in Abu Dhabi. The Qawasim begin attacking British shipping in the gulf as protection from outside interference with Arab trade. The region of the lower gulf is called the "Pirate Coast" by the British as a result.
1744	Muhammad ibn 'Abd al-Wahhab established in Najd, or Central Arabia, in the oasis Dar'iyah and allies with the al-Saud, who founded the first Saudi State.
1749	Al Bu Sa'idi dynasty is established in Oman as both the imam and the sultan.
1797–1802	Expansion of Saudi authority in Qatar, Bahrain, and the lower gulf, but it comes into conflict with Oman; in the Hejaz and Iraq, with the Ottoman authorities.
1802	Saudi/Wahhabi expansion into the Hejaz attacks the authority of the Ottoman sultan, and plans are made with Muhammad 'Ali, governor of Egypt, to deal with the threat.
1803	Saudi expansion includes the entire Arabian Gulf coast and tries to force the Omanis to pay tribute. The Qawasim, as the main local rivals of the Omani sultans, ally themselves closely with the al-Sa'ud family and begin the Buraimi dispute that lasts into the twentieth century.
1811–1818	Egyptian-Turkish troops invade the Hejaz, and then the Najd, and take the Saudi capital of Dar'iyah and end the first Saudi state.
1812–1820	Conflict between the British based in India and the Qawasim leadership result in numerous clashes

Timeline of Important Events xxv

	between British and Arab fleets. The Qawasim are called pirates, and the lower gulf is deemed the "Pirate Coast" by the British. In 1820, an expedition is launched against Ras al-Khaimah that ends with a treaty signed by the local rulers of the seven sheikdoms of what eventually would be called the United Arab Emirates, as well as those of Qatar and Bahrain. The British change the designation of the region to the "Trucial Coast" or "Trucial Oman."
1824	Turki ibn 'Abdallah reestablish the second Saudi state, with the capital located in al-Riyadh.
1835	Britain requires that the gulf shaykhs sign agreements of peace between themselves to end local wars that disrupted trade and sea shipping.
1836	The al-Rashid of the Shammar tribe establish a pro-Ottoman force and anti-Saudi force in northern Arabia based in the oasis of Ha'il. They become the major threat to Saudi survival.
1867	Shaykh Mohammed al-Thani of Qatar signs a treaty with the British that recognizes Qatar's independence from Bahrain.
1871	The Ottomans assert authority over al-Ahsa and the 'Asir. This limits the power of the Saudi state.
1872	Shaykh Jassim bin Mohammed al-Thani signs a treaty with the Ottomans and begins a policy of playing the British off against the Ottomans.
1892	Britain signs a number of treaties with various gulf leaders accepting British protection against the Ottomans.
1893	The Rashid take al-Riyadh and force the al-Sa'ud family to seek protection with the shaykh of Kuwait, Mubarak al-Sabah.
1896	Mubarak al-Sabah assassinates his kinsman Mohammed and is quickly recognized by the British. Mohammed was pro-Turkish and pro-Rashid to the point that Mubarak decided to assassinate him and seek the protection of the British. Negotiations at that time decided that Kuwait was independent of Iraq and was left out of

an essential survey in 1913 of the Ottoman Province of Basrah. Kuwait's independence is not recognized by Iraq until the 1960s.

MODERN PERIOD (TWENTIETH AND TWENTY-FIRST CENTURIES)

1902	'Abd al-'Aziz ibn Sa'ud retakes al-Riyadh from the Shammar.
1903	'Abd al-'Aziz ibn Saud takes the title of sultan of Najd and begins the conquest of Saudi Arabia. The third Saudi state begins.
1914–1918	World War I. Britain and France fight the Ottoman Turks and the Germans in the Middle East.
1915	'Abdullah bin Jassim al-Thani oversees the withdrawal of Turkish forces from Qatar.
1916–1918	The Arab Revolt against the Ottoman Turks led by the sharif of Makkah, but many Arabs stay loyal to the Ottomans.
1922	Britain gets the Trucial shaykhs to sign an agreement that excludes other countries from oil concessions in the lower gulf.
1928	Shaykh Shakhbut ibn Sultan becomes the amir of Abu Dhabi after eliminating his uncle Saqr bin Zayed. This incident of bloodshed inside the family prompts their mother, *Shaykhah* Salamah bint Buti, to extract the promise that none of her sons would kill a brother for the leadership position.
1931	Oil is discovered in Bahrain.
1932	King 'Abd al'Aziz names his country the Kingdom of Saudi Arabia.
1933	First oil concessions in Saudi Arabia.
1939	Shaykh Shakhbut of Abu Dhabi signs a seventy-five-year agreement with Britain excluding all other countries from oil exploration in his sheikdom. This was to stop American interest from gaining favor with the Abu Dhabi after they began exploring for oil in Saudi Arabia. First oil discoveries in Qatar,

	but they are not developed due to the outbreak of World War II. First oil concessions in Abu Dhabi, but the area is disputed by Saudi Arabia.
1939–1945	World War II. Oil production is stopped during the war years.
1946	Shaykh Zayed becomes governor of the Eastern Province of Abu Dhabi based in al-Ain.
1952	Fujairah is recognized as the seventh member of Trucial Oman. First meeting of the heads of the seven Trucial Oman states. Saudi Arabia occupies the village of Hamasah in the Buraimi Oasis.
1955	The Trucial Oman Scouts reoccupy Hamasah in Buraimi.
1958	Oil is discovered and developed in Abu Dhabi at Umm Shaif.
1962	Oil exports begin from Abu Dhabi.
1966	Shaykh Zayed ousts his brother Shaykh Shakhbut in a bloodless coup over setting a proper budget for Abu Dhabi. True to his promise to his mother, *Shaykhah* Salamah, no harm comes to Shakhbut, and he is allowed to return and live out his life in al-Ain.
1968	Great Britain realizes it cannot continue a military presence in the gulf and announces its withdrawal timetable. This comes as a shock to the Trucial Omani leaders.
1971	British troops begin withdrawal from the Trucial States, Oman, and Southern Yemen. Iran occupies the three islands, Abu Musa and Greater and Lesser Tunb. The United Arab Emirates are formed of six of the Trucial states. Qatar and Bahrain elect to stand apart as independent, as does Ras al-Khaimah. Abu Dhabi's oil wealth provides 80 percent of the new country's income.
1972	Soon after the formation of the United Arab Emirates (in December 1971), Ras al-Khaimah decides to join the union (in February 1972) for greater diplomatic pressure on Iran to give up the occupied islands in the gulf.

Timeline of Important Events

1974	King Faysal of Saudi Arabia and Shaykh Zayed of Abu Dhabi (and president of the United Arab Emirates) meet and sign the Treaty of Jiddah that ends the Buraimi dispute. Saudi Arabia withdraws from Buraimi/al-Ain but takes the oil field at Khor al Udaid. Shaykh Zayed is reported to have remarked that the bit of land was not worth going to war over, and the loss of one oil field would not hurt the United Arab Emirates. This means that Qatar only has a land border with Saudi Arabia.
1980–1988	The Iran-Iraq War ends, with both sides returning to the prewar borders, but with massive loss of life on both sides. The United Arab Emirates forgives huge financial debt owed by Iraq.
1981	The Gulf Cooperation Council (GCC) is formed by Saudi Arabia, Kuwait, Bahrain, Qatar, the United Arab Emirates, and Oman.
1985	Emirates Airline (Dubai) is founded, the first airline of the United Arab Emirates.
1990	Iraq invades Kuwait and sets off a series of changes in the Middle East. The United Arab Emirates stands with the other GCC members against Iraq, and though military recruitment was brisk, some people in the United Arab Emirates remain pro-Saddam Hussein.
1991	The U.A.E. military is stationed with other Arab troops (from Syria, Egypt, and Saudi Arabia) in the front against Iraq. The private bank, Bank of Credit and Commerce International, fails due to financial mismanagement, and Shaykh Zayed comes to the rescue, issuing a fifty-million British pound payout.
1996	The United Arab Emirates establishes a permanent constitution for the country, and Abu Dhabi becomes the official capital. The United Arab Emirates recognizes the Taliban government of Afghanistan and is one of three states that does, Saudi Arabia and Pakistan being the other two.
1999	Luxury class hotel Burj al-Arab opens for business in Dubai.
2003	Etihad Airways (Abu Dhabi) is founded.

Timeline of Important Events

2004	Shaykh Zayed passes away, and his son Khalifa becomes the next president of the union, as well as leader of Abu Dhabi.
2006	First elections are held for the Federal National Council. Women are allowed to run for, and are elected to, office.
2011	The Arab Spring comes to the gulf, with Saudi and Emirati police sent to help subdue the protests in Bahrain.
2015	The tallest building in the world, Burj Khalifa, is finished in Dubai. Costing 1.5 billion USD to build, it stands 828 meters (2,717 feet) tall and contains a hotel, restaurants, offices, and private apartments. Dubai becomes the single largest postmodern city in the world. Saudi Arabia and the United Arab Emirates join the war in Yemen sparked by the Arab Spring for the forced withdrawal of Ali Abdallah Salih as president and the refusal of many in Yemen to accept the leadership of Abd al-Rabbuh Mansur Hadi.
2017	The United Arab Emirates joins with Saudi Arabia and Bahrain in the boycott of Qatar. Saudi Arabia demands that the government of Qatar restrict the news coverage of the Arab world's single most influential news station, al-Jazeera because its coverage of the Saudi Crown prince has been too detailed for comfort. In addition, Qatar supports different Islamist groups in Syria.
2018	The United Arab Emirates begins a withdrawal from the Yemen conflict and trains local Yemeni troops to stand in for U.A.E. troops. The United Arab Emirates declares its support for the war and Crown Prince Mohammed bin Salman but decides to withdraw some of its troops. South Yemen (Aden and the Hadhramaut) declares its independence from unified Yemen and thanks the United Arab Emirates for its support.
2020	Although the United Arab Emirates' health service is one of the best worldwide, COVID-19 strikes the gulf. As of June 2020, the number of people with the virus is 36,559, with 19,153 recovered cases. The

number of deaths is only 270. The United Arab Emirates has the most extensive testing rate per capita in the world and it, along with its excellent level of health care and extreme care of closing its borders, meant the virus is contained. The United Arab Emirates closed its borders on March 19 and were closed except for nine destinations in Australia, the United States, and Europe with stringent check-in rules.

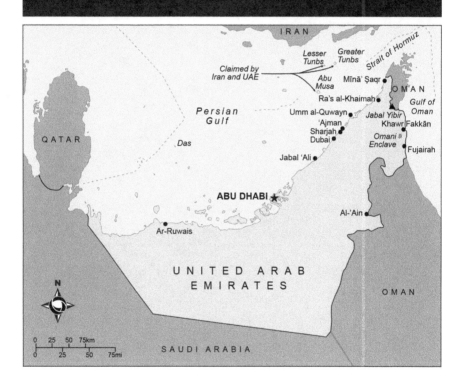

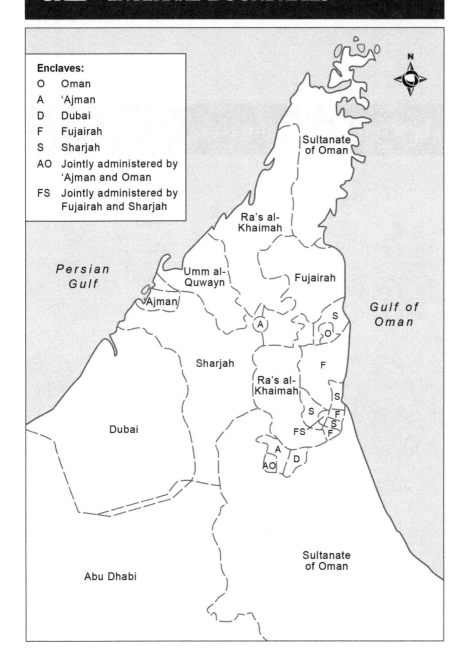

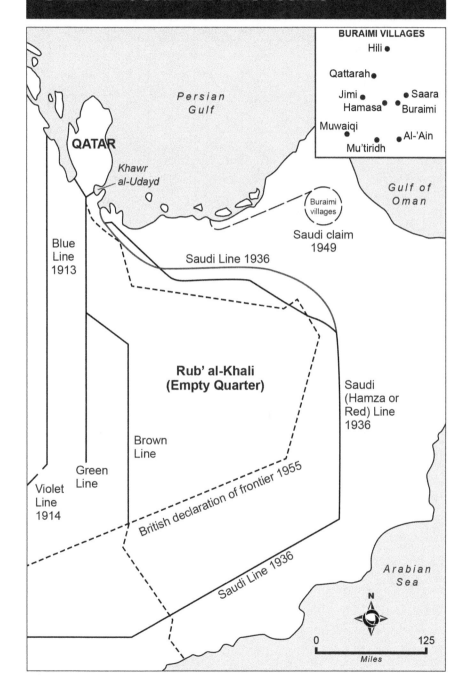

1

The United Arab Emirates: The Land and the People

The United Arab Emirates (U.A.E.) is both an old and new country. Today, the U.A.E. borders Oman and Saudi Arabia, and a bit of Saudi territory separates it from Qatar. While the exact country did not exist before independence from Great Britain as a protectorate, it has a long history that stretches back to the third millennium BCE. Emirate means "princedom" in Arabic, *imarah* in singular form and *imarat* in plural form. The dry, desert conditions of today did not exist in the ancient past, and the entire peninsula was covered in lush greenery, with rivers flowing into the sea. The desert began to grow one hundred thousand years ago during a wet phase of the planet Earth. This wet phase in the Arabian Peninsula was caused by an intensification of the monsoons in the Indian Ocean that pushed deep into the peninsula, but this came to an end during the Neolithic period (which lasted from around 10,200 BCE to 2000 BCE), when the climate shifted, and the deserts began to grow. The rivers of the peninsula became seasonal dry beds, called wadis in Arabic, many of which no longer run water today. The lush vegetation died out, leaving only tough, drought- and salt-resistant varieties, and the wildlife died as well, though Arabia was home to several species of African savannah animals that lasted until they were hunted to extinction when rifles replaced lances and bows. These included the ostrich, leopard, and cheetah, which were killed off just after World War I.

When the United Arab Emirates became independent in 1971, Qatar had already decided not to be part of the union and became independent on its own in 1970. The other emirates, a total of six, formed a union with Abu Dhabi, the richest and largest in area of them, as the leader. The seven emirates that form the United Arab Emirates include Abu Dhabi (the largest in the area), Dubai, Sharjah (spelled *al-Shariqah* but pronounced al-Sharjah), Ajman, Umm al-Quwain, Ras al-Khaimah, and Fujairah. Abu Dhabi is the wealthiest, having the largest amount of oil and the most active oil wells, with Dubai and Sharjah next in wealth. The two poorest of the emirates and dependent on money grants from Abu Dhabi are Ras al-Khaimah and Fujairah. Fujairah is the poorest of the modern emirates, with a mainly Bedouin population that was only recently able to claim independence from Sharjah. Ras al-Khaimah was the last of the seven emirates to join the United Arab Emirates in 1972, one year after the others joined the union.

THE SEVEN EMIRATES

Abu Dhabi

Abu Dhabi is the largest of the emirates, consisting of 87 percent of the total area of the United Arab Emirates, or 26,000 square miles (67,340 square kilometers), and it is the richest of the emirates, having most of the oil wealth. Its population is 3.2 million or 34.7 percent of the total population (9.5 million in 2018 according to Infographics[1]), making it the second-largest emirate in population. The territory is mostly desert and/or salt flats called *sabkha* in Arabic that separates Abu Dhabi from Saudi Arabia and Qatar. In the desert are two large oases, Liwa and Buraimi, which attracted settlers and produced one of the major exports before oil: dates. Buraimi lies at the foot of an outlying spur of the al-Hajar Mountains called Jabal Hafit, which serves as a water source for extensive date groves. The great amount of water was noted in 1840 during a visit by the British officer, Captain Atkins Hamerton, who also described the use of *aflaj* (underground channels) that brought the water some fourteen hours to the date groves.[2] Of the some six hundred varieties of dates know in the Arab world, Abu Dhabi's oases produce two to three hundred varieties of different

The United Arab Emirates: The Land and the People

The al-Hajar Mountains, in the region that is jointly administered by Sharjah and Fujairah. (Courtesy of John A. Shoup)

types of sugar content. Dates and pearl diving were the main economic activities in Abu Dhabi until in the 1930s, when cultured pearls were introduced to the world market by Japan. Cultured pearls took over the market, but this was soon replaced by oil. In the 1930s, foreign companies began to explore for oil, but commercial production was suspended until after World War II. In 1958, oil fields were discovered, first off the island of Umm Shaif and, in 1963, on Zakum Island. In the 1960s, five oil fields had been discovered, and Abu Dhabi became an oil-exporting country.[3] Today, Abu Dhabi has some one thousand producing wells, which provide for much of the infrastructure and development projects not only for Abu Dhabi but for all seven emirates.

In 1971, the British withdrew from the gulf, and the United Arab Emirates became independent. The leader of Abu Dhabi, Shaykh Zayed became the president of the association, and Abu Dhabi (the town) became the provisional capital. In 1996, it became the permanent capital due to the efforts of Shaykh Zayed in creating the country. Abu Dhabi spends it great wealth on projects in the country and, through the Abu Dhabi Fund for Development, provides funds for development programs throughout the Arab and Muslim world. The Abu Dhabi National Oil Company plays a major role in providing jobs for Emiratis, as does the Abu Dhabi Investment Authority, which invests oil monies in projects that will last once oil is no longer a source of wealth. Although Abu Dhabi offers Emirati nationals free housing, education, and medical treatment, its record for nonnationals, in particular Indian, Pakistani, and Filipino wage earners, is dismal. In 2019, Abu Dhabi declared the month of February the Month of Tolerance to celebrate the pope's visit to the Arabian Peninsula. The crown prince of Abu Dhabi, Mohammed bin Zayed, also invited Dr. Ahmad al-Tayeb, the shaykh al-Islam from al-Azhar University in Cairo, the main university of Sunni Islam, to the same events. The Emirates, as a whole, wants to become a beacon for religious tolerance in the Arab and Muslim world, challenging Saudi Arabia, Qatar, and Iran.

Dubai

Dubai has the largest population of any of the seven emirates but is the second largest in area, consisting of 1,505 square miles (3,900 square kilometers) that covers the coastal area, some of the inland desert, and the oasis of Hatta as an enclave on the border with Oman. Its population is estimated to be 3.32 million or 37.5 percent of the total for the country. Much of its population is composed of nonnationals, and again, Indians and Pakistanis form the greatest share of the people living in both the city of Dubai and the emirate. Dubai was founded in 1833 by the Al Bu Falasah subsection of the Bani Yas tribe that left Abu Dhabi. From fairly early times, Dubai had a multinational population of Arabs, Persians, and Baluchis and was more strongly attached to the pearl trade than was Abu Dhabi. The entrepreneurial spirit of Dubai began early, and it has the largest suq or traditional market in the United Arab Emirates, located in Deira, the heart of old Dubai. It has a large gold market, as well as a pearl market, a remnant of the older trade in pearls.[4] A natural creek or inlet from the gulf served as a harbor and split the city of Dubai, with half in Deira, and the other across the creek in Bur Dubai. Bur Dubai served as the main port in the past and Fahidi fort, the headquarters of the Al Bu Falasah of the Bani Yas, and home to the Maktoum family that produced the family of shaykhs.

In 1938, the ruler of Dubai had to allow the private sector to take over social services for the emirate due to the world depression and the loss of revenue caused by cultured pearls. This caused a rift in the ruling council, which was made up of mostly Iranian merchants (mostly Hawali Sunni Arabs) and Bedouin tribesmen who were loyal to the ruling shaykh, Sa'id ibn Maktoum. Sa'id was seen by the British as a reformer, and they supported him for being a force for modernization. In 1958, he was succeeded by his son Rashid, and Dubai became the model for the quick modernization and development in the gulf. Improvements along the creek that gave the city its maritime nature gave birth to such improvements as a modern harbor, electricity, telephone, and an airstrip that became an international airport in the 1960s. Medical services and education were improved with the assistance of British technical staff that helped bring technical education to the gulf. Oil was discovered in 1966, and in 1969, the first oil was exported, giving added income to the strong maritime economy of the emirate. Today, oil finances the improvements and modernization drive of the shaykh. Dubai has the second-most proven oil reserves after Abu Dhabi. With its oil wealth, it has been able to afford its massive growth and, today, has the world's largest collection of postmodern architecture. It is also one of the few gulf states that has tried to preserve it pre-oil heritage. The wind-tower houses in al-Bastakiya (a mainly Persian area of Bur Dubai) were restored, and now the district is open to specialty shops, coffee shops, and restaurants. Although cultural heritage now plays a major role in Dubai, it pales in comparison to Sharjah's commitment to its cultural heritage.

Today, Dubai is a progressive state with liberal laws about foreign investment, and much of its population is made up of nonnationals. It hosts a number of educational and medical institutions with access to the most modern technology and with a large staff of British, American, Canadian, and Australians in addition to highly trained staff from India. Dubai allows them to build places of worship for Christians, Hindus, Buddhists, and Jews, so it sees itself as a leader in tolerance in the Arab and Muslim world. The shaykh of Dubai, Muhammad bin Rashid, as the vice president of the United Arab Emirates, helped host the Catholic pope Francis during his visit in February 2019. In addition, Dubai has focused on festivals, including the month-long shopping festival that brings in tourists from European countries, such as the newly wealthy Russians. In order to assist the new Russian tourists, the emirate produced signs in Russian script and provided Russian-speaking guides. It also hosts major film festivals, as well as the world's richest horse race and other sports events, including golf and tennis tournaments, that bring in top names and a large viewing crowd. The emirate provides hotel accommodations and is close enough to Sharjah that it can take the spillover tourists from Dubai.

Dubai is also home to a number of "cities" or centers concentrating on a particular profession, such as Dubai Media City. The Dubai Media

City is a 100 percent duty-free area where the company owners can be 100 percent foreign. It hosts a number of professional organizations, such as television stations, news media of various types, advertising agencies, and publishers. It is an expression of Dubai's commitment to a "knowledge-based" economy—and is seen as a gender-neutral zone where female Emiratis can obtain work after they finish their studies. Dubai's success has led to other emirates adopting a similar stance toward moving forward to the digital age.

Sharjah (al-Shariqah)

Al-Shariqah is pronounced *al-Sharjah* in the local dialect of Arabic, where the "qaf" is pronounced as a "jim." Sharjah lies at the old front line between the Bani Yas of Abu Dhabi and Dubai and the emirates controlled by their rivals, the Qawasim or Qasimi lineage (see chapter six). Sharjah is fairly large, 1,004 square miles (2,600 square kilometers) in size. It is similar to its neighbor Dubai, made up of coastal region of creeks with a desert inland, and isolated pockets on the Indian Ocean side separated by Omani and other Emirati territory in Khor Fakkan, Kalba, and Dibba. The shallow creeks or *khawr* in Arabic allowed the emirate to develop sea trade and protected it from attack by deep ocean vessels. Its population has long consisted of Arabs, Persians, and Hawali Arabs who lived on both shores of the gulf. It is nearly as multinational as Dubai but did not pursue quick modernization as Dubai did. Today, its population is 1.5 million, or 16.2 percent, of the total for the entire country, with most living in the capital city. The majority of the population is made up of nonnationals, with Persians being an important part of the community. Oil was discovered relatively late, in 1973, and production and export began in 1974 off the island of Abu Musa, shared with Iran. In 1984, Iran stopped the transfer of Sharjah's share of the oil produced due to the costs of the ongoing war with Iraq and the fact that Sharjah backed Iraq. Fifty percent of the oil belongs to Iran, while three other emirates share the oil—20 percent to Sharjah, 20 percent to Umm al-Quwain, and 10 percent to Ajman. Since the first discovery of oil in Sharjah, other fields have been found, even inside the capital city itself, but Sharjah's oil and gas reserves (discovered as late as 1992) are not as large as those of Abu Dhabi or Dubai.

Sharjah also went through a period of rapid development, and most of the old town, made of coral rock, was destroyed and replaced with modern buildings of cement and glass. However, starting in the 1990s,

Sharjah began a program to rebuild a number of its historic buildings. Using foundations and pictures, they have been successful in not only restoring but also rebuilding those using traditional methods. Suq al-Arsah, the oldest suq in the emirates, was rebuilt and reopened, including a number of shops selling traditional, handmade objects as well as both a coffee house and a restaurant of gulf foods. Suq al-Arsah has become one of the showcases of traditional *Khaliji* (meaning gulf) culture, and the government of the Sharjah uses it for several cultural events and banquets. In the 2000s, the project of rebuilding old Sharjah continued with other places, such as the Sharjah Art Foundation and the sites it supervises. Such places recall the blending of desert Bedouin culture with that of the seafaring shipping of Sharjah's past. Sharjah also boasts one of the most colorful markets, called the Blue Suq, from its use of mostly blue tile from Iran. Unlike the modern shopping malls of Dubai, the Blue Suq or, as it is officially called, the Central Market, uses the design of a more traditional market and has shops selling everything from cameras and computers to Persian rugs, antiques from Iran, India, and the gulf to traditional styles of clothes. For visitors to the emirates, the Blue Suq offers more than the modern shopping malls in Dubai and adds to the experience. It has been surpassed today by the rebuilt and renovated Suq al-Arsah with its shops of Persian carpets and antiques.

Unlike most of the rulers of the seven emirates, the shaykh of Sharjah, Dr. Sultan III bin Muhammad, is keenly aware of the importance of education. He holds a PhD (1983) from Exeter in the United Kingdom in history and another PhD (1999) from Durham University, also in the United Kingdom, in political geography of the gulf. He has authored several books on the history of the gulf region and is the president of a number of universities in Sharjah. He carries on the educational emphasis that started in 1953 by Shaykh Khalid when Sharjah founded the first school in the United Arab Emirates. He uses his doctorate as one of his titles along with those associated with being the ruler of the emirate. In addition, he has founded the Sharjah University City, where six universities and colleges are housed, along with many of their faculty. He distinguishes his emirate with fewer leisure activities than are allowed in neighboring Dubai. In fact, "frivolous" activities for youth that are allowed in Dubai, such as arcade games, are against the law in Sharjah because they divert attention from studies—part of Sharjah's decency laws, which are the strictest in the emirates. Nonetheless, Sharjah is a favored place for families to live, away from the lights and activities of Dubai. It is also cheaper to find living space in

Sharjah than in Dubai; thus, many who work in Dubai prefer to live in Sharjah and the other nearby emirates, such as Ajman.

Ajman and Umm al-Quwain

Ajman and Umm al-Quwain are the two smallest of the seven emirates, with Ajman being only 260 square kilometers (100 square miles) and Umm al-Quwain 750 square kilometers (289 square miles). Both have little to no oil wealth, and they depend on gifts of money from Abu Dhabi after the pearl trade ceased to be a major source of economy. Ajman has two places that are famous for agricultural production, Masfout and al-Manama, both inland enclaves. Both Ajman and Umm al-Quwain were recognized in 1820 by treaty with Great Britain, but there is little information on them before that time.

Ajman's ruling family is of the Nu'aym (the same as the Na'im tribe that was involved with the disputes in Buraimi and Hatta in the past, being strong supporters of the Wahhabis of Saudi Arabia). Population wise, both are tiny in comparison to the big three, Abu Dhabi, Dubai, and Sharjah; Ajman's population is 540,000, and the population of Umm al-Quwain, the smallest in population of the seven, is only 80,000. Ajman's population had a recent growth spurt due to its government's attempt to lure families away from Dubai by developing similar types of high-rise living spaces. This put a strain on the tiny emirate's natural resources, which includes one of the few remaining natural groves of mangrove trees used as wood for traditional ships, called dhows in English. As of 2021, the government has not curbed development, which continues to threaten the natural environment. It is hoped by some that Sharjah's experience in its loss and regaining of its heritage will influence Ajman.

Ras al-Khaimah

Ras al-Khaimah is one of the most ancient of the emirates and, along with Sharjah, is the home of the Qawasim or Qasimi lineage that ruled much of the area since the sixteenth century. It is the site of the lower gulf's major city of Julfar that was abandoned in the eighteenth century, and Ras al-Khaimah became an important place during the period of warfare with the British in the nineteenth century. Ras al-Khaimah became the main headquarters of the Qawasim leadership. Today, the emirate includes 656 square miles (1,699 square kilometers) and has a population of 390,000. Ras al-Khaimah has been under the control of Sharjah several times in its history, with the Qawasim leadership moving to Sharjah, such as between 1900 and 1921. Historically, Ras al-Khaimah was a much more important place than most of the rest of the United Arab Emirates, with a number of sites located in the northeast, including Julfar and Dibba, the site of a major battle in the early Islamic times. It was also invaded in the distant past by Iran and was a battlefield between Iran and Oman in the eighteenth century. In the nineteenth century, the Qawasim fleet operated out of Ras al-Khaimah and proved to be major foes for the British East India Company. A war erupted that lasted until the imposition of a peace treaty in 1820. For the first time, the numerous emirates along the lower fringe of the gulf were grouped together as Trucial Oman or the "Omani" emirates that agreed to peace with Great Britain.

Ras al-Khaimah lost its importance to Sharjah, as leadership of the Qasimi family moved to Sharjah and Ras al-Khaimah became a dependent of Sharjah. It regained its independence in 1869 but lost it again between 1900 and 1921. Like the other emirates, its economy was based on pearling, fishing, and agricultural production, but in the 1930s, the economy suffered from the loss of pearl sales due to cultured pearls dominating the market. In 1971, Ras al-Khaimah lost two islands in the Persian Gulf to Iran, the Lesser and Greater Tumb, and the dispute remains unsettled. In 1971, Ras al-Khaimah joined the United Arab Emirates because the country's leaders were committed to the return of the two islands, and this was reconfirmed in 1972. Control of the Tumb islands was among the reasons why the emirates supported Iraq in its war against Iran. Ras al-Khaimah has little oil but does have several oil- and gas-refining plants. It also hosts the largest cement factory and rock quarry in the emirates.

Ras al-Khaimah has one of the largest suqs in the country that offers traditional pottery, knives called khanjars, and traditional walking sticks/axes called *jirz* in Arabic that have been attested to an ancient history in Oman. Such items are sought after by the Shihuh who live in the nearby Musandam Peninsula of Oman. The *jirz* are also used by most people in the United Arab Emirates for traditional dances, but few use them daily. The Shihuh, though, use them as identity markers to differentiate them from other groups in the United Arab Emirates and Oman.[5] The Shihuh are south Arabians with an added mix of Baluchis from across the Straits of Hormuz (both Iran and Pakistan), and they speak a form of south Arabian that varies enough from the north Arabian language that the two languages are mutually unintelligible. The *jirz* is an ancient weapon with finds of ax heads that date back to

1800 BCE made of bronze, while today they are made from steel. They not only are used as Shihuh identity but also replace the khanjar (dagger) used by most men in the United Arab Emirates and Oman.

Fujairah

Fujairah was the last of the seven emirates to join the union and did not decide to join until 1972. Fujairah was controlled by Sharjah until 1879, when the leader of the Sharqiyin tribe of Bedouin, Hamad bin 'Abdullah, was recognized as an independent ruler by the British and the region free of control by the Qasimi ruler of Sharjah. In 1952, due to a dispute between Ras al-Khaimah and the British, Fujairah's shaykh could offer his lands for oil exploration and use as a refueling station for the Royal Air Force, giving Fujairah not only recognition but also actual independence from the Qawasim. Fujairah is 1,166 square kilometers (450 square miles), with a population of 250,000 people. Until the 1970s, the economy was based on pearling, agriculture, and pastoralism. The Sharqiyin tribe used to move between Oman and Sharjah

A house in Fujairah. Fujairah has more rain due to the monsoon weather patterns, and traditional houses need a steep A-frame. The sides are made of mud-covered stone. The base, which is exposed to rainwater, is made of a high layer of stone. (Courtesy of John A. Shoup)

and Fujairah but were based in Fujairah. The emirate has very little to no oil reserves and depends on Abu Dhabi and Dubai for wealth from oil sales. The Sharqiyin are among the largest of the Bedouin tribes in the United Arab Emirates, after the Bani Yas of Abu Dhabi and Dubai. Relations between the Sharqiyin and the Qawasim were frequently bad, with the Sharqiyin shaykhs determined to give the Qawasim leadership of both Ras al-Khaimah and Sharjah a difficult time, as noted by Heard-Bey.[6] Fujairah is the only one of the seven emirates that make up the United Arab Emirates that faces the Indian Ocean, and its lands form a barrier between the Musandam Peninsula and the rest of Oman. Its territory is also broken by oases that belong to Sharjah or Oman or are administered by both Fujairah and Sharjah.

GEOGRAPHICAL FEATURES OF THE U.A.E.

Today, there are three main features of the United Arab Emirates: the desert, the mountains, and the sea, both the Persian/Arabian Gulf and the Gulf of Oman (part of the Arabian Sea). The entire country consists of 83,600 square kilometers (32,278 square miles), about the size of the state of South Carolina. The three geographical features have significant influences on the way of life the people living in the United Arab Emirates.[7] The desert is a major part of the geography and influences the lives of the people of the region. A large part of the United Arab Emirates is desert and lies just to the northeast of the vast Empty Quarter or Rub' al-Khali in Arabic. The Rub' al-Khali has a hyperarid climate, with an average of only 36 millimeters (1.4 inches) of rainfall a year. Temperatures reach an average of 47°C (117°F), with summer temperatures reaching a maximum of 51°C (124°F) during the day. The desert is large; in fact, it is one of the largest sand deserts in the world at 1,000 kilometers (620 miles) long and 500 kilometers (310 miles) wide. It serves as a natural border between Saudi Arabia, Oman, and the United Arab Emirates, with only a few Bedouin tribes (the al-Murrah, Awamir, Rashid, and Manasir) crossing it for raids in the past, and no one living in it year-round. Beyond the stretches of the Rub' al-Khali, desert forms the vast majority of inland areas of the emirates, accounting for two-thirds of the territory of the seven states.[8] The desert has been the home of Bedouin tribes since pre-Islamic times. The great Rub' al-Khali was not crossed by Europeans until 1931, first by Bertram Thomas, who traveled with Bedouin companions from Salalah in Oman to Qatar. He was followed in 1932 by Harry (St John) Philby, who approached it from Riyadh in the north, and in 1946–1947 and in 1947–1948 by Wilfred Thesiger, also from Oman.[9] Thesiger's trips have become the stuff of legend, and his original 1960 publication *Arabian Sands* is a classic in his deep descriptions of the southern Arabian Bedouin. Bedouin preferred to cross between Oman and the emirates, where nature provided a wadi system that connected Oman via the towns of Nizwa, Bahla, and Ibri to Buraimi. Along the coast, travel was difficult, as the salt marshes of Sabkhat Matti formed a natural barrier that nearly ran from the Persian/Arabian Gulf coast to the Rub' al-Khali.[10] Even today, the borders with Oman and Saudi Arabia are fluid, since there are no regular patrols and, on occasion, foreign employees on camping trips in the United Arab Emirates are picked up by Saudi border patrols for "crossing illegally" into Saudi territory in the Liwa region. Bedouins have dominated the oases in the United Arab Emirates. The main oases are Liwa, al-Ain/Buraimi, Dhaid, and Hatta (actually located in the al-Hajar Mountains). They are fed by underground water and irrigated by *aflaj* (singular *falaj*), underground irrigation canals whose concept was brought to Oman by the Iranians in the pre-Islamic period. Al-Ain/Buraimi is the most productive of the oases and among the largest, with lush gardens of palm trees that provide important shade for other truck garden (ground) crops such as melons, cucumbers, and tomatoes, in addition to abundant date production. Further development is possible by using the available sources of groundwater that have been surveyed, and plans have been made to expand the amount of water available.[11]

The sea is the second important geographical feature of the United Arab Emirates. The coast is occasionally penetrated by creeks called *khawr* in Arabic, or narrow inlets of brackish sea water from the gulf that are not connected to dry stream beds. They allow shallow draft (traditional craft) access, and with offshore shoals, they gave protection from the larger crafts used by European navies. In the past, they were lined with mangrove forests that provided shipbuilding materials, as well as hiding for pirate activities. Seasonal pearl fishing was an important part of local income until the 1930s, when artificial pearl manufacturing killed the market in the gulf. The local pearl industry survives today, but synthetic pearls produced in places such as Japan make natural pearls less in demand. Local consumers of pearls still prefer natural pearls for jewelry. Pearling was done in the Arabian/Persian Gulf, and the Straits of Hormuz (also spelled *Hormuz*) connect the Arabian Gulf with the Gulf of Oman on the Omani side. The straits separate Oman (the Musandam Peninsula, which pushes north to create the narrow Straits of Hormuz, is ruled by Oman) from

Baluchistan, Iran, by a distance of 46 kilometers (28.5 miles). Due to the vast amount of oil shipped through the straits, it is one of the most important seaways of today. The straits are controlled by Iran but are shared with Oman and the United Arab Emirates. Fujairah, Sharjah, Ajman, and Oman administer the Gulf of Oman side of the emirates in a confused mix of contested lands. The tip of the Arabian Peninsula, the Musandam, is under Omani administration. While the Gulf of Oman shore is often rough, with steep mountains rising abruptly from the coast and penetrated by Scandinavian-like fjords, the Arabian Gulf side is gentle, with inlets called "creeks" (*khawr* in Arabic) that were frequently blocked by sandbars. The shallow nature of the creeks did not allow heavy, oceangoing vessels easy access and, thus, gave rise to the pirate activities the coastal settlements were known for until the early nineteenth century. Settlements began along the creeks that have become the major cities of today. Fishing and pearling were important to the economy of places such as Dubai, Sharjah, Ajman and Ras al-Khaimah but a bit less so for Abu Dhabi, which controlled large oases in the interior that exported dates.

The mountains form a single range rising from the Straits of Hormuz and running along the eastern side of the emirates into Oman, where it becomes Jebal Akhdar. In the emirates, the mountains are mainly called Jabal Hajar, and parts of them, such as the Ru'us al-Jibal (meaning mountain peaks) rise to over 2,000 meters (6,562 feet).[12] The highest peak in Jebal Akhdar reaches 3,000 meters (over 9,842 feet) in height but catches little rain. Rainfall averages 107 millimeters (just over 4 inches), making agriculture difficult. In addition, the mountains have little to no topsoil but consist of bare, exposed rock. Where erosion has caused deposits of soil along valley floors, agriculture is possible with irrigation. The mountains are cut by deep, dramatic valleys, which made travel difficult until the twentieth century introduced motorcars and paved roads. The region was among the least accessible to the outside and allowed the Ibadi Khawarij to exist from the early Islamic period. In addition to the main chain of mountains, there are outliers such as Jabal Hafit, which is 1,000 meters (3,280 feet) in height and a full 10 kilometers (just over 6 miles) in length.[13] The mountain is shared by the United Arab Emirates and Oman.

PEOPLE

The people of the United Arab Emirates are divided first into nationals and nonnationals, with nationals numbering some 1.4 million people out of a total of 9.5 million people for the country (according to 2018 estimates), or only around 11.48 percent. Those of Indian and Pakistani origin form the majority nonnationals (27.49 percent Indian and 12.69 percent Pakistanis). It is estimated that nationals form between 11 and 40 percent of the total population (depending upon which agency is collecting the data), with most nonnationals living in the three richest emirates, Abu Dhabi, Dubai, and Sharjah. Nonnationals are comprised of Europeans, Americans, and Australians, who are among the smallest in number but account for many in highly skilled professional positions. Indians, Pakistanis, Afghans, and Bangladeshis occupy many of the lower-level skilled positions and even some of the highly skilled professions, such as teachers, university professors, and doctors. Other East Asians provide much of the skilled labor for construction and domestic labor, while other Arabs occupy some of the other needed professional positions, such as teachers and university professors. Unlike Oman and Bahrain, there is no attempt to employ Emiratis in all positions, though businesses must have an Emirati as the head of the company. Employees come from the vast Asian labor pool as well as from the Arab world and Europe and North America. Nationals are encouraged by the government to find useful jobs in the economy, but many tend to prefer to work as the boss rather than as skilled labor. Therefore, among the comments made by visitors to the United Arab Emirates is that they do not meet Emiratis. Hotel desk clerks are Lebanese, Syrian, or Egyptian; taxi drivers are Indian, Pakistani, or Afghan; and checkout clerks in stores or restaurant waiters are Indian or Syrian.

Emiratis number between one and two million and are divided into two major groups, *hadr* or settled townspeople or villagers, and *badw* or Bedouin. This is the classic division of the Arab world and, unlike in Syria or even Saudi Arabia, the *badw* do not hold the socially superior position in the lower gulf, the *hadr* do.[14] In addition, all tribes are divided between Yamani (called Hinawi in Oman) and Nizari or Qaysi (called Ghafiri) in Oman.[15] Although the two have a long rivalry, in Oman, there is also cooperation between them, and the division is of less importance, with frequent alliances between tribes with different origins.

Each of the emirates is dominated by specific tribes linked to the ruler. In Abu Dhabi, the dominant group are called the Bani Yas. They arrived in the seventeenth century and quickly took over the region. The town of Abu Dhabi was founded in 1761 when a water source was located on the island, and by 1793, the settlement had become the seat of the Al Bu Falah leadership of the Bani Yas.[16] (The rulers of Abu Dhabi belong to the subtribe called the Al Bu Falah.) Dubai became independent in 1833 when the leadership of Al Bu Falasah exercised their authority with the assent of the Al Bu Falah shaykhs of Abu Dhabi. The close relationship between the al-Nahyan of the Al Bu Falah and the Maktoum of the Al Bu Falasah has been maintained throughout history with only brief interruptions. Other tribes in Abu Dhabi are the Manasir, the Dhawahir, the Manahil, the Rashid, and the Afar, which are all Omani groups. The Awamir and the al-Murrah are associated with Saudi Arabia today, but they have sections that used to spend part of the year with their camels near Liwa oasis. Some tribesmen of the Awamir and Manasir claim both Saudi and Emirati citizenship because they used to migrate between al-Ahsa oasis or Qatar and Liwa, owning date gardens in both places for generations.

The northeastern emirates are governed by the historic Qasimi (plural, Qawasim) tribe that formed a unified front in the eighteenth and nineteenth centuries. The Qawasim were of Huwali origin or of Sunni Arabic–speaking people who lived both in Iran and the Arabian Peninsula of the gulf. The Qasami *shuyukh* (plural of shaykh) dominated the north and used Bedouin tribes in the north against the expansion of the Bani Yas. Until the British forced an end to the piracy of the Qawasim, the shaykhs ruled from near where Ras al-Khaimah is located today, from the town of Julfar. At one time, they controlled the entire Musandam Peninsula, taking the region from the sultan of Oman, and also towns in southern Iran, Qeshm, and Lingah where they drew a great deal of wealth from trade. Fujairah had its own tribal leader of the Sharqiyin tribe, the second largest tribe in the United Arab Emirates after the Bani Yas. Sharqiyin control was recognized by the British in 1952 against Qasimi claims to the region.[17] The emirate was confused by the Sharqiyin *shuyukh* submitting the authority at different times to the Na'im of Buraimi, as well as by the Bani Yas of Abu Dhabi and tax collectors of the sultan of Oman, who were allowed uncontested access to villages in Fujairah. Other tribes in the northern part of the country adhere to the Al Ali, who make up nearly the entire emirate of Umm al-Quwain, the Za'ab, Tanaij, Naqbiyin, Ghafalah, and the Bani Qitab. A few other small tribal groups, such as the Al Bu Shamis and the Shihuh of the Musandam, played important parts in the disputes between emirates that lasted until the mid-twentieth century by providing armed men for one side or the other.

In addition to Arab peoples, Baluchis, who are from southern Iran/Pakistan and have lived in the United Arab Emirates and Oman for generations, comprise some 5 percent of the total population of the United Arab Emirates. The majority serve in the armed forces of the country, seen as an honorable profession that many nationals aspire to do. Most came originally from Makran, Pakistan, which was part of the overseas possessions of the sultan of Oman. Since Oman still owns places intermixed with villages that adhere to different emirates, some two hundred to four hundred and sixty thousand live in the United Arab Emirates. They are Sunni and have integrated into local society, speaking Arabic and adopting Arab national clothes. They are not distinguished from their Arab neighbors and intermarry with them but have their own family names to note that they are Baluchi. Hindu merchants settled in the commercial centers generations ago and are called *khojah* in the United Arab Emirates. They have not integrated into local society, travel back to their "homeland," and speak their Indian languages. They were granted protection by the British, which caused legal problems later for this small group of people in the United Arab Emirates.

The majority of Emiratis (nationals) are Arab and Sunni, but there are large minorities of Persian-speaking Shi'ites, where they make up between 5 and 8 percent of the population. In Sharjah, Persian speakers make up enough of the merchant class that it is possible to shop in the market using Persian only. Unlike Sunni mosques, Shi'ite mosques are often closed to outsiders, even to other (non-Shi'ite) Muslims. This is to prevent any problem between Sunni and Shi'ite communities, since Shi'ites differ in their prayer in small but important ways. They carry a small stone called a *khaki pak* or "holy rock" made of baked clay from the places of martyrdom in Iraq of Imam Hussein and Imam 'Ali, Karbala and Kufa, or the nearby cemetery of Najaf, Iraq, where 'Ali is buried.[18] During prayer, they place this piece of baked clay where they touch their foreheads to the ground rather than on a carpet or even on the earth as Sunnis do. As well, views on the Prophet's wives differ from Sunnis, who called A'ishah the mother of Muslims, while Shi'ites take 'Ali's side against her in a dispute between these two historic figures.

The population of the United Arab Emirates varies greatly between the various emirates, and each has a different profile of nonresidents. Dubai has one of the highest numbers of nonnationals, while smaller emirates such as Umm al-Quwain have among the highest percentage of nationals. Each emirate takes its own census and does not cooperate with the others to provide accurate numbers globally, which is why total numbers vary. For example, many of Dubai's nonnationals live in Sharjah because it is cheaper and housing is more available than in Dubai, but how are these people counted? While they are residents of Sharjah, they work in Dubai and can be counted in both censuses or ignored in both. Generally speaking, the United Arab Emirates has one of the largest numbers of nonnationals among the Gulf Cooperation Council member states; some 80 percent of residents are nonnationals. As noted above, the largest number of residents are from India and Pakistan, forming 50 percent of the country's inhabitants, and other Asian countries are heavily recruited for jobs Emiratis refuse to do because they are too "low," both socially and economically.[19] In essence, these are jobs held by slaves in the past and, in local culture, because people are paid to do these jobs, they are seen as not even being at the level of slaves. Former slaves have honor in that they are a reflection of their owner's honor, while foreign workers have no honor and because they are paid for the work they do, and so, they do not reflect their employer's honor. Today, former slave populations living in the United Arab Emirates work in the military or in other such jobs, maintaining their special connections with the families of the ruling class.

Almost all the emirates have their own universities, but the oldest is the University of the United Arab Emirates that opened in 1977 and is located in al-Ain in Abu Dhabi.[20] It promotes a highly technical course of study with an Arab and Islamic context. The Higher Colleges of Technology is a Canadian organization that has set up a number of campuses throughout the country. It opened the first four campuses in 1988 but subsequently established campuses in almost all seven emirates.

EDUCATION

Originally, the United Arab Emirates had only the *kuttab* or primary level of Islamic education. The children were taught to read and write using one book, the Qur'an, and if and when they memorized sections of it, they were rewarded with a special ceremony.[21] Modern education took hold in the country in the middle of the twentieth century, with Shaykh Zayed introducing modern schools in al-Ain first. He also pushed for girls to go to school, and this helped the United Arab Emirates have among the highest rates of female registrations in universities.[22]

The United Arab Emirates has had amazing growth in education; today 93.2 percent of the population is literate. This should be compared with the 1975 statistics, when the population was 53.5 percent literate.[23] Today's rate is one of the highest education figures in the world for both men and women over fifteen (adult literacy). The United Arab Emirates has placed educated women in what are seen as gender-neutral jobs, such as those that use a computer, but they also employ women in the police, border control, and in other services that need a woman to respond to particular needs. Most Emiratis attend college or universities, but it is nearly impossible for them to fail. Instead, institutions of higher learning find ingenious ways to not fail students but also not pass them on to higher levels. It is one of the failures of Shaykh Zayed's in not promoting internal competition in schools.

The University of the United Arab Emirates opened in 1977 with a registered enrollment of six hundred students.[24] Modern technology is studied with an Arab and Islamic context. Today, it has a large student body from throughout the United Arab Emirates, and around 50 percent of students are women.[25] Specialized universities opened in the 1980s with the Canadian consortium the Higher Technical Colleges. In 1988, they opened four campuses in various parts of the United Arab Emirates, and they have grown in number since. They offer what would be called an associate degree in the United States and Canada, and places are open for government employees, health workers, and businesspeople.[26] The Higher Technical Colleges now offers a four-year full degree, as well as a one- or two-year associate degree.

The emirate of Sharjah takes pride in its drive to be the "cultural capital" of the United Arab Emirates, with the shaykh president of the emirate's universities. His own PhD is from Exeter in Great Britain in history and politics, and he has published his dissertation as a refutation of the region's name of the Pirate Coast. He places a very high value on education, and the University of Sharjah opened in 1997. It was started with the assistance of the American University in Cairo and offers similar degrees. It is a private university, and it is located in the University City compound in the main city of Sharjah. At the same time, there is another university located in a different campus but in the same general neighborhood, the American University of Sharjah. Both are chaired by the ruler, Sultan bin Muhammad al-Qasimi.

GOVERNMENT AND HUMAN RIGHTS

The government of the United Arab Emirates is a confederation of independent hereditary monarchies brought into the union by a constitution. The country is a constitutional monarchy, but the monarchs are absolute rulers in their own territories. The constitution itself does not apply that much to the individual citizens, but there is free travel between the seven states. The government is under the shaykh of Abu Dhabi, being the richest and largest of the emirates, as the president of the country. The vice president and prime minister positions are held by the shaykh of Dubai. The council of ministers includes the other *shuyukh* and members of the royal families of the seven emirates. They hold power and are not elected. Elections are for the forty-seat National Council, but it is an advisory council only. Half its members are elected via an electoral college.[27] However, the supreme power is held by the Supreme Council, made up of absolute monarchs, which is set in the constitution of the state.[28] As such, the independence of each of the emirates is fully allowed, but aspects, such as a national defense force, foreign policy, national bank/printing of money, and national budgets, are left to the Federal Supreme Council. It is governed by the national constitution that was accepted in 1996 but was first proposed before independence in 1971. It remained provisional until a decision was made on the national capital; in 1996, Abu Dhabi was chosen, and a new city, to be called Karamah, was abandoned.[29] The vice president and office of prime minister is named as the ruler of Dubai. The other royal families have a share of the seats on the Federal Supreme Council but are also in the cabinet of ministers. The elected body of the National Council is selected from the names nominated by the electoral college, which is a select body of men and women from all seven emirates. The inclusion of women is due to the influence of the royal women, especially those of Abu Dhabi's ruling al-Nahyan family.[30] The National Council reviews the laws, and though it has no power to reject them, they can call them into question if it thinks they go against Islam.

The legal system in the emirates is based on Islamic law in all seven of the emirates, even though there is a bit of difference between interpretation. Extreme punishment or *al-Hudud* is given for crimes such as fornication, murder, theft, adultery, and even homosexuality, which is considered a crime.[31] The United Arab Emirates has a poor reputation in human rights, and according to the Human Rights Scorecard, it ranks toward the bottom in most of rights. It ranks 120 out of 179 on respect for civil liberties, it ranks 6 out of 7 on political right, and 115 out of 142 on discrimination and social abuse.[32] The United Arab Emirates does place fairly well in some of the aspects of the scorecard, such as freedom from arbitrary or unlawful depravation of life, freedom of religion, and freedom from corruption. Most family laws, such as marriage, divorce, alimony, and custody of children, are handled by Islamic courts. This has caused some friction that has come to light even within the glittering world of the royals, with a divorce case between the shaykh of Dubai and his Jordanian wife, Princess Haya.

To be a recognized citizen in the country, one must obtain a *khulasat al-qaid* or family book, which makes citizenship an exclusive right controlled by the ruling elite and to the tribes that inhabited the area before oil. This was to keep full citizenship limited to a small group when 84 percent of its population is nonnational.[33] It is possible for nonnationals to obtain a passport but not full citizenship.

The United Arab Emirates has a bad record when it comes to treatment of its "guest workers" from India, Pakistan, Afghanistan, and Southeast Asia. It has not signed any of the international conventions to protect the status of the workers and uses arbitrary punishments to keep them under control. This was made evident in the American film name *Syriana* (released in 2005) about a fictional Arab gulf state where the Pakistani workers had to get new jobs within a short time when the old ones were terminated. They had no rights and were subject to police abuse. Any criticism of the ruling families is against the constitution of the state, and there have been several trials of people because of this. One activist, Ahmed Mansoor, received ten years in prison for "defaming" the country.[34]

ECONOMY

The economy of the United Arab Emirates is based on oil production today, as it was on pearls and dates in the past. The economy suffers with the fall in oil prices, and Abu Dhabi agreed to pay 5 percent of all government employees' salaries. The other six emirates, in particular Dubai and Ras al-Khaimah, initially refused to pay their share. Dubai went through a near crash in 2009, but Abu Dhabi stepped in and saved the situation with its vast wealth. Dubai had to request a standstill (suspension) in debt repayment, as the national agency for investment, Dubai World, needed to suspend payments for six months. Abu Dhabi agreed to pay $10 billion to the Dubai government, to be paid out as Islamic bonds called *sukuk* to the creditors, for the Nakheel housing project built on a man-made island.[35] In thanks, Dubai changed the name of its world's tallest tower from Burj Dubai to Burj Khalifa. Dubai continued to emphasize the non-oil segment of its economy that is based on its promotion of enterprise. It is a good place for business start-ups, as it gives incentives for new enterprises.

There are specialized places called "cities" where everything from media to universities are able to have a place.

Abu Dhabi remains the richest of the emirates, but this capital city remains second in population. Dubai is the largest city with the largest international recognition. Abu Dhabi has date production along with vast oil fields. Dates remain an important crop but can in no way match oil for wealth. The people of Abu Dhabi also own herds of camels that are now used for racing. Individual camels can be worth $55,000 each, with stud camels worth as much as $5 to $30 million.[36] These fortunes are the draw for people to continue raising camels, and Abu Dhabi has a long tradition of raising livestock. There are local markets, but Emiratis face strong competition from Oman.

Other emirates produce vegetables and fruit in intensive farms in places such as Masfout and al-Manama in Ajman. They produce berries and fruits such as lemons, pineapples, and papayas. Both Masfout and al-Manama are called the breadbaskets of the United Arab Emirates, and they produce mostly for the local markets. Dates used to be among the major produce of the emirates, but as already noted, they have been replaced by oil. Other sources of income include a large cement factory located in Ras al-Khaimah.

NOTES

1. "United Arab Emirates Population Statistics," Global Media Insight. Accessed January 31, 2019. https://www.globalmediainsight.com/blog/uae-population-statistics/.

2. Hellyer, Peter and Buckton, Rosalind. *Al Ain: Oasis City*. Dubai: Motivate Publishing, 1998.

3. Higgins, Carla. "Abu Dhabi (Emirate)," in *Saudi Arabia and the Gulf Arab States Today: An Encyclopedia of Life in the Arab States*, edited by Sebastian Maisel and John A. Shoup. Westport, CT: Greenwood Press, 2009.

4. Higgins, Carla. "Dubai," in *Saudi Arabia and the Gulf Arab States Today*.

5. Richardson, Neil and Dorr, Marcia. *The Craft Heritage of Oman*, vol. 1. Dubai: Motivate Publishing, 2003, 78–81.

6. Heard-Bey, Frauke. *From Trucial States to United Arab Emirates*. Dubai: Motivate Publishing, 2004, 93.

7. Ibid., 6.

8. Ibid.

9. Thesiger, Wilfred. *Crossing the Sands*. Dubai: Motivate Publishing, 2006, end map.

10. Heard-Bey, 30.

11. Hellyer and Buckton, 17.

12. Heard-Bey, 8.

13. Hellyer and Buckton, 70.
14. Carter, J. R. L. *Tribes in Oman*. London: Peninsular Publishing, 1982, 12.
15. Ibid., 12.
16. Heard-Bey, 44.
17. Ibid., 71.
18. Glassé, Cyril. *The Concise Encyclopedia of Islam*. New York: HarperCollins, 1989, 365.
19. Mehler, Carl, et al. *National Geographic Atlas of the Middle East: The Most Concise and Current Source on the World's Most Complex Region*, 2nd edition. Washington, DC: National Geographic, 2008, 58.
20. Hellyer and Buckton, 50.
21. Sondheimer, Rachel. "Education," in *Saudi Arabia and the Gulf Arab States Today*, 140.
22. Ibid., 141.
23. "United Arab Emirates—Adult (15+) Literacy Rate," Knoema: World Data Atlas. Accessed June 24, 2020. https://knoema.com/atlas/United-Arab-Emirates/topics/Education/Literacy/Adult-literacy-rate.
24. Hellyer and Buckton, 50.
25. Ibid., 50.
26. Ibid., 51–52.
27. Morton, Michael Quentin. *Keepers of the Golden Shore: A History of the United Arab Emirates*. London: Reaktion Books, 2017, 214.
28. Ibid., 213.
29. "Constitution of the United Arab Emirates," World Intellectual Property Organization. Accessed June 24, 2020. https://www.wipo.int/edocs/lexdocs/laws/en/ae/ae030en.pdf.
30. Morton, 205.
31. Ibid., 215.
32. "United Arab Emirates—Human Rights Scorecard," CJPME Foundation: Human Rights Report Series. Accessed June 24, 2020. https://d3n8a8pro7vhmx.cloudfront.net/cjpmefoundation/pages/101/attachments/original/1471374145/UAE_Chart_2015-11-16-v2.pdf?1471374145.
33. Morton, 212.
34. "United Arab Emirates Jails Activist for 10 Years for 'Defaming Nation,'" BBC News Services, May 21, 2018. https://www.bbc.com/news/world-middle-east-44317613.
35. Morton, 208.
36. Kracha, Bassima. "Identity 2016: Camel Racing, a Market Worth Millions," BBC News Services, April 1, 2016. https://www.bbc.com/news/business-35935661.

2

A Land Called Magan: Early Antiquity (5000–300 BCE)

The history of the United Arab Emirates extends back to the Neolithic period, when the first traces of man's occupation have been found. The Arabian Peninsula had a green period when large rivers flowed into the surrounding seas and into lakes that have subsequently become sandy deserts. Due to the lowering of the sea levels during the last Ice Age, the Arabian/Persian Gulf became a large, green valley, with the Tigris and Euphrates Rivers flowing to the Arabian Sea at the Straits of Hormuz today.[1] Remains of early man in the peninsula date back to 127,000 years ago in places such as Jabal Faya, showing a close connection with early cultures in the Nile Valley. Flint tools are not only like those of the Nubian tradition, but they are also exactly the same technology. How people came from Africa to the peninsula is an unanswered question, but they most likely came across at the narrow Bab al-Mandab, only twelve miles (nineteen kilometers) wide. From Yemen, they would have had a fairly easy path across a verdant landscape filled with running streams, natural springs, and wildlife to hunt until they reached the equally narrow Straits of Hormuz, with only thirty-four miles (fifty-five kilometers) to cross into Asia. Initially, it was supposed that early humans followed the shoreline, but recent excavations prove that instead, they followed a more inland route because they did not need to rely on fish, and there was plenty of food and water inland that could be utilized.[2] Approximately seventy-five thousand years ago, due to the strength of the last Ice Age, so much water became locked up in ice that sea levels dropped, leaving a strip of green land along the combined Tigris and Euphrates River that flowed into the Arabian Ocean. Humans expanded beyond Arabia into Asia and perhaps as far as Australia before approximately ten thousand years ago, when the sea began to rise and reclaim the Arabian/Persian Gulf. This may have inspired the story of the great flood of the "Epic of Gilgamesh" that lives on today as the story of Noah.[3]

Recent archeology indicates that the early inhabitants of the region (United Arab Emirates) used seasonal settlements along the coast and further inland to exploit different environments. Because they had domestic animals, sheep and goats, they seemed to have arrived in the region of the United Arab Emirates from the north, perhaps from Syria or Iraq. The presence of sheep indicates a northern origin because sheep are not found among the wildlife in the peninsula, while there are numerous wild goats found in local fauna. A northern place of origin is also supported by the type of flint tools early inhabitants made, which are similar to those in Palestine and Syria. Archeological finds, such as pottery fragments, also link them to the Ubaid culture (65,000–38,000 BCE) of early Iraq.[4] The ruins of these early settlements date back to 5000 BCE, the date of the first settlements in the area, and some, such as Akab and al-Madar, have large collections of dugong (a type of manatee) bones, indicating a workstation where many of the sea animals were killed and processed for food.[5] This indicates that the settlements were temporary but were used again and again over a long period of time, making them different from the other settlements, such as at Umm al-Nar, Tell Abraq, and Shimal.

BRONZE AGE (3300–1200 BCE)

In the 4000s BCE, sailors from Sumer began to explore the gulf region and came upon three places mentioned in the early written texts: Dilmun (Bahrain), Magan (Oman), and Melukha (Pakistan's lower Indus Valley). Each provided Sumer with specialized products: Dilmun provided pearls, coral, tortoise shell, and dried fish; Magan provided copper, dorite stone, hardwood, and onions; while Melukha provided carnelian, lapis lazuli, ivory, hardwood, tin, gold, and copper.[6] Both Dilmun and Magan become more important and more active in trade by 3200 BCE and developed settled sites. In the United Arab Emirates, sites inland at Jabal Hafit have been identified from that date (3200 BCE) and lasted until 2000 BCE. At Jabal Hafit, ancient copper mines have been discovered, as well as along Wadi Jizzi, which forms a natural road deep into Oman, and the mines remained open until 1600 CE.[7] Nearby are other numerous ruins that are part of the Umm al-Nar civilization at Hili and at Qarn Bint Sa'ud, with the ruins in Hili among the most impressive in the area. Hili includes not only tombs with grave goods but also a tower tomb in stone with engravings on it that represent large cats (lions or cheetahs); humans, including a figure leading a donkey; and gazelles. Dated to 2250 BCE, it was among the world's oldest carvings until the recent discoveries of the temple art at Göbekli Tepe in southern Turkey that dates back to over 9000 BCE and Çatalhöyük, also in Turkey, with wall art that dates to before 7000 BCE. Nonetheless, Hili remains an important site for archeology in the Arabian Peninsula, and in addition to the stone tower tomb, it contains a number of round brick-built tombs.

Umm al-Nar not only was in touch with ships from Sumer, Dilmun, and Melukha but also developed its own ships that, according to pictorial representations, were distinctive. Dilmun's ships had both high-curved bows and sterns, while those from Magan had a high-curved bow with a triangular sail. This is different from those depicted from Sumer, Dilmun, and Melukha, which have square sails. The ships from Melukha and Magan were made of reeds or, more likely, sewn wooden planks, much like the dhows of the later gulf Arabs. Smaller coastal vessels were made of bound reeds, like those depicted in ancient Egypt, and these, called *badan* or *shu'i*, can still be found along the coast of Oman for coastal fishing.[8] Another small boat for coastal fishing and transportation built and used in the Musandam Peninsula is called a *batil*, but it is a wooden-plank constructed vessel rather than one made of bound reeds. The lack of detailed representations makes it hard to conclusively make many statements about shipbuilding in Magan, as there is, so far, only one representation on a pendant from Tell Abraq dated about 1000 BCE. However, sewn-plank vessels are attested to in Sumer from 3000 BCE, and it is not hard to conceive that the technology spread to other gulf cultures. There is ample information on the construction techniques for building sewn-plank vessels from Arabia and Mesopotamia, including early Greek and Latin texts on Red Sea and gulf ships, as well as a detailed description from Sumer dating to the Third Dynasty of Ur.[9] What is unusual is the shape of the Magan sail. In Pakistan, Iran, Bahrain, and Iraq, the sails are depicted as being square, but the Magan lateen sail is triangular. If the depiction is correct, this is the oldest depiction of the lateen shape and may indicate the use of the lateen/triangular sail in the gulf long before the accepted beginning of the sixth century CE by Arab seamen. The sail in question is drawn as tied down to the bow of the ship, corresponding directly with how later Arab seamen secured the sails of their ships.[10] Further archeological evidence needs to be found to verify the use of the lateen sail as early as the Umm al-Nar and Wadi Suq traditions in the gulf.

In the United Arab Emirates, Umm al-Nar progressed into the Wadi Suq culture (2000–1300 BCE), which was more dependent on terrestrial domestic livestock for their main food supplies; sea animal sources remained important to their overall diet. Despite the change in the overall food supplies, maritime sources were still important, but as the climate changed to its less-hospitable environment, dependence on domesticated animals and oasis agriculture became the pattern of life that lasted until the middle of the twentieth century. Oases, with their constant supplies of water, needed to be managed and stored for continued agricultural production. Dates quickly became an important source of subsistence, with places such as al-Ain becoming important communities. Patterns of life remained seasonal, with movement between inland and coastal settlements, but permanent settlements in places such as al-Ain were linked to copper mines in Wadi Jizzi and Oman. These mines allowed for the use of copper and bronze implements, with tin being supplied from Melukha. Remains of Wadi Suq culture include a large field of some sixty tombs at Qarn al-Harf. These are large tombs containing the bodies of children, men, women—up to fifty people in a single tomb. The site was disturbed by building a road around Ras al-Khaimah. Finds included silver jewelry that have images of lions, bulls, and dogs—but not of camels yet.

IRON AGE (1300–300 BCE)

The Iron Age in the gulf dates from 1300 to 300 BCE and brought not only the development of weapons and tools but also agricultural developments such as the *falaj* (plural *aflaj*) that became the mainstay of oasis agriculture. The Iron Age brought outside interest that included conquest, and the Assyrians were among the first to envision the need to control the region. While the Assyrians launched military expeditions against the Arabs in the northern Peninsula, in 640 BCE, the king of Izke (perhaps modern Izki in Oman), Pade, surrendered his kingdom to the Assyrian king Ashurbanipal (ruled 667–626 BCE), and ruled as a vassal of Assyria.[11] Although the Assyrian text mentioned in the book by Potts noted above does not mention the name Magan, it does state that Izke is a city in the region the Assyrians called Qade, which is the Akkadian name for Magan. This is clear from inscriptions from Iran that refer to the region as Maka in Persian (older Magan) and notes that in Akkadian it was called Qade. Pade sailed from the southern region of the gulf first to Dilmun (Bahrain) and then proceeded up the gulf to Babylon and then by boat to the Assyrian capital city of Nineveh (near modern Mosul). His visit and submission to the Assyrian king is noted on the walls of the Temple of Ishtar. While the Assyrians launched and continued to launch military campaigns against the northern Arabs (even deep into the desert), they never bothered to attack either Dilmun or Magan but did maintain diplomatic and trade relations with the lower gulf.

The Iron Age also introduced two other important elements to society in the peninsula. The first was the domestication of the camel, which contributed to long-distance trade, and the second was the introduction of the *aflaj* system of underground canals that allowed for better water delivery to oasis agriculture. The camel was first domesticated in Yemen and was not that important for the region of the lower gulf until the arrival of Arab tribes in the second half of the first millennium BCE.[12] Camels were domesticated between 2500 and 1500 BCE in the southern part of the Arabian Peninsula, most likely in the region of the Hadhramaut of Yemen or Dhufar in Oman. Numerous clay models of camels were found at Muwailah, indicating that camels were used for transporting goods before they were used for riding.[13] Clay figurines of camels were also part of the trade between southern Arabia and the north, as Yemeni/Omani figures of camels that date to 1000 BCE have been found in Mesopotamian sites.[14] Some of the artistic representations indicate harnessing for these animals—the south Arabian saddle, called a *fulani*, which seats the rider behind the hump and is used in Yemen, Oman, and the lower gulf. The saddle is secured by a small wooden tree called a *shadad* that is placed in front of the hump on a woolen saddle blanket called a *bidad* (that can be very decorative), which is tied to a cinch that goes around the girth of the animal. The cinch is called a *ghurdah*, and the secondary cinch is called a *ziyar*; both are attached to a small wooden piece that connects the tree together. The riding pad, called a *mahwi*, is then attached by ropes to the saddle tree.[15] This is a precarious seat and makes it difficult to maintain the rider's balance when controlling the animal using a long stick. Later, the north Arabian saddle was developed, which secured the rider on top of the hump and gave both greater control and balance to the rider. The oldest pictorial representation of the north Arabian saddle, called a *shadad*, is found at Tell Halaf in Syria, dating to 900 BCE.[16]

More importantly for the region is the importation of the *aflaj* system from Iran. Iran established its control over the United Arab Emirates and Oman shortly after the expansion of the first Persian Empire by Cyrus (625–600 BCE) or his son Cambyses (600–559 BCE). By the time of Darius I (ruled 521–486 BCE), the region was under ethnic Persian governors or satraps. The Persian period is better known due to the numbers of written documents that passed back and forth between the capital, Persepolis, and the region, which were written in Elamite. The region contributed troops to put down rebellions in the empire but outside of Maka (Maciya), or Mazun, the modern states of Bahrain, Qatar, and the United Arab Emirates. Contact with Iran was through the gulf port city of Bushehr or the Shatt al-Arab waterway and then to Persepolis. The local Arab population served as troops using local weapons (a bow and a straight, short sword) and dressed in local, distinctive dress (a leather cloak and a short wrap-around kilt or skirt, not unlike the dress of the southern Bedouin from Wilfred Thesiger's day). In 480 BCE, they participated in the Battle of Doriscus against the Greek Delian League in Asia Minor under the command of Xerxes I (ruled 486–465 BCE) on his way to crushing the Greek city states. Trade with India, the East Indies, and China continued with items such as cinnamon and nutmeg, considered by the Greeks to be from Oman but which came from modern Indonesia. In fact, when Alexander the Great conquered Persia, on his return from the Indus River, one of his generals, Nearchus, was sent by ship. Near Hormuz, he sighted the Musandam Peninsula. Later Europeans confused the name Maketa, Maceta, or Macae with the spice nutmeg, and in German, it is called *muskatnuss* or *Musqat nut*, as it was supposedly from the mountains behind Muscat.[17]

Some *aflaj* from the Iron Age still provide water to groves of date palms, such as Falaj al-Saruj, which serves the oasis city of al-Ain.[18] Both the United Arab Emirates and Oman have systems that date to the Persian period and one in Nizwa, the Falaj Daryush, named for the Persian king Darius. Iran seems to be the home of the technology that has come to be associated with Omani agriculture. Clearly, in Oman, with the United Arab Emirates historically connected to Oman, the *aflaj* have allowed oasis agriculture to flourish in the interior and allowed an increase in population. Recent archeological investigation in al-Ain has pushed back the date of the oldest *falaj* to 1000 BCE, dating it to the end of the Bronze Age/start of the Iron Age rather than from the later Persian occupation.[19] If the *aflaj* system is an indigenous invention, it begs the question of why it did not spread until the Persian occupation. More archeological work needs to be done to bring this period into greater light.

NOTES

1. Morton, Michael Quentin. *Keepers of the Golden Shore: A History of the United Arab Emirates*. London: Reaktion Books, 2017, 10.
2. "First People: Out of Africa," PBS, December 6, 2015, video, 8:09. Accessed January, 28, 2019. https://www.youtube.com/watch?v=2mpkn7AEAvU.
3. Morton, 11.
4. Ibid., 12.
5. Potts, D.T., et al. *Waves of Time: The Marine Heritage of the United Arab Emirates*. London: Trident Press, 1998, 10, 16.
6. Vine, Peter. *Bahrain National Museum*. London: Immel Publishing, Ltd., 1993, 48.
7. Hellyer, Peter and Buckton, Rosalind. *Al Ain: Oasis City*. Dubai: Motivate Publishing, 1998, 31.
8. Richardson, Neil and Dorr, Marcia. *The Craft Heritage of Oman*, vol. 1. Dubai: Motivate Publishing, 2005, 270.
9. Potts, et al., 38.
10. Ibid., 39.
11. Ibid., 40.
12. Bulliet, Richard W. *The Camel and the Wheel*. New York: Columbia University Press, 1990, 45.
13. Morton, 22.
14. Bulliet, 77.
15. Dickson, H. R. P. *The Arab of the Desert: A Glimpse into Badawin Life in Kuwait and Sau'di Arabia*, 3rd edition. London: George Allen and Unwin, 1983, 186; Richardson, Neil and Dorr, Marcia. *The Craft Heritage of Oman*, vol. 2. Dubai: Motivate Publishing, 2005, 334–336.
16. Bulliet, 80.
17. Morton, 47.
18. Hurriez, Sayyid Hamid. *Folklore and Folklife in the United Arab Emirates*. New York: Routledge, 2002, 13.
19. Morton, 20.

3

Arrival of the Arab Tribes and Persian Rule: Later Antiquity (300 BCE–620 CE)

During the Persian period (300 BCE–620 CE), a number of Arab tribes moved into the region from the north and were divided into the classical Arab divisions, the Ghafiri or Qaysi (associated with lineages in the north) and the Hinawi or Yamani (associated with lineages from Yemen).[1] Among the various tribes mentioned in classical works by authors such as Pliny the Elder in his *Natural History* and in later Arabic sources are the Hinawi Azd, who became the local power during the Sassanid era (ruled by the Jalanda dynasty). The Sassanid era dates from 224 to 650 CE. These tribes frequently engaged in raids and counterraids. In Syria, the division between these two major sections of Arab tribal groups was important until the first part of the twentieth century. In Oman and the lower gulf, the division was not that important, and groups allied themselves to members of different lineages for reasons such as commercial interest or for shared grazing lands. It is noted that the first of the Arab tribes that arrived in the lower gulf region were the Azd, who came from Yemen at about the time the great dam at Ma'rib fell, around 120 CE.² These tribes in the lower gulf depended more on camels, domesticated first in Yemen and spread throughout the Middle East and North Africa, with camel saddles appearing around 1200 BCE. Arab troops were depicted in ancient art as two riders per camel, one sitting in front of the hump, using a long stick to guide the animal, and one, armed with bow and arrow and a long, straight sword, riding behind the hump. As time went by, better equipment was invented. In Oman and the lower gulf, the rider remained behind the hump with harnessing, called a *fulani*, developed for firmer seat and better control. In the north, a new type of saddle, called a *shadad*, was invented that placed the rider on top of the hump, giving a much firmer seat on the animal and greater control.³

Despite Persian control over the lower gulf and Oman, contact between Hellenistic and Roman Middle Eastern cities was fairly steady, with coins based on Greek coins minted in the lower gulf town of al-Dur. Among these coins is an imitation of Alexander the Great's coins with the name Abiel replacing that of the Greek word for ruler, *Basilius*. Because the name Abiel can be both male or female, it is not certain if the region had a dynasty of men or women rulers or even how many Abiels there were. Much of the archeological evidence comes from the northern emirate of Ras al-Khaimah, with sites such as al-Dur and Mleiha. Al-Dur contains a great deal of archeological remains and has produced a number of coins, indicating trade with Rome. Rome was the main enemy for the Iranian Parthians and Sassanids, yet it is evident that trade with Rome for local items, such as pearls and coral, was important. In addition, Greek and Roman geographers produced maps and books with descriptions of places in the peninsula. These include Theophrastus (370/2–286/8 BCE), Strabo (64 BCE–21 CE), and Pliny the Elder (23–79 CE), as well as Claudius Ptolemy (100–170 CE). These works drew on the eyewitness accounts of Alexander the Great's general Nearchus, though the original account no longer exists. They also drew on the accounts of merchants who traveled either to the gulf or dealt with traders who did. The *Periplus of the Erythraean (Red) Sea* gave descriptions of places along the Red Sea, the east coast of Africa, and the coast of the Arabian Peninsula. From Oman, the Romans were interested in frankincense, while from the gulf waters, their interests were pearls and coral. While these classical sources name numerous places and tribal groups along the coast, the one that stands out is Kadaei, which seem to be the same as Qade in the Assyrian texts.

SASSANID PERIOD (224–650)

In 224 CE, Ardashir (died in 242) overthrew the Parthians and began the Sassanid period, which lasted until the conquest of Iran by Islam. The Sassanids quickly took control over the trade routes from China, India, and Oman to Rome. Shortly after establishing the Sassanid state, Ardashir embarked on the conquest of Oman and established a military governorship at Rustaq.[4] The Persians called the region that includes today's United Arab Emirates Mazun, and there are references to it as *Mo-xun* in Chinese sources from the *New History of the Tang Dynasty* by Jia Dan (730–805 CE). Romans were interested in the goods from South Arabia, what they called Arabia Felix, and the new emperor, Augustus Caesar, organized a military expedition in 24 BCE under the command of Aelius Gallus.[5] Gallus was aided this by the Syllaeus, a leading citizen of Petra, and launched an army of ten thousand men, first in ships along the Red Sea, and then overland along the Hadhramaut coast.[6] The guide supplied by the Nabateans was blamed for leading the poorly prepared army into the worst of desert conditions. Many of the soldiers died, and the army eventually turned back after reaching the city of Mariama, called Mariaba by the Romans. Despite the harsh conditions of the south Arabian deserts, Romans still believed the cities were wealthy and adorned with "the most beautiful of temples," according to Aelius Gallus's eyewitness reports that served as the information for Pliny the Elder.[7] The expedition of Aelius Gallus ended in disaster (being lost in the desert with numerous men dying of thirst or due to Bedouin raids) with no tangible goods to prove victory, even though he claimed victory over large numbers of Bedouin tribes. In the end, his army made it back to the Red Sea coast to take ships back to Egypt, and Rome never again attempted to invade Arabia. Rome was the main customer for goods either from Oman or imported to Oman from India and the East Indies. Omani merchants kept the sources for their goods a secret, and Rome thought all the products were from Oman. The Omanis spread stories, such as that the incense made from the sap of trees, so important to Roman religion, were protected by swarms of winged snakes. Snakes also played a part in Aelius Gallus's account of life in the desert, and such stories were considered to be true.

Among the stories that survived into the present day is that of the lost or vanished city of Ubar. Its location was swallowed up in the vastness of the desert, but it was reputed to be the most important trade city in south Arabia. In the Qur'an, the city was destroyed for not obeying the word of God and being full of pride. "Consider how the Lord dealt with 'Ad, and the people of Iram [or Aram], adorned with lofty buildings the like of which has not been seen" (*surah* 89 *the Dawn* lines 6–7). The city, or its surrounding region, was called Wabar/Ubar, and sometime around 300 CE, it was no longer an important trade city. However, two centuries before, the geographer Claudius Ptolemy (died c. 170 CE) placed it on his map as Omanum Emporium. Around the time the city vanished, the frankincense trade with Rome collapsed. In 1991, the British mercenary and explorer, Ranulph Fiennes, who had served in the Omani army against rebels in Dhufar in the 1960s, claimed to have found the lost city. Having developed a major interest in the city and its legends during the war, he returned to a likely place, Shisr and found materials that date to the Roman period, as well as broken pieces of pottery from Greece, Syria, and China. According to the archeologist working with Fiennes, the city sank due to overuse of the water table, compounded by an earthquake.[8] Despite the numerous finds, the identity of the mysterious city is still in question, though for Fiennes, the city is Ubar.

During the Persian period, Rome was a serious rival, first for the Parthians and later for the Sassanids. In the north, this rivalry frequently erupted into warfare in places such as Syria and Armenia. As the Roman Empire coalesced into the Western Empire and the Eastern Empire, later called the Byzantine Empire, the rivalry became one between Christianity and Zoroastrianism. Zoroastrianism is the ancient religion of Iran, whose founder/prophet was Zoroaster (lived between 628 and 551 BCE), based on the concept of good and evil. Good was the god Ahura Mazda, and evil was the god Ahriman, and people had to keep the balance between them. Zoroastrianism is accepted in Islam as a revealed religion with beliefs similar to Christianity.

With the conversion of Ethiopia to Christianity, Ethiopia became an ally of Byzantium in their conflict with Iran and, as such, interfered in Yemen and Oman for the Byzantines. Around 500 CE, a Syrian monk named Faymiyun introduced Christianity to the Najran in southern Arabia. Most Christian communities in Arabia were of Syrian Monophysite origin that eventually was persecuted by the Greek Orthodox Church. From 428 to 431 CE, the patriarch of Constantinople was Nestorius, who adhered to a form of Christianity that denied the dual nature of Christ. This view was opposed by Cyril of Alexandria, and eventually, Nestorius was declared a heretic, and his followers fled to places such as Persia, seeking protection in Iran and the Arabian Gulf. The community in Najran was persecuted by the Jewish king of Yemen, Dhu Nuwas (ruled 522–525 CE), and he ordered the death of a large number of them om 523 CE. Faymiyun was most likely a member of the Nestorian Church, but the death of large numbers of Christians at the hands of a Jewish king in Arabia was beyond the tolerance of the Byzantine emperor Justin I (ruled 518–527). One man, Daws ibn al-Tha'laban escaped and appealed to the Byzantine emperor, Justin, for aid.[9] Byzantine turned to Christian Ethiopia rather than sending its own troops. Ethiopia responded by sending an army of seventy thousand men under the command of Abraha (a variant of Abraham), and they defeated Dhu Nuwas. According to legend, rather than face defeat, Dhu Nuwas spurred his horse into the Red Sea and disappeared.

Christian Ethiopia faced Iran across the frontier of Yemen, and eventually, the two powers clashed over the control of Oman. Persia had become a friendly power to the Nestorian Church and allowed it to set up monasteries and churches throughout the empire and beyond to Central Asia and India. Since the Nestorians were primarily from Syria, they used Syriac, a form of Aramaic, in their liturgy. As such, languages such as Mongolian and Turkic were written in Syriac script well into the Islamic period, when Arabic script eventually became the most used. The gulf had a number of Christian communities, including several bishoprics, such as in Bahrain, which referred to both the island called Bahrain and the coastal region of Saudi Arabia.

Recently, archeological excavations in the al-Ahsa region uncovered a Christian church. In the lower gulf, on the island of Sir Bani Yas, the site of a Nestorian monastery was found in 1992. The ceramics found at the site helped date it to the sixth century CE and include representations of grapes and crosses in stucco. In addition, manuscripts, such as *Chronicle of Seert*, composed in 1036, mentions the life of Abdisho, who journeyed to the island called Yamama (Bahrian), where he converted and baptized a number of local people.

The founding of the Nestorian Church dates to the synod held at Markabata in Iraq in 425/424.[10] The church asserted its independence from the patriarch of Antioch and Constantinople. The synod also recognized the region of the lower gulf and Oman as Bet Mazunaye (Bayt Mazun) and nominated bishops in 544, 576, and 676.[11] The contact between today's regions of the United Arab Emirates and Oman with India, in particular Kerala, is attested to in a number of inscriptions in Pahlavi (the script used in Sassanian Iran). The Iranian city of Bushehr was called Rev-Ardashir and served as an important emporium in the gulf, with strong connections to both the lower gulf and India.

In the conflict between Iran and Ethiopia, Iran established firm control over the lower gulf and Oman, and eventually, the Ethiopians had to retreat to Africa in 575 CE. Arab legend surrounds the final year of Ethiopian control over Yemen and the heroic figure of Sayf ibn dhi Yazan, who has become the subject of an epic poem. His story was popular with coffeehouse storytellers. Sayf supposedly sought Byzantine aid against Ethiopia. The Byzantines refused him assistance, and he then turned to Iran. The Persian king, Khosrow Anushirvan (or Kisra Anusharwan, ruled 531–571 CE), sent troops to support the Arabs against the Ethiopians. In 575 CE, Shah Hormuzd IV sent eight hundred men under Wahraz (or Wihraz) who defeated the Ethiopians. Sayf became the satrap for the Persian shah, and Yemen fell under Persian control. In 628 CE, the Persian satrap of Yemen, Badhan, accepted Islam, and Yemen became the strongest supporter of the new religion.

NOTES

1. Carter, J. R. L. *Tribes in Oman*. London: Peninsular Publishing, 1982, 15.
2. Hellyer, Peter and Buckton, Rosalind. *Al Ain: Oasis City*. Dubai: Motivate Publishing, 1998, 37.
3. Dickson, H. R. P. *The Arab of the Desert: A Glimpse into Badawin Life in Kuwait and Sau'di Arabia*, 3rd edition. London: George Allen and Unwin, 1983, 184–187.
4. Potts, D. T., et al. *Waves of Time: The Marine Heritage of the United Arab Emirates*. London: Trident Press, 1998, 62.
5. Taylor, Andrew. *Travelling the Sands: Sagas of Exploration in the Arabian Peninsula*. Dubai: Motivate Publishing, 2004, 13.
6. Hitti, Philip K. *History of the Arabs*. New York: Palgrave Macmillan, 2002, 61.
7. Ibid., 62.
8. Taylor, 155.
9. Hitti, 62.
10. Potts, et al., 66.
11. Ibid., 66–67.

4

Rise of Islam and Khawarij Oman (620–1600)

For centuries before the country was formed, the United Arab Emirates was considered to be a part of Oman or the kingdom of Hormuz, which was located across the straits of Hormuz and was part of Iran. A separate identity did not begin until much later, in the eighteenth and nineteenth centuries, when several "pirate" states existed. In the nineteenth century, these small states warred with the British East India Company's shipping in the Indian Ocean, and in 1820, the British forced them to sign a treaty of peace. With this peace, the Trucial Oman was born, which eventually became the United Arab Emirates in 1971. The United Arab Emirates did not exist before that time, and events in the lower gulf region are recorded as events in Oman. Thus, this author will use the term Oman here to mean the region of the lower gulf and not the country of Oman only. More confusion is added to this, as the Arabian Sea shore of the United Arab Emirates is a disputed area between various Emirates and Oman even today.

LIFE OF THE PROPHET MUHAMMAD AND THE WARS OF *RIDDAH* (570–633)

The religion of Islam began when the angel Gabriel (*Jabra'il* in Arabic) first appeared to the Prophet of Islam, Muhammad ibn 'Abdallah, in 610 CE. Muhammad was from the ruling Quraysh family of Makkah (Mecca) and was born around the year 571, which is when the Ethiopian general, Abraha, tried to expand out of Yemen into the Hejaz or western Arabia. According to the Qur'an, Abraha and his troops were driven back by an immense flock of birds that dropped stones on them (*surah* 105 *al-Fil* lines 1-5). Both of Muhammad's parents died when he was still a child, and he was raised by his grandfather, 'Abd al-Muttalib, and then by his paternal uncle, Abu Talib.

The new religion borrowed from both Judaism and Christianity. According to popular legend, during a commercial trip to Syria when Muhammad was twelve, a Christian monk named Bahria recognized him as the future prophet of the religion of God. As the Prophet, he taught ethical behavior and not to cheat widows and orphans of their inheritance. Initially, many of the revelations warned of the last days and final judgment. Eventually, he gathered a following, which angered the ruling Quraysh and resulted in the persecution of his followers. Seeking refuge from the persecution, he sent some of his followers to Ethiopia under the rule of a "righteous" and Christian king, who protected them from the Quraysh. In 620, the two main tribes of Yathrib (now called Medina from the Arabic *al-Madinah al-Munawwarah* or the Enlightened City) came to appeal for Muhammad's intervention in their long and dangerous dispute. Muhammad sent his followers to Yathrib, and this began the Islamic calendar or the Year of the Hijrah (meaning the Year of Migration). The people of Yathrib opened their doors to the migrants from Makkah and were called the ansar (supporters), and the people from Makkah became the muhajirun (emigrants). Those who were too weak for the trek remained in Makkah, and the Quraysh took heavy revenge on them. As a result, the Prophet allowed an expedition against the yearly trade caravan to Syria, but the Makkans organized an expedition against the fledgling state in Medina, and the two met at the wells of Badr in 624. The small army of Muslims defeated a much larger force of Makkans and their Bedouin allies, and a number of leading members of the Quraysh tribe died in the fighting.

The Makkans took revenge for their defeat at Badr with their victory over Muhammad and his followers at Uhud, outside of Medina, in 625, but the Makkans did not follow up their victory by attacking the town. Muhammad won another victory in 627 when, at the advice of a Persian convert named Salman, the Prophet defeated again a much larger army composed of the Quraysh, Bedouin allies, and Ethiopian mercenaries (called the *ahzab* or confederates) by digging a trench around Medina. The besiegers withdrew after a month with little loss of life but the Jews of Madinah were persecuted as a result because some of them seemed to side with the Makkans.

In 628, Muhammad led his followers to Makkah and, in a last-minute effort to spare Makkah from a possible conquest, the Quraysh offered a truce. Muhammad reached close to Makkah at the wells of Hudaybiyah, only 14½ kilometers (or 9 miles) from Makkah. During the truce, Muhammad was accepted as God's messenger by some of the Quraysh upper class, such as Khalid ibn al-Walid and 'Amr ibn al-'As, who were destined to become important commanders in the expansion of Islam into Syria and Egypt. In 620, the Persian satrap of Yemen converted to Islam and brought much of southern Arabia with him. Tribes from Oman and Hadhramaut declared for Muhammad and his religion. In 632, the Arab tribe of Azd under the Julandah family drove the Sassanids out of Oman and the lower gulf, yielding to the Arabs the cities of Dibba and Julfar.[1] Yemen remained faithful to Islam, but many Bedouin tribes that submitted to Muhammad, not as the messenger of God but as the leader of a new and growing political state in Arabia. In 630, the Quraysh broke the truce, and Muhammad took Makkah without a fight. In 632, the Prophet died in Medina, the capital of his state, and was succeeded by his close friend Abu Bakr. Almost immediately, many of the Bedouin tribes broke with the new religion. This is referred to as the Ridda Wars or the Wars of Apostasy. Several new prophets arose with the support of particular tribes. The Tayy, Asad, and Ghatafan followed Talhah, while the largest group of Bedouin followed Sajah, a female soothsayer who was perhaps a Christian, and her husband Musaylimah. The support for the rebels came from Bani Hanifah and the Bani Tamim. The rebels defeated two Muslim armies that were sent to bring an end to their apostasy. Those from the Persian Gulf coast from Bahrain to the Hadhramaut followed the prophet al-Aswad. Among them was the Azd tribe, whose people chose between 'Amr and Gaifar, the brothers who had ruled them under the Sassanids before the conversion to Islam, and the new prophet Laqit ibn Malik dhu al-Taj. Eventually, Abu Bakr chose Khalid ibn al-Walid to put an end to the apostasy, and he cornered the prophet Laqit and his Bedouin supporters at Dibba. The town of Dibba lies at the foot of the Musandam Peninsula, where steep mountains meet a flat plain and where the Sassanids chose to build one of their forts control the lower gulf and Oman. Dibba lies deep in today's United Arab Emirates, and the approach was difficult, made so by the Persians in defense of the town. The march to Dibba was difficult, and Khalid left stragglers behind to meet the army of the false prophets. During the battle, the course of the fighting seemed to go against Khalid, but as the day progressed, the stragglers caught up with the main body of the army and turned the tide. Laqit was killed, as were ten thousand of his men, while Khalid and the Muslims lost a large number of those who had memorized the Qur'an that it seriously threatened the survival of the new state.[2] The Day of Dibba marked the end of the Ridda Wars and returned the peninsula to Islam.

However, along the gulf coast, the Nestorian Christian community continued well into the Islamic era. Not only did the Sassanids help with its continuity, but the Nestorians were also able to expand into India and Central Asia, and the Indian Nestorians helped maintain the churches and monasteries in the gulf for decades. Being "people of the Book," the Nestorian Christians were not persecuted by the Muslim rulers, and they were able to survive at least until the end of the Umayyad dynasty (661–750) that ruled from Damascus. The Umayyads were generally tolerant of Christians and Jews inside their new empire, and several of their rulers or caliphs (*khulafa'*) had Christian boon companions, especially famous poets such as al-Akhtal al-Taghlibi.

With Islam secure in the entire peninsula, forces of Islam pushed out into Byzantine and Sassanid territories. The two great powers of the time had fought and finally concluded an exhausting war between them in 628, with Byzantium the winner. Smaller Arab armies took advantage of the exhaustion of the two powers to defeat their armies, first in Palestine and Syria (between 633 and 640), and then in Iran (between 634 and 643).[3] The Julandah family, who had helped push the Iranians out, stood with Islam against the false prophets, and once they were defeated, the brothers once more exercised the authority given to them by the new government. Oman was assigned to the governor of Bahrain, who left it mostly to its own self-government under the Julandah family, who gained control over the various tribes in Oman and the lower gulf. The tribal structure of Oman was clearly maintained in that the Julandah regained control over the Azd and their allies once both the Persians and the Arab governments weakened. When the conflict arose over the leadership of the new Muslim state between the forces that supported 'Ali ibn Abi Talib and those that supported the old Quraysh leadership under Mu'awiyyah ibn Abi Sufyan, Oman remained out of the conflict but was influenced by it. A party of followers of 'Ali refused to recognize his agreement to arbitration with Mu'awiyyah and withdrew from both parties, thus becoming the Khawarij (singular Kharaji) community of Islam. The Khawarij held to the early democracy of Islam under the Prophet and the election of his successor or *khalifah* rather than based it on his blood relatives (the Shi'ite stance) or on the old pre-Islamic Quraysh leadership (the Sunni stance). The theology of the Khawarij was the product of 'Abdallah ibn Ibad al-Tamimi, who died in 708 and whose democratic ideals were embraced by the Bedouin in the peninsula.[4] In 657, Kharajites from Iran fled to Oman from persecution by the Umayyads (the rulers of the Muslim empire based in Syria), and the Ibadi belief spread rapidly. In 749, the first Ibadi imamate was founded with Nizwa as the first seat of local power.[5] Today, Oman is the only Arab state that is officially Ibadi Khawarij rather than Sunni or Shi'ite. The Julandah fought several Umayyad armies sent against them. The Julandah were generally defeated, and in 684, the Umayyads succeeded in imposing their rule in the lower gulf.[6]

THE UMAYYAD DYNASTY (661–750) AND THE ABBASID DYNASTY (750–1258)

The Umayyads were determined not to lose Oman and landed troops on the lower gulf coast at Baynunah and Julfar. With the collapse of the Umayyads, the power of the Khawarij was consolidated in Oman, and the Ibadi evolved. In the eighth and ninth centuries, the Abbasids (750–1258) sent troops to bring an end to the tribal problems in Oman and enforce Sunni Islam. The conflict between the Arab tribes in the Omani hinterland had increased, with no force strong enough to bind them together. In 751, the tribal leadership in Oman elected the first imam of the Julandah dynasty to rule instead of the Abbasid *khalifah* in Baghdad. The Abbasids came to crush the Julandah state three times, in 840, 850, and 892. The Abbasid *khalifah* al-Mu'tadid (892–962), in a period of revival of imperial power, sent General Muhammad ibn Nur with a large force of men (supposedly twenty-five thousand armed warriors) to reconquer Oman and the lower gulf.[7] Muhammad ibn Nur was abusive to the local people, using torture as a means of both suppressing local support for the Julandah family and enforcing laws from Baghdad. As a result, local people rejected Abbasid rule and adhered to the Khawarij belief and support for the Julandah family.

The extreme Qaramitah movement found favor among the Bedouin around the middle gulf region and with the poor in Iraq and eventually spread from southern Iraq to include much of the peninsula and rural Syria. Founded in 874 by Hamdan Qarmat, a student of Abdallah who delineated the belief of the Sevener or Isma'ili Shi'ites, the Qaramitah, as their followers came to be called, were known for their communist-like beliefs with a radical theology that has come to be called "Bolsheviks of Islam."[8] They took the oasis of al-Ahsa under the leadership of Sa'id al-Hasan al-Jannabi and, in 903, took Oman.[9] Al-Jannabi was succeeded by his son al-Tahir, who conquered Makkah and removed the Black Stone (*al-Hajar al-Aswad*) from the Ka'abah in 930. The Black Stone was believed to have been sent by God—al-Rahman—to Abraham, who used it as a foundation of the building. It was replaced when the Ka'abah was rebuilt by the ruling Quraysh tribe of Makkah when Muhammad was thirty-five years old. The stone was one of several meteorites that were worshipped in pre-Islamic Arabia and is the only one that was maintained after the rise of Islam. In 683, it was cracked and broken into three pieces, and today, it is in seven pieces, held together by a silver frame.[10] The Black Stone remained in al-Ahsa until the Isma'ili *khalifah* al-Mansur (ruled 946–953) of the Fatimid dynasty (ruled from Tunisia and then Cairo from 921 to 1171) asked for it be returned in 951.[11] The Qaramitah state fell but was replaced by the power of the Isma'ili doctrine, which was like a wave over the Islamic world until the Sunni revival under the Seljuq Turks (ruled 1037–1194).

The Qaramitah invaded the lower gulf in 925 and ruled for sixty years before Oman and the lower gulf fell in 966 under the rule of the Persian Buyids/Buwayhids (932–1062), who were Shi'ites and had control over the Abbasid khalifahs as well.[12] The Buyids claimed descent from Sassanid kings, and Ahmad al-Buwayh captured Baghdad and the *khalifah* al-Mustakfi (ruled 944–946) in 945. The Buyids originated in northern Iran and took (conquered) cities as they moved south and eventually took Baghdad. While the khalifah was a Sunni, the Buyids were Shi'ite, and this marks the lowest point in Abbasid pride and power. The Buyids extended their control over Oman and the Straits of Hormuz, ensuring the passage of trade goods from India and Indonesia to Iraq and then the West. The Abbasids had favored the Red Sea and ports in Egypt, and during their time, the gulf suffered from a decline in local economics. Under these new Persian rulers, Jumeirah (near Dubai) grew as an important port where its inhabitants traded pearls for other imported goods from India, Indonesia, and China. Pearls became the region's most important trade good and the basis of the local economy. In 1055, the Buyids lost to the Sunni Seljuq Turks (1040–1194), who smashed their military power in 1060. The Great Seljuqs ruled until the death of Sanjar in 1157 and, like the Buyids, they controlled the Straits of Hormuz beginning in 1055.[13] While Julfar and Tawam rose in importance and power, Dibba slipped back into obscurity after the Battle of the Day of Dibba. Julfar may have been located close to the contemporary site of Ras al-Khaimah; its exact location is thought to be Tall Kush or the nearby site of al-Mataf.[14] Julfar was very important in the Middle Ages and was an important producer of pearls. The name has since been extended over the entire coast of today's United Arab Emirates. The local leader was called the amir of Julfar and eventually ruled as a vassal of the king of Hormuz. The region had an economic boom after international trade was diverted away from the Red Sea and Egypt to the gulf. This was due to the Seljuqs and, later, to the Mongols/Ilkhanids (1256–1353). Following the collapse of the Ilkhanids, Iran broke into smaller political entities, and Hormuz was able to control the straits and international trade for the next three hundred years.[15]

THE SAFAVIDS (1501–1747) AND THE PORTUGUESE (1505–1622)

Hurmuz or Hormuz in Iran became one of the most important ports in the lower gulf and traded with India and China. Hormuz became the object of the envy of Persian rulers, and the Safavids (1501–1747) tried to take it in rivalry with Portugal. Portugal became interested in Hormuz and its dependencies as early as 1515. Portugal entered the Indian Ocean and into the competition for international trade with the voyages of Vasco da Gama and Pero de Covilha in 1487.[16] In 1490, the Portuguese arrived off the coast of Oman under Pero de Covilha, and their target was the city of Hormuz. Hormuz had developed a reputation for wealth, and in the thirteenth century, the Italian traveler Marco Polo visited the city twice, describing it as a rich trading port with incredible goods. The city had developed with trade for luxury goods from India, Indonesia, and China with its shops overflowing with silks, cotton prints, pearls, and valuable and rare spices for Europeans. Venice considered the city to be a rich emporium trading in pearls from the gulf and other goods from India, making it an important base for the Portuguese. In 1505, the Portuguese attacked Arab shipping on a large scale, inflicting great damage to both ships and

The al-Budyah Mosque (also called the Ottoman Mosque), located in Fujairah, may be the oldest mosque in the country, as it dates back to 1446. Its two accompanying watchtowers (one is in the photo) date to around the same time. In 2018, a one-thousand-year-old mosque was found in al-Ain, but it is in ruins. The al-Budyah mosque remains the oldest still in use in the United Arab Emirates. (Courtesy of John A. Shoup)

goods. In 1507, Afonso de Albuquerque inflicted heavy defeats on the king of Hormuz and captured the ports of Khor Fakkan (in the United Arab Emirates) and Muscat (in Oman).[17] De Albuquerque's fleet was composed of seven ships armed with the latest canons and a crew of five hundred men, but after capturing Hurmuz by force, he was forced to withdraw due to a mutiny by his own men.[18] In the same year, the wazir of Hormuz, *Khwaja* (Hoja in modern Turkish) 'Ata, convinced the Portuguese to attack Bahrain to gain control over trade in the Gulf, but the attacking force ran into Persian resistance under the Safavid shah Isma'il I (ruled 1501–1524). In 1508, the Portuguese sailed back to Socotra, off the coast of Oman, in order to prepare for another attack on Bahrain, but it also gave Bahrain time to also repair its defenses. In 1514, the Portuguese fleet under the command of Pero de Albuquerque, the nephew of Afonso, sailed into the gulf and, by chance, took some twenty ships that the Persians had captured from the ruler of Hormuz. However, the Portuguese returned to Goa rather than continue on to Bahrain. In 1515, Afonso returned to retake Hormuz and Julfar, which remained under the Portuguese until 1622.[19]

In 1521, the Portuguese tried to conquer Bahrain in order to control trade in the gulf. The Portuguese were assisted in this attempt by the shah/king of Hormuz, who had a longtime plan to bring Bahrain under his control. The troops from Hormuz were commanded by *Ra'is* Sharaf, who had harbored a great hatred for the Bahrain leader, Muqrin ibn Adjwad ibn Zamil, since the attempt to conquer Bahrain by *Khawja* 'Ata failed in 1511.[20] Muqrin thought the invasion of 1521 was not a serious threat, only a raid, and he was wounded and died a few days later. In order to have proof of Muqrin's death, the Hormuzian commander, *Ra'is* Sadradrim, cut off his head and brought it back with him to Hormuz.[21] In 1523, the Portuguese were driven out of Bahrain, but in the same year, they returned with a nephew of the shah of Hormuz, Badr al-Din, who was installed as the governor. He eventually fell out with the Portuguese, who sent a fleet against the island, and in 1529, Badr al-Din left Bahrain for Iran. He was followed by Jalal al-Din Murad Mahmud, who ruled the island for more than forty-seven years and maintained good relations with the Ottomans, who were extending control over both the Red Sea and the gulf. In 1559, the Portuguese defeated a Turkish fleet based in Basrah in Iraq. Portugal was driven out of Bahrain in 1602, but it was Iran, under shah 'Abbas I (ruled 1587–1629), that took the island. Iran was a rival of the Ottomans, who had built up their military presence on the mainland and remained in control of the Arabian Peninsula's southern gulf coast. Bahrain remained firmly under Persian control and expanded its military presence by building the Arad Fort in Muharraq Island in 1635. Portugal tried to retake the island, but their attack on Arad Fort resulted in a Portuguese defeat in 1635.

The Portuguese built a series of impressive forts along the coast of Oman, but the Ottoman Turks sent a fleet into the gulf to defeat them, and in 1552, the fleet under the command of Piri Reis (a famous Ottoman admiral) took many Portuguese positions. The Ottomans were defeated in 1546 near Diu in India, but their interest in Oman and Yemen remained. In 1548, the Ottomans conquered Aden from the Portuguese, and in 1552, they besieged the forts at Muscat, forcing the troops to surrender. The Ottomans did not stay in Muscat but continued into the gulf to control the trade network of ports along the coast. Their main goals were Hormuz and Bahrain, which fell to the Ottomans in the same year. Ottoman fleets raided Portuguese India in 1553, but in the same year, the Portuguese defeated an Ottoman fleet in the Indian Ocean. In 1581, the Ottomans once again took the city of Muscat under their admiral Ali Bey, but they lost it again to the

Portuguese in 1588.[22] The Portuguese presence in Oman has left few remains behind other than the massive forts, among the best examples of fortification of the time. Forts in today's United Arab Emirates built by the Portuguese include those in Julfar, Dibba, Khor Fakkan, and Bidiya, but the best examples of Portuguese military construction are in Oman at Sohar and Muscat.[23] These Portuguese forts served as models for those built by the Arabs in place such as Abu Dhabi, Dubai, Ajman, Umm al-Quwain, and Ras al-Khaimah. The Arabs had to take the power of European cannons mounted on ships into account in order to build forts that could resist them.[24] Local Arabs used cannons before the arrival of the Europeans, but the power of the European cannons was beyond the power of those cast locally. European cannons captured in battle were mounted on Arab fortifications, and Portuguese cannons can still be found today in places such as Dubai.[25]

In 1586, the Portuguese brought the Italian architect, Giovanni Battista Cairati, to design their new forts in Oman.[26] Italian design was considered to be the best by Western Europeans, and the parts were made in the Portuguese possessions in West Africa, numbered, and shipped for assembly in East Africa and Asia. In 1622, Hormuz was lost to a coalition of Iranian, Omani, and English forces, and this marked the end of Portuguese control of the gulf. In 1650, the Omanis took the forts of Muscat and nearby Muttrah despite heavy losses due to the firepower of the forts' cannons. The Arab forces lost between four and five thousand men, and the fort at al-Mirani (called Capitan by the Portuguese and built in 1586) fell when the governor, with his forces reduced to a mere sixty or seventy men, surrendered it. Afterward, the governor leaped to his death; his body smashed on the rocks below.[27] Nearby, the twin fort to al-Mirani (built in 1588), called al-Jilali by the Omanis and Joa by the Portuguese, fell once al-Mirani was captured. In the same year, the Omani leader, Sultan bin Saif I (ruled 1649–1679) was declared the ruler of Oman by the Khawarij scholars in Nizwa, thus starting a new dynasty.[28] Muttrah is a classic Arab fort, though its two towers were built by the Portuguese. It fell to the Ottomans twice (in 1552 and 1581), and the Omanis took the city in 1654, ending the Portuguese period in regional history. Oman continued to challenge the Portuguese, taking much of the East African coast form them and driving them out of the Indian Ocean by 1698.

NOTES

1. Potts, D.T., et al. *Waves of Time: The Maritime History of the United Arab Emirate*. London: Trident Press, 1998, 72.

2. Morton, Michael Quentin. *Keepers of the Golden Shore: A History of the United Arab Emirates*. London: Reaktion Books, 2017, 30.

3. Hitti, Philip K. *History of the Arabs*. London: Palgrave Macmillan, 2002, 153, 157.

4. Ibid., 247.

5. Higgins, Carla. "Oman," in *Saudi Arabia and the Gulf Arab States Today: An Encyclopedia of Life in the Arab States*, edited by Sebastian Maisel and John A. Shoup. Westport, CT: Greenwood Press, 2009, 340.

6. Hellyer, Peter and Buckton, Rosalind. *Al Ain: Oasis City*. Dubai: Motivate Publishing, 1998, 37.

7. Morton, 32.

8. Hitti, 444.

9. Ibid., 445.

10. Glassé, Cyril. *The Concise Encyclopedia of Islam*. New York: HarperCollins, 1989, 77.

11. Hitti, 445.

12. Morton, 33.

13. Khalili, Nasser D. *Islamic Art and Culture: Timeline and History*. Cairo: The American University in Cairo Press, 2008, 20. The Seljuqs continued to rule from Konya in Turkey until 1307.

14. Potts, et al., 77.

15. Ibid., 80.

16. Vine, Peter, editor. *Bahrain National Museum*. London: Immel Publishing Ltd., 1993, 89.

17. Morton, 34–35.

18. Ibid., 35.

19. Ibid., 36.

20. Vine, 91.

21. Ibid., 93.

22. Dinteman, Walter. *Forts of Oman*. London: Motivate Publishing, 1993, 20.

23. Potts, et al., 86.

24. Ibid., 87.

25. Ibid., 82.

26. Dinteman, 20.

27. Ibid., 20.

28. Ibid., 23.

5

Islam and the International Rivalry of Portugal, Iran, Ottoman Turkey, and Oman (1600–1700)

DEFEAT OF THE PORTUGUESE

As noted in the previous chapter, Portugal was a major player in the Indian Ocean and in East Africa beginning at the end of the fifteenth century until nearly the end of the seventeenth century—over 150 years of control over not only the sea routes but also many of the ports. Portugal seized ports along the coast of Oman in the sixteenth century, but lost them twice to the Ottoman Turks, in 1552 and again in 1581. The Ottomans attacked the forts in Muscat in 1546 and shelled them but did not follow up with an occupation. The Portuguese made an alliance with the independent king of Hormuz, across the straits in Iran, and organized the forts under the Portuguese governor of India. Trade with Oman and the gulf (then considered to be part of Oman or Hormuz, as noted in the previous chapter) brought their interest in occupying the main ports of the gulf, with Bahrain as the main prize. The Portuguese control lasted, as noted above, for 150 years before they were pushed out and replaced by the Omanis.

Oman was, at first, subdued by the firepower of the Portuguese and by their mastery of sailing. Portuguese ships and cannons were superior to those of the Arabs, and only the ships of the Ottoman navy reached a similar level. However, the Ottomans had limited interest in the Indian Ocean. After the war, which lasted from 1534 to 1566, the Ottoman fleet in the Indian Ocean was defeated, and they no longer challenged the Portuguese beyond the Red Sea and the gulf.

The Ottomans were involved in a number of regional conflicts with the Persians, the Ethiopians, and in Europe, and affairs of the Indian Ocean were of interest to certain grand wazirs (chief ministers of state) but not to others. In 1567, under the leadership of the Wazir Sokollu Mehmed, the Ottoman fleet invaded Sumatra and formed a strong bond of friendship with the sultan of Acheh. In the same year, a Zaydi imam (a religious leader of the Fiver Shi'ites) began a rebellion in Yemen, forcing the Ottoman fleet to return to deal with the insurrection. The problems in Yemen were due to the behavior of the Ottoman governor, who extracted huge amounts of money as taxes from the local people as the Ottomans prepared for the expansion into the Indian Ocean. While Sokollu Mehmed was able to satisfy the needs of the Yemeni people, his government became embroiled in a conflict in Europe with Russia, Venice, and the Holy League (most of the Italian states, the pope and the Knights of Malta) that resulted in the defeat of the Ottoman fleet at Lepanto in 1571. Nonetheless, within a year, the Ottoman Mediterranean fleet was rebuilt and able to carry out campaigns that took Cyprus from the Venetians in 1572 and conquered Tunisia in 1574. In the meantime, the Portuguese were seen as a minor irritant in the far southeast. In 1581, a combined Ottoman/Egyptian fleet sailed out of the Red Sea and reduced the forts to rubble in Muscat, which a small Turkish garrison occupied for eight years before the Portuguese returned to retake it.

In Ethiopia, the Muslim (Somali) leader, Ahmad ibn Ibrahim al-Ghazi Gran (ruled 1527–1543), threatened the Coptic Christian kingdom and received help from the Ottomans. During the time of the conflict, it was called the Abyssinian-Adal War. The Muslim sultanate of Adal was based in the town of Harar, and Ahmad's predecessor was killed in battle against the Abyssinian (Ethiopian) forces. Ahmad defeated a much larger Ethiopian force, which proved his Somalis were a match for a much larger force of Ethiopians. With the help of the Ottomans, he conquered much of the territory of Ethiopia. In the end, the Ethiopians obtained aid in the form of men and materials from the Portuguese under Cristovoa da Gama. In 1543, the Muslim forces under Ahmad ibn Ibrahim were soundly defeated by the Ethiopians, and the Ottomans withdrew up the Red Sea coast into Sudan. Ahmad was killed, and the subsequent rulers of Adal were weakened to the extent that they were no longer a threat to Ethiopia. However, Ethiopia was also greatly weakened, and the Portuguese extended their control inside Ethiopia. In 1624, the Ethiopian king converted to Roman Catholicism, which turned his people against him and the Portuguese missionaries. In 1632, the next king returned to the Coptic faith and expelled the Portuguese priests.

In the gulf, the Portuguese were unable to hold Bahrain due to local resistance as well as both the Persians and the Ottomans, who blocked Portuguese progress up the gulf. The Ottomans gained control over the Arabian Peninsula along the gulf coast from the important oasis of al-Ahsa to the Shatt al-Arab waterway, and the Persians controlled the north shore of the gulf and organized the Bahraini resistance to European presence on the island. In 1602, the Safavid shah 'Abbas I (ruled 1587–1629) took the island from the Portuguese, and the Europeans began a slow retreat from the gulf. The major port of the northern shore of the lower gulf, Hormuz, maintained its independence from the Persians, and its satellite state of Julfar (located in today's United Arab Emirates) remained tied to it. The Portuguese built forts along the Arabian Sea/Indian Ocean coasts of today's United Arab Emirates and Oman but treated the population with harsh measures, including torture, turning the local people against them.[1] The Portuguese ruled Hormuz from their base in India, but in 1622, a combined force of Persian and British troops forced them to surrender the city.[2] Nonetheless, they held on to Julfar and built a new fort in 1631, no doubt hoping to use it as a base from which they would recapture Hormuz.[3] However, a new force arose in Oman, the Ya'rubah or Ya'rub, a lineage that was of Hinawi origin, which turned the tide against the Portuguese.

The Ya'rubah first took control of inner Oman, an area that never fell to the Portuguese, and became the leaders of Oman's Khawraij community. The Ya'rubah was an old tribal group in Oman, arriving from Yemen in pre-Islamic times. Ya'rubah, the founder, arrived around 794 BCE, a descendant of the Qahtans—a Hinawi tribe. They arrived from Yemen around the time the Azd, another Hinawi tribal group, arrived in Oman.[4] The Ya'rubah grew in power, and by the time of the Portuguese occupation, they formed a strong army based on the Khawarij imamate of Nizwa. In 1633, the imam Nasir ibn Murshid seized the fort at Julfar, freeing the lower gulf from the Europeans.[5] Other Portuguese forts on the Indian Ocean coast at Khor Fakkan, Fujairah, Dibba, and Kalba also fell to Omani forces, and Suhar fell to the Ya'rubah in 1643. In 1650, a new imam, Sultan bin Saif (ruled 1649–1679), came to power, and he mobilized his forces against the twin forts in Muscat, which fell in the same year. Armed with swords and shields, the Omanis lost some four to five thousand men in the attack, but according to an English author, they were not shaken and remained on the attack until the Portuguese surrendered.[6] With the fall of Muscat, the Portuguese were pushed out of Arabia, ending their 150 years of occupation. The Ya'rubah followed them to East Africa and continued to inflict defeats on them.[7] In 1698, the Portuguese were driven out of Kenya when Omani forces took the port city of Mombasa and the nearby island of Zanzibar. Oman built up an empire that covered much of East Africa, in particular the Swahili coast, and parts of India. With the Portuguese pushed out of most of the Indian Ocean trade, both Holland and Britain were able to force their way into the region. The Dutch East India Company (formed in 1602) and the British East India Company (formed in 1600) took over much of the former Portuguese trade in the Indian Ocean, and the British supplied men and cannons to the conquest of Hormuz. The Dutch were forced to close their factory in Bushire in 1759.[8]

The Dutch established a trading post up the upper gulf, near Basrah, in 1635, but it did not disturb either the Ottomans or the Safavids. In several naval victories over the English, the Dutch maintained their trade in the gulf and access to Iranian goods. In 1651, the imam of Oman, Sultan bin Saif, visited their trading post on the Iranian side of the gulf. He offered to arrange for the Bani Yas to provide camels for the land transport of goods from Basrah to the lower gulf.[9] The Dutch were in an argument with the Iranian port authorities over duties over Persian silk, the Dutch rejected the offer. This was among the first mention of the Bani Yas, a Bedouin tribe that had migrated from Oman and came to live around Liwa oasis.[10] They and most of their allies are Hinawi tribes. The designation of Hinawi and Ghafiri emerged with Oman's civil war that ended the Ya'rubah dynasty in 1749.[11] The Ya'rubah civil war erupted at the death of Sultan II bin Saif in 1718, and the leadership of his young son, Saif II bin Sultan, who was only twelve years old, was contested by Muhammad bin Nasir of the Bani Ghafir tribe. The Ya'rubah had the support of the Hinawi faction, led by Khalaf ibn Mubarak of the Bani Hina. The conflict quickly became a civil war, with tribal confederations supporting one side or the other. In 1737, now grown to manhood, the young Saif II asked for help from the Persian shah Nadir (ruled 1737–1747). Nadir Shah agreed to help and assembled an army that soon occupied Julfar and Khor Fakkan and marched against Buraimi oasis. The Persians defeated the Ghafiri tribal forces in Oman but retired to Julfar, where they launched a new invasion in 1741. In the meantime, a new contender for the imamate arose in the person of Ahmad ibn Sa'id of the Al Bu Sa'idi lineage of Hinawi origin. In 1749, the main Ghafiri contender sought refuge in the Omani town of Suhar, and Ahmad ibn Sa'id refused to hand him over to the Persians. Instead, he formed a coalition of anti-Persian forces made up of factions from all of Oman's tribes and eventually gained independence from the Persians. Although he did not have the full support of the Ghafiri faction, he did have the Hinawi uluma and the merchants from the coast, as well as most of the Ghafiri uluma.

RISE OF THE ARAB SHEIKDOMS IN THE LOWER GULF

The Bani Yas have become one of the most important tribes in the lower gulf. At the heart of the tribe is the Al Bu Falah lineage, which includes the al-Nahyan family, the rulers of Abu Dhabi. As noted above, the Bani Yas seem to have appeared in the distant mists of time, with their name already associated with the island of Sir Bani Yas in a 1580 account of the Venetian jeweler looking into the viability of the pearl trade. He called the island Sirbeniast. Oral tribal history claims the tribe arrived from the Najd (central Arabia) and that the leader, named Yas, dug a well at Liwa. The tribe congregated around him there, making it their chief location, as well as a main producer of dates. The tribe was both sedentary oasis farmers and nomadic Bedouin, shifting between the two main forms of subsistence, with Liwa's fresh water being a major draw for them. The Bani Yas are referred to in early works on the Ya'rubah civil war, and in 1624, the Bani Yas welcomed the contender Nasir ibn Qahtan, who had to retreat from Oman into what is today the area of Abu Dhabi. In the battle between the forces near al-Shayb, the Bani Yas leaders Saqr ibn Isa and Muhammad ibn Isa were killed.[12] The Bani Yas emerged in the eighteenth century as one of the two major powers in what came to be called the United Arab Emirates, gathering smaller tribal groups under their protection.

The second power in the lower gulf region also emerged from the Arab tribes living in the area of Julfar; they were the Qawasim or Qasimi. The Qawasim arrived in today's United Arab Emirates between the fourteenth and eighteenth centuries, perhaps from the Najd (Central Arabia), but their origin is lost in time.[13] More recently, their origin goes back to a Qawasim who set up his tent near Julfar, which came to be called *Ra's al-Khaimah* or Head or Spit of the Tent, which became the modern town of Ras al-Khaimah. Unlike the Bani Yas, who continued living as nomads or seminomads, the Qawasim quickly took to the sea and established themselves as sailors, traders, and pearl divers. The Qawasim belong to the Ghafiri division of Arab tribes, as do most of the people from the northern region of todays United Arab Emirates. When both the Persians and the Omanis left Julfar in 1633, the Qawasim in Sharjah and the new settlement of Ras al-Khaimah took control.[14] They used the Ya'rubah civil war to expand their area, taking over islands in the gulf and the trading center of Lingah in Iran, as well as areas along the Indian Ocean/Arabian Sea coast. Lingah was an important trading center for the British to access Iranian silks and other items, and this led to the confrontation between the British and the Arabs of today's United Arab Emirates.

SHIPBUILDING IN THE GULF

Generally speaking, shipbuilding in the gulf is based on the dhow, a ship with lateens (triangle sails). The term *dhow* is not used in Arabic but seems to be based on the Persian or Indian (Hindi) word *daw,* which has become common in English to refer to the traditional Arab form of ship.[15] There are a number of ship types with different functions, but all are distinguished by having a light draft, making even larger ones able to move close to the shore; they don't need a deep port. Thus, the shallow creeks or *khawr* along the lower gulf, among them Dubai and Sharjah, were used to build protected ports that became havens for pirates. Sharjah became one of the major political centers of the Qawasim, along with the northern ports of Julfar and Ras al-Khaimah; all of them were along shallow creeks that were developed into important ports. Shipbuilding techniques along the gulf were exported to India and East Africa. They used mangrove wood that still grows wild in the creeks near Ajman as well as along the East African coast. In addition, other woods such as teak were used in the construction of the ships. Rather than nailing the planks together as was done in European shipbuilding, the planks were sewn together using rope made of fibers from date palm, and the ropes were caulked with tar and fish oil. The construction allowed the ship's sidings to move with the currents and waves, giving the whole structure the ability to stay afloat without a deep keel. The ships are highly maneuverable and very fast, making them perfect for lightning raids against other types of vessels. Ships built with this sewn form of construction are called *mtepe* in Swahili and quickly replaced older outrigger canoes once trade with Arabia began.[16] The above-water portions of the ships are covered in a protective layer made of shark's oil, while the area below the water is covered in lime and sheep's fat.[17]

Of the several types of ships built, the *batil* was preferred by the pirates because it was fast, manned by sails and oars, and maneuverable.[18] Its bow was long and narrow, with fine lines that made a sharp cut in the water. It had a distinctive shape, with a bow piece in the form of a fiddle. The stern was high, with a horse's head carved on it, and the rudder had a horse's tail carved on it. This was, perhaps, because of the use of horses in battle due to their quick maneuverability and speed. A *batil* did not have a large carrying capacity, and once the British forced a treaty on the gulf states, they were rarely used other than by admirals of pearling fleets. The warships were fitted out with deck cannons mounted in the fore and aft of the ships, again, for lightning strikes similar to land warfare by cavalry. Although the *batil* were large ships, they were not built to haul freight, and two types of large, ocean-worthy ships were built, the *baghlah* and the *bum*. The Arab merchants of the gulf preferred—and still prefer—the *bum* over the *baghlah* because the *bum* has finer lines and does better in the open ocean. Although the *bum* is slightly smaller, its shape allows for it to carry loads of up to three hundred tons.[19] The *baghlah* had a square back, used as a room by the captain, and the outside had lavish decorations carved into the wood, including designs that are suspected to be copies of those used by the Portuguese centuries ago. For example, the mid-twentieth century British explorer Wilfred Thesiger noted that some of them had the Latin letters IHS inscribed on the high, carved sterns, which he supposed were initially in imitation to Portuguese galleons.[20]

Most ships meant for the pearling fleets are smaller, but they are still sleek for quick maneuverability. Like the larger war and cargo ships, they are equipped with sails, usually two, and oars for when the winds fail to fill the sails. The larger cargo ships often have three sails in addition to oars. The two ships most used by pearling fleets were and still are the sambuk and the *shu'ai*, with, as noted above, only the admiral in a *batil*. The sambuk is the larger of the two types, and to allow for the crew's movements on board, the entire deck is flat. It allows for the easy use of oars, often needed when the fleet is together and individual ships need to make quick turns. The main difference between the two types is that the sambuk has a different shape and the size of the bow/stem piece, which is somewhat thick at the bottom and rises to a sharp end that is painted. The *shu'ai's* bow piece is a bit taller and thinner, making the ships easy to identify in profile. The sambuk is used only for pearling, while the smaller *shu'ai* is used both for pearling and fishing. In addition, like the *batil*, the sambuk's stern is decorated with wood carvings, making it an elegant craft.

Dickson states that in the past, Kuwait was known for the best ships because the wood was allowed to dry thoroughly before being cut into planks for new ships.[21] Nonetheless, nearly all of the ports along the gulf—on both the Arab and the Persian shores—still have shipbuilding harbors. Abu Dhabi has an active one, as do Qatar, Bahrain, and Basrah in Iraq. Ships were, and are, also built along the Swahili coast of East Africa and in India. Despite statements made in the 1940s and 1950s predicting the end of traditional shipbuilding, the craft continues in Oman, the United Arab Emirates, Qatar, Bahrain, Kuwait, and southern Iraq. Today, many of the ships that put into harbor in the United Arab Emirates have flags from East Africa (Somalia, Kenya, and Tanzania) and Iran. Traditional shipbuilding is still a needed craft, as ships carry cargo to and from the traditional ports that were established centuries ago.

NOTES

1. Potts, D. T., et al. *Waves of Time: The History of the United Arab Emirate.* London: Trident Press, 1998, 83.
2. Morton, Michael Quentin. *Keepers of the Golden Shore: A History of the United Arab Emirates.* London: Reaktion Books, 2017, 36.
3. Potts, et al., 87.
4. Carter, J. R. L. *Tribes in Oman.* London: Peninsular Publishing, 1982, 15, 118.
5. Morton, 36.
6. Dinteman, Walter. *Forts of Oman.* Dubai: Motivate Publishing, 1993, 20.
7. Hurreiz, Sayed Hamid. *Folklore and Folklife in the United Arab Emirates.* New York: Routledge, 2004, 20.
8. Al-Qasimi, Sultan bin Muhammad. *The Myth of Arab Piracy in the Gulf.* New York: Routledge, 1998, 1.
9. Morton, 37.
10. Hurreiz, 20.
11. Heard-Bey, Frauke. *From Trucial States to United Emirates.* Dubai: Motivate Publishing, 2004, 275, 277.
12. Morton, 40.

13. Hurreiz, 21.

14. Potts, et al., 90.

15. Shoup, John. "Dhow," in *Saudi Arabia and the Gulf Arab States: An Encyclopedia of Life in the Arab States*, edited by Sebastian Maisel and John A. Shoup. Westport CT: Greenwood Press, 2009, 111.

16. Middleton, John. *African Merchants of the Indian Ocean: Swahili of the East African Coast*. Long Grove, IL: Waveland Press, Inc., 2004, 10.

17. Dickson, H. R. P. *The Arab of the Desert: A Glimpse into Badawin Life in Kuwait and Sau'di Arabia*, 3rd edition. London: George Allen and Unwin, 1983, 213.

18. Ibid., 217.

19. Ibid., 219.

20. Thesiger, Wilfred. *Arabian Sands*. London: Longmans, Green and Co., 1960, 219. (See also the photo of the stern of a ship in Thesiger, Wilfred. *Crossing the Sands*. Dubai: Motivate Publishing, 2006, 137.)

21. Dickson, 216.

6

The Pirate Coast and the British Trade with India (1700–1820)

THE BANI YAS BEDOUIN TO 1820

The eighteenth century saw the rise of different local powers in the lower gulf, with the Qawasim in Ras al-Khaimah and the Sharjah, and the Bani Yas in Liwa, Abu Dhabi, and Dubai. Fujairah emerged under the Sharqiyin tribe that broke from the Qawasim in the nineteenth century. The Sharqiyin are the second-largest tribal group in the United Arab Emirates today; only the Bani Yas are larger.[1] They are of Bedouin origin and, with allied tribes, dominate the Shamaliyah, the northeastern coast between the two areas that belong to Oman, the Musandam in the north and Khor Kalba in the south.

The Bani Yas broke into major lineages, each centered on what eventually became the cities of Abu Dhabi and Dubai. The Al Bu Falah descend from Falah, who lived in the eighteenth century. From him descends the al-Nahyan, named for one of his sons.[2] The al-Nahyan become the paramount shaykh of the Bani Yas tribal group; although each lineage had their own shaykh elected from their own lineage, the al-Nahyan were seen as the head of the entire tribe. Dhiyab bin Isa al-Nahyan became the shaykh of the entire Bani Yas in the eighteenth century, and the town of Abu Dhabi was founded during his time. Abu Dhabi's current location was an uninhabited island, cut off from the mainland by a shallow lagoon that was easy to wade across most of the day, until high tide, when the amount of water increased. In recent years, the lagoon is crossed by two bridges, but in the past, the places where it could be crossed were protected by armed guards in watchtowers. In 1761, a group of Bani Yas tribesmen were on the island hunting deer or gazelle when one of them came across a freshwater spring. Among the tribesmen were members of the Al Bu Falah who settled there, and thus, the town of Abu Dhabi (or "he of the deer") was born. The Al Bu Falah built a watchtower next to the well, and people came and settled nearby. In an alternative story, the first to find freshwater on the island was a fisherman who settled there and founded the town. Whether it was founded by a fisherman or by a band of Bedouin hunters, Abu Dhabi's freshwater source attracted settlers. The crossings onto the island were protected by watchtowers manned by Bedouin guards who trained their rifles on each caravan coming to the island. The main crossing was at al-Maqta', and a modern bridge follows the path across the lagoon. In the past, the crossing was considered dangerous, with any careless step causing a camel and its load of goods to be lost to the water. Another watchtower protected the eastern approach to the island at Batin.

Shaykh Dhiyab spent only a few months of the year on the island, and the oasis of Liwa remained the capital of his territory. Some four hundred homes built of palm fronds housed Liwa's population of fishermen and pearl divers or workers on pearling ships. In 1793, Dhiyab was assassinated by his cousin Hazza during an argument. Hazza tried to take over the leadership of the Bani Yas, but Dhiyab's son Shakhbut, with the support of the tribal members, became the new shaykh. Hazza went into exile, and his followers were killed by Shakhbut's men. In 1795, Shakhbut left Liwa and set up his residence in Abu Dhabi, making it his new capital. He built his fort at the site of the first tower at the freshwater spring, which, over the years was expanded. Today it is called Qasr al-Hosn. It served as the center or power until the current century.

The Bani Yas tribe was plagued with intrigue by various members, each vying for control. In 1816, Shakhbut was deposed by his own son, Muhammad, but Muhammad was deposed by a younger brother named Tahnun. In 1818, Muhammad sought refuge in Doha (in Qatar) and bided his time while his younger brother, Tahnun, remained shaykh. In 1824, Muhammad, in alliance with the Manasir, who still occupy the area between the United Arab Emirates and Qatar, attacked Abu Dhabi, but Tahnun repelled them. Tahnun was a firm ally of the sultan of Oman and was aided by the Awamir who lived across the desert from Liwa to Laila in Saudi Arabia to just north of the Rub' al-Khali, or Empty Quarter. Shakhbut remained an important voice in the Bani Yas tribe, acting in place of his son and even signing treaties in his name.

In 1833, Tahnun was killed by two of his brothers, Khalifa and Sultan. To secure his position as shaykh, Khalifa sought aid from the new power in Arabia, ibn Sa'ud. Muhammad thought this was his chance to take back his position, but Shakhbut supported the two younger sons against Muhammad.[3] This did not end the plots, and eventually, there was a plot against Khalifa by his cousin and led to Khalifa taking bloody revenge against those who plotted the coup. This ultimately split the family and resulted in the move of some thirty-seven hundred Bani Yas to Bur Dubai, where they set up a new settlement, under the leadership of the Al Bu Falasah, shaykh Maktoum bin Buti. This move placed a Bani Yas settlement in close proximity to their enemies, the Qasim in Sharjah. Only the *khawr* or creek (it is actually a shallow saltwater inlet from the gulf) separates the two, and even today, it serves as the border between the two emirates.

The Bani Yas sought closer connections with the sultan of Oman in order to protect themselves from the Qasimi of Sharjah and Ras al-Khaimah, while the Qasimi sought closer connections with the al-Sa'ud to counter the spreading Bani Yas. In 1802, the Wahhabi, as the Qasimi form of fundamentalist Sunni Islam came to be called, appeared in Buraimi (al-Ain) oasis to challenge the sultan of Oman and the Bani Yas tribe. The Ottoman Turks were alarmed by the growing power of the al-Sa'ud family and their attacks on Muslims who had not converted to their fundamentalist outlook. They and their governor of Egypt, Muhammad Ali, sent his son, Ibrahim Pasha, with enough troops to end their "outrages" against pilgrims to Makkah (Mecca). In 1818, the Egyptian forces overwhelmed the al Sa'ud tribal forces in their Najdi stronghold and brought an end to the fist Saudi state.[4] In order to respond to the threat posed by the Egyptian/Turkish troops, the Sa'udi leader, Muhammad al Sa'ud, was forced to give up concerns in Buraimi and the attempt to bring Oman under his control.

The Omani sultan, Sa'id bin Sultan (ruled 1804–1856) expanded his state into the Dhufar, and parts of the East African coast were freed of the Wahhabi threat.

THE QAWASIM EMPIRE UNTIL 1820

The Qasimi were bitter rivals of the Bani Yas and represented the more settled parts of the coast and inland villages. The *khawr* is the setting for a number of skirmishes between the Bani Yas and the Qasimi of Sharjah. The Qasimi, it is said, are of the Huwala Arab tribes that moved back and forth from Siraf in Iran to the Arab side of the gulf. They belong to the Ghafiri coalition of tribes that inhabit the area north of the *khawr* at Dubai. They have a strong urban merchant class that deal in pearls and trade with their own powerful fleet of ships. Even today, Huwala families make up a powerful merchant class in the gulf from Kuwait to Bahrain and south into Qatar and the United Arab Emirates. They are Sunni Muslims and have lost power in Iran but remain the main international trading class on the Arab side of the gulf and into East Africa. The first mention of a Qasimi shyakh is in 1718 when the amir of Julfar (Ra's al-Khaimah), Rahma bin Matar, is

The Shindagha Fort in Dubai was once used as the residence of the shaykhs of Dubai and is now partially open as a museum. (Courtesy of John A. Shoup)

noted by the Dutch in dispatches.⁵ In 1720, the Qawasim seized the port of Basaidu on the island of Qeshm, seriously affecting the collection of taxes by the Persians and the British.⁶ This led the British East India Company to send a military expedition against the Qawasim in 1727 to force them to return what they considered to be their share of customs taxes collected.⁷ This began the nearly century of intermittent warfare between the British and the Gulf Arabs.

WAHHABI INFLUENCE IN ARABIA AND THE QAWASIM EMPIRE

In 1800, a new power burst into the political landscape of the lower gulf. Troops sent by the amir of the Najd, central Arabia, forced the Na'im and Dhawahir tribes to surrender their portions of the important oasis of Buraimi to 'Abd al-'Aziz ibn Sa'ud (ruled 1765–1803). Ibn Sa'ud was the leader of a new religious movement that was based on a strong, fundamentalist belief in Sunni Islam, popularly called Wahhabism, named after its founder, the religious scholar Muhammad ibn 'Abd al-Wahhab (1703–1791). The Wahhabis themselves reject the name Wahhabi and, instead, refer to themselves as the Muwahidun or Unitarians. They condemned the lax practice of Islam by many Sunnis, rejected the beliefs of the Shi'ites, and set about trying to force others to follow their form of fundamentalist Islam. They followed the fundamentals of Islamic law as laid out by ibn Hanbal (780–855), founder of one of the four schools (*madhhab*, or madhab, in singular and *madhahab* in plural) of Sunni Islam. Initially, they had success in overrunning the oasis of al-Ahsa on the gulf coast in 1780, and then were able to invade and take the cities of Karabala (in Iraq) in 1801 and Mecca in 1803. Like the Qaramitah in the past, they were able to find support from the Bedouin tribes in the Najd and, more importantly, from the settled oasis farmers. Their movement was supported by converts in Oman, Ibadi Khawarij, who already followed a very strict version of Islam, as well as those who converted due to their military success. In Buraimi, they found support from the Qawasim and the Na'im and enmity from the sultan/imam of Oman and his Bani Yas allies.

The founder of the Wahhabi movement, Muhammad ibn 'Abd al-Wahhab, was born in 1703 in the central Arabian (Najd) village of Uyayna. He was from the settled oasis farmer origin (not a Bedouin, as is often mistakenly said), and early in his studies, the works of the Hanbali (one of the four schools of Sunni Islam) scholar ibn Taymiyyah (1263–1328) influenced his interpretation of religion. Ibn

Taymiyyah wrote religious decisions for the Sunni mamluks against other Muslims, who were seen to be not following Islam as they should. Normally, it is consider illegal to war against fellow Muslims, but ibn Taymiyyah allowed it, making him popular among the fundamentalists, such as Islamic State in Iraq and Sham (ISIS) and al-Qaida, today. 'Abd al-Wahhab targeted practices that were "un-Islamic," such as building tombs for saintly men and visiting them and charms for health or good luck. Both ibn Taymiyyah and 'Abd al-Wahhab had a special dislike for Shi'ites, calling them *ahl al-bida'a*, or people of innovation.

In 1744, he established a strong tie with Muhammad al Sa'ud in the Sa'udi town of Dar'iyah, also in central Arabia, after being forced out of his natal town of Uyayna. The two leaders, one religious and the other political, set about the origins of Saudi Arabia, and the small Saudi state quickly gained in economic strength. The new political entity began its program of jihad or religious war of expansion. By 1792, the Najd of Uyayna was in Sa'udi-Wahhabi hands, with the major towns of Riyadh, Kharj, and Qassim surrendering to Saudi control.[8] In 1780, the Saudis brought the gulf oases and the island of Bahrain under their rule, and the path to the lower gulf and Oman was open to them. The initial success continued with the conquest or pillage of the Iraqi town of Karbala in 1801, surrender of Taif in 1802, and conquest of Mecca in 1803. In 1808, 1810, and 1812, Baghdad was threatened by Saudi forces, and in 1810, villages in southern Syria were also raided by them.[9] In 1800, they arrived in the Buraimi oasis and planned to use it as their base to invade Oman.

The Ottomans had enough of the Saudis and, in 1811, sent the governor of Egypt, Muhammad 'Ali, to deal with them. The Saudis had taken both of the holy cities of Medina and Mecca, preventing Muslim pilgrims from Syria and Egypt entering. The Ottoman sultans had inherited the caretakership of the two cities from the mamluks, and the Saudis now threatened this important status. Muhammad 'Ali sent his son Tusun with an army, and by 1813, Mecca and Taif were free from Saudi control. The Egyptian forces pushed into the Najd, but Tusun was unable to force the Saudi leader, 'Abdallah (ruled 1814–1818), to negotiate an end to the conflict. In 1816, Muhammad 'Ali recalled Tusun and replaced him with another son, Ibrahim. Ibrahim quickly put 'Abdallah under siege and, in 1818, conquered and put to flame and sword the town of Dar'iyah.

In the lower gulf, the Saudi forces built one of the major forts in the oasis of Buraimi, from which they commanded the military governorship. With Qawasim and Na'im support, they gained control over most of the gulf coast by 1803 and even attempted the conquest of Oman.[10] Starting in 1812, the Ottomans turned to the new and energetic governor of Egypt, Muhammad'Ali, who invaded the Hejaz to take back the cities of Mecca and Medina, which was accomplished in 1813, as noted above. In 1818, the Egyptian forces, led by Ibrahim, captured the capital of the first Saudi state at Dar'iyah (near Riyadh) and captured the amir 'Abdallah. 'Abdallah was sent to Cairo and then on to Istanbul, where he was executed. The Egyptian forces destroyed the town of Dar'iyah and burned the date groves to break the power of the Saudis.

The Wahhabis rose again under the leadership of Turki bin 'Abdullah (ruled 1824–1834) and regained most of their territory until between 1835 and 1840, when the Egyptians and Ottomans retook control of central Arabia. In the gulf, the British contained the Wahhabis. In politics and history of the lower gulf, the Saudi's claim to Buraimi continued to plague the Bani Yas' leadership and the sultan of Oman until 1974, when King Faisal agreed to end Saudi claims and recognize United Arab Emirate and Omani claims to the oasis. Although the Na'im tribe adopted the Wahhabi doctrine, they turned against the Saudis in 1868 and threw their weight behind the Bani Yas' shaykh. Later, the Na'im occasionally backed the sultan of Oman and his claims to a share of the oasis.[11]

BRITAIN IN THE LOWER GULF

The last power to enter the gulf was Great Britain. England opened a trading post in the lower gulf in 1600 in competition with the Dutch and the Portuguese and gave aid to the Arabs and Persians to drive out the Portuguese, as noted above. The Dutch remained the main rival for trade with Iran for silks and other costly luxury goods, and in 1616, the English were given the rights to open a factory (trading house) by Shah 'Abbas I (ruled 1588–1627) in Iran.[12] The English forced the other Europeans to leave, and the last were the Dutch, who were forced to give up to the English in the numerous wars between the two powers. By 1800, the English were the main European power in the gulf and fairly soon fell into conflict with the Qawasim of Ras al-Khaimah. The British named the lower gulf the Pirate Coast or Pirate Oman.

The Qawasim became jealous of the English traders in the gulf, even though the English paid well for the pearls from Ras al-Khaimah and Sharjah. In 1778, a three-day battle between an East India Company ship and the Qawasim ended with the capture of the English vessel.[13] The Qawasim justified the seizure of the ship on the grounds that it was flying an Omani flag, and the Qawasim were at war with Oman at that time. The Omani sultan Sayyid Sultan bin Ahmad (ruled 1792–1804) was an ally of the English, and the Qawasim were concerned about British involvement in the war. The Omanis wanted to gain control of the entire gulf and engaged in a war not only against the Qawasim in the lower gulf but also against the 'Utub Bedouin tribes in the upper gulf, who gained control from Qatar to Kuwait. The British, in their Persian base of Bushire, encouraged British ships to fly the Omani flag as a degree of protection, but the 1778 Qawasim seizure of a British ship began a long period of warfare.

The Qawasim demanded a ransom of 4,000 rupees for the crew, ship, and cargo (perhaps some $60,000 U.S. today). A year later, in 1779, the East India Company ships the *Success* and the *Assistance* fought off separate attacks, but neither attack could be attributed to the Qawasim. However, in 1790, the British ship the *Beglerbeg* was captured off the coast of Musandam, and in 1797, the ship *Bassin* fought a day-long battle with a fleet of Qawasim ships and was captured. The shaykh Saqr bin Rashid al-Qasimi of Ras al-Khaimah protested that the attack was a "misunderstanding" and that the Qawasim had nothing against the British, who were their "honorable friends."[14] Also, in 1797, the British ship the *Viper* was attacked by a Qawasim fleet under Salih, the nephew of shaykh Saqr, while riding at anchor in the port of Bushire on the Iranian side of the gulf. The attack was beaten off after an attempt to board the ship; again, the excuse for the action by the Qawasim was that the British were allied with Omanis, and shaykh Saqr claimed that Salih had acted on his own without his knowledge.

The Qawasim allied themselves with the Wahhabis when they invaded Buraimi in 1800. The Wahhabis' plan was the conquest of the Arabian Peninsula, and the Al Bu Sa'idi of Oman stood in their way, both religiously and politically. The British signed a treaty with the Omanis and, thus, became the enemies of the Wahhabis and the Qawasim. British trade in the gulf included arms with Iran and with the pro-British Arabs along the gulf coast. Shaykh Saqr died in 1803 and was succeeded as ruler by his son Sultan. He contested control of Buraimi with the Bani Yas, as well as with the Omanis. In 1804, the Omani sultan Sayyid bin Ahmad died at sea and left Oman weak, and the Qawasim took advantage. They joined with the Arab Bani Mu'in tribe on the gulf island Qeshm and, with their Arab relatives in the Iranian port of Lingah, they took the Omani port in Iran called Bandar

'Abbas and the upper gulf island of Kharg, off the coast of Iraq. The Qawasim blocked the Omani fleet in their harbors as they had been blocked in the past by the Omanis. They then attacked two British ships in late 1804, capturing both the *Shannon* and the *Trimmer*. Both were refitted and reused by the Qawasim as part of their fleet, but the ships were privately owned by the East India Company representative in Basrah. The ships' owner, a private citizen who worked for the East India Company, had built up his personal fleet of transportation ships in the gulf, and the two that were taken were his ships rather than the company's ships. The result was that in 1805, the Qawasim were banned from Indian ports under British control. Sultan al-Qasimi began to lose control over other tribes because of the extortion in taxes by the Wahhabis in Buraimi and due to the arrival of a strong British fleet in the gulf.

Napoleon's campaigns in Europe caused Britain fears in the east, especially when Russia went to war with Iran. The British resident in Muscat, Oman, decided to propose a peace with Sultan, and it was signed in Bandar 'Abbas in 1806. Britain gave up the cargo of the captured ship *Trimmer* and allowed Qawasim ships to trade at British ports, in exchange for ships under the British flag and Britain's allies being given free sailing in the gulf. Sultan did not consult his Wahhabi allies, and they rejected the treaty. However, the British also made the Qawasim promise to give them a three-month warning should the jihad at sea begin again against foreign ships and made them agree to pay 30,000 Maria Theresa thalers or dollars if they broke the treaty. The Maria Theresa thalers or dollars were minted in Austria starting in 1741 and served as a standard weight of silver up to the present day, weighing 23.389 grams or .752 troy ounces. It is used to weigh silver jewelry being sold in Oman, the U.A.E., and other Middle Eastern countries today. The Arabs call it Abu Rish because of the double-headed eagle of the Hapsburg dynasty on one side of the coin; it has a very buxom portrait of the Austrian monarch on the other and, long after her death, the coin is minted and circulated today.[15]

In 1808, the Qawasim broke the treaty and attacked the ship *Lively*, but the attack was repulsed. The Qawasim dispatched a fleet of some twenty ships into the Arabian Sea for a major attack on the Indian Ocean shipping, and in the same year (1808), two dhows attacked the British ship *Fury*, which were again beaten off. Later the same year, the British ship the *Neptune* was attacked but was able to escape. Again, the British ship the *Sylph* was attacked and nearly taken, with great loss of life, until the fellow ship the *Nereide* arrived in time to rescue the *Sylph*

Dhows with fish traps made of woven metal wire. (Courtesy of John A. Shoup)

and drive off the attack. Sultan's power base was slowly eroded away, and in 1808, the Wahhabi governor of Buraimi appointed another as the shaykh along the Arabian Sea coast in Fujairah, Khor Fakkan, and Dibba. In addition, in 1809, shaykh Sultan and two of his qadis, or religious judges, were called to the Najd to defend themselves against the alleged charges of not sharing the British ships' cargos and not paying enough zakat, as demanded by both the Wahhabi qadi to the lower gulf and by the Wahhabi governor of Buraimi.[16] In his absence, Sultan nominated his brother, Hasan, as the shaykh of Ras al-Khaimah. Hasan and another brother Ibrahim considered themselves to be true believers in Islam, and Hasan deemed himself to be the *Amir al-Mu'minin*, or "commander of the faithful," and nominated Ibrahim as the commodore of the Qawasim fleet against the foreigners and nonbelievers. At the same time, the British planned an invasion of the lower gulf to end Qawasim interference in East India Company's trade.

In spring 1809, the Qawasim fleet attacked the British ship *Minerva*, which put up a two-day running fight. It was overcome and captured with loss of life among the crew, and an Englishwoman, Mrs. Robert Taylor, was captured and held for ransom.[17] She was ransomed for a sum of 1,000 Maria Theresa dollars.

Following this attack, the British East India Company planned a punishing raid into Qawasim territory. The commander in charge was told to not engage with any Wahhabi forces but only with forces of the

Qawasim. In the fall of that year, sixteen ships and a ground force of thirteen hundred troops arrived off the coast of Ras al-Khaimah. The ships intercepted the *Minerva*, now acting as a vessel of the Qawasim fleet, and captured and burned it. The fleet then bombarded the town, while, inside the fort, the leadership of the Qawasim met to decide what action to take. The men decided to fight but sent the elderly, women, and children to hide in the nearby palm grove. In the morning, the British troops landed and, with the support of cannons offloaded from some of the ships, they defeated the Qawasim forces and overran the town and put it to the torch. They also destroyed fifty ships of the Qawasim fleet. The British then returned to their ships and left to deal with the Qawasim forces in Lingah. They found the port deserted but destroyed some twenty ships in the harbor. On the island of Qeshm, the tribal leader of the Bani Mu'in decided to surrender the town of Lift after some eighty tribesmen were killed or wounded in the bombardment of the town.

The British fleet then cruised the gulf, attacking any and all ships flying the Qasimi flag, and destroyed some destroyed vessels. The British banned trade with the Qasimi and, in particular, trade in the teak wood needed to rebuild their fleet with wood imported from Africa. In the meantime, shaykh Sultan returned from the Najd, and in 1814, with renewed help from 'Abdallah ibn Sa'ud, the Qawasim were again able to take to the sea. However, the Qasimi ruler of Sharjah, Sultan ibn Saqr, withdrew his support for Ras al-Khaimah and joined with the ruler of Oman, Sayyid Sa'id, in an effort to overthrow Ras al-Khaimah's control over the lower gulf. Between 1812 and 1814, Oman launched three expeditions against Ras al-Khaimah but failed to destroy the Qawasim fleet. The British, as allies of the Omanis, felt sure that recent attacks on ships flying the British flag were the fault of Hasan ibn Rahma and his representatives in the gulf. When the ship *Ahmad Shah* was attacked, blame fell on Hasan and Ras al-Khaimah. The *Ahmad Shah* was a native ship flying the British flag, and when it ran aground near Qeys Island, it was first looted by people under the control of the shaykh of Charak. Part of the loot taken was a shipment of horses that were brought to Ras al-Khaimah, but Charak was under the Persian king's authority. Hasan denied any involvement with the incident but did admit to allowing his ships to raid the coast of Sindh, which was not under British control. Neither the amir of Najd and Hasan wanted to anger the British and agreed to pay restitution for any British ship that was attacked by his fleet. In 1814, Hasan's representative, Hasan ibn Muhammad ibn Ghayth, was authorized to sign a peace agreement with the British agreeing not to attack ports in India or ships flying the British flag, and the Qawasim fleet would fly a special flag. The agreement was ratified in India by the East India Company, and a ship was sent to Ras al-Khaimah. Upon reaching Tunb Island, the British ship was visited by the shaykh of Sharjah, and then proceeded on to Ras al-Khaimah, but it was attacked in the harbor. Hasan later claimed that the attack was done by Na'im tribesmen from Ajman, a separate tribal group under the control of the Qasimi of Ras al-Khaimah.

In 1815, men of the Bani Yas seized control of a native ship flagged with a British flag, and then brought it to Sharjah. Shaykh Sultan seized the ship and refused to return it or pay for its cargo. In 1816, three British ships were attacked, and most of the crews were killed by Qawasim ships in the Red Sea. This caused the British to claim that Ras al-Khaimah broke the 1806 treaty, and the British attempted to demonstrate their displeasure. However, the British ships could not come close enough to the shore, and their cannons either did not reach the walls of the fort or proved ineffective. The crowd watching on shore cheered, angering the British even more. In the end, the British had no choice but to retreat. The British vowed that something would be done to end the piracy of the Qawasim once and for all.

By 1819, the British and their Omani allies were ready to invade and destroy Ras al-Khaimah. The British provided some three thousand men and a fleet of three British naval warships, nine East India ships, and twenty transport ships. They were to meet an Omani fleet of seventy ships and some four thousand armed tribesmen, who would arrive by land, in addition to six hundred men who would arrive with the fleet. The British fleet arrived in late November, and three Qasimi ships that were trying to make the harbor were intercepted. The sultan of Oman's ships reached Ras al-Khaimah the next day, and the landings of troops were unopposed. They marched to the city. Hasan ibn Rahma was greatly weakened by the defection of Sharjah and Ajman and the Egyptian destruction of the Sa'ud power in the Najd. Nonetheless, he decided to fight with his four thousand men, armed with muskets and cannons. After three days, the walls were breached, and Hasan's brother Ibrahim died trying to retake a bastion. Hasan entered negotiations with the British commander, but these failed. In the meantime, the heavy guns were disembarked from the ships that lent aid to the attack, and the walls of the fort were breached. The British flag was raised above the fort, and the battle ended. The population retreated across the *khawr* and escaped to the nearby mountains, leaving the British with a deserted town. The British seized sixty ships and numerous cannons and destroyed them all, leaving a smoldering ruin. Hasan then appeared in the British camp to ask for peace. As the peace deal was hammered out between the Qasimi leader and the British, the British fleet moved up and down the entire length of the gulf and destroyed what was left of the Qawasim Empire. Ports, fortifications, and ships were destroyed and left in smoking ruin. In the meantime, after the fall of Ras al-Khaimah to the British, the Omani land army arrived. Slowly, one by one, each of the shaykhs signaled their surrender, and even the Bani Yas shaykh Shakhbut and the leader of the 'Utub Bedouin on Bahrain wanted to be included to ensure they were distanced from any connection with the Qawasim. In total, six shaykhs of the lower gulf signed the treaty, and these formed the Trucial Oman States that formed the United Arab Emirates with the addition of Fujairah in 1952.[18] In July 1820, the British withdrew to India, leaving a small garrison to maintain the peace. As a result, Omani merchants were very happy, as they were able to trade in the gulf again, unopposed by the Qawasim.[19]

The Qawasim were defeated in battle, and their shipping was restricted to small crafts that could not be used as war vessels. The British enforced a new flag on the rulers of the lower gulf; instead of the all-red flag of precious years, the new flag was white, with a red square in the middle. The leadership was lost by Hasan, and he was replaced by Sultan ibn Saqr, who also ruled two smaller Qasimi sheikdoms. Some raiding by the Bani Yas continued in the gulf, but by 1835, this also ended in a maritime truce. In 1853, Britain imposed a total truce on the sea (but not on land) in return for British protection from the Ottomans and the Persians.

NOTES

1. Heard-Bey, Frauke. *From Trucial States to United Arab Emirates*. Dubai: Motivate Publishing, 2004, 72.
2. Morton, Michael Quentin. *Keepers of the Golden Shore: A History of the United Arab Emirates*. London: Reaktion Books, 2016, 40.
3. Ibid., 45.
4. Maisel, Sebastian and Shoup, John A. *Saudi Arabia and the Gulf Arab States Today: An Encyclopedia of Life in the Arab States*. Westport, CT: Greenwood Press, 2009, 389.
5. Morton, 54.
6. Heard-Bey, 280.
7. Ibid., 280.
8. Al Rasheed, Madawi. *Politics in an Arabian Oasis: The Rashidis of Saudi Arabia*. New York: I.B. Tauris, 1991, 32.

9. Ibid., 33–34.
10. Heard-Bey, 278.
11. Ibid., 60–61.
12. Al-Qasim, Sultan Muhammad. *The Myth of the Arab Piracy in the Gulf.* New York: Routledge, 1988, 1.
13. Morton, 55.
14. Ibid., 55.
15. Ibid., 58.
16. Ibid., 59.
17. Ibid., 60.
18. Ibid., 63.
19. Heard-Bey, 283.

7

Trucial Oman and the Discovery of Oil (1820–1971)

TREATY OF 1820 AND MARITIME TRADE IN THE GULF

The war of 1819–1820 ushered in a period of peace and trade to the gulf, establishing the region as a special one that eventually developed into the United Arab Emirates and calling the various small states that signed the treaty the Trucial States or Trucial Oman. The British forced the Qawasim forces of the lower gulf to surrender but allowed Omani merchants to safely access the Persian Gulf and allowed other Arabs from the north secure passage into the Indian Ocean. The Qawasim considered the British a major competitor for trade in the Indian Ocean and the gulf, but this ended with their defeat by the British. The Hinawi ruler of Oman and his Hinawi allies in Dubai and Abu Dhabi also signed the treaty. The treaty was signed in Ras al-Khaimah by Hasan ibn Rahma, followed by Qadib ibn Ahmad of Jazirat al-Hamra, Shakhbut bin Dhiyab for Shaykh Tahnun of Abu Dhabi, and Husayn ibn Ali of Rams. The leader of Dubai sent his uncle, Muhammad ibn Hazza, to sign the treaty in Sharjah, as did the representative sent by the shaykh of Bahrain. The rulers of Ajman and Umm al-Quwain signed the treaty aboard a British ship a few months later—marking the first time these two emirates were recognized as being independent. The maritime peace brought a period of relative prosperity to the gulf as a whole and allowed the pearl trade to flourish. In 1823, Qeshm was evacuated by the Qawasim, and in 1825, a British resident, called a native agent, was installed in Sharjah by the government of Bombay (for the East India Company).[1] As in other parts of the expanding British Empire, a native agent was often a local ruler rather than a British citizen, and in the case of the gulf, he was an Arab under the command of the British agent located in Bushehr, across the gulf in Iran. The treaty allowed for the eventual unity of the region, which included Bahrain and Qatar, to join the United Arab Emirates in the twentieth century, but both Bahrain and Qatar decided to be their own independent states. In addition, the coinage along the gulf coast was the Indian rupee, but in the interior, the Austrian Maria Theresa thaler remained in use until the twentieth century. British India became the de facto ruler of the gulf, both on the Persian and the Arabian shores.

The Maritime Treaty was enforced, and local Arab rulers came to see the British as a system of justice they could turn to when conflict between Arab neighbors loomed. With the peace, the pearl industry grew and needed protection, which was covered in a separate peace treaty that declared that the months used for pearling season, May to November, were to be free of conflict between the Arab rulers and their captains.[2] This was expanded in 1843 with a ten-year truce between the Arab states. This led to a stabilization of relations between the Ghafiri Qawasim and the Hinawi Bani Yas, the two main rivals in the region. Warfare on land was allowed, but on the seas, the British maintained peace. Some breaches of the maritime treaty did occur between the rivals, but in general, they were of the nature of tribal *ghazw* or raids not unlike those between tribal groups on land. In 1853, the British resident in Bushehr proposed a permanent peace, and between May 4 and 9, 1853, all the local leaders signed the treaty.[3]

The British turned their attention to the slave trade, and though they brought an end to the trans-Atlantic trade by 1833, it remained a problem, with the Spanish and Portuguese remaining the most important offenders. Britain passed the antislavery act in 1807 and, in 1833, passed another antislavery act that was to be enforced in the territories under the control of the East India Company and the British government. Special deals were made with Oman, and Oman sent a representative to East Africa to help ensure that no European or European ship would be allowed to traffic in slavery. African slaves were needed to help produce the agricultural output of Oman and its African dependencies, and in the Arab sheikdoms in the gulf, their labor was needed for the production of pearls. They staffed pearling ships and worked as divers to collect the natural pearls. Much of the warfare was sparked by competition between Arab states and in the recovery of debts between citizens of the different states rather than attacks on foreign shipping. Nonetheless, the British were anxious about the trade in African slaves that were sent to Arabia. In 1822, the British signed a treaty with the sultan of Oman that banned the sale of slaves to Christians. In 1838–1839, they forced the sultan of Oman to agree to allow the British the right to stop and search ships thought to be carrying slaves and allowed the British to seize cargos of slaves. In 1847, the sultan agreed to stop and seize any Omani ship carrying slaves from any port, and in 1856, the Omani leader agreed to turn over to the British any slave brought into his territories. In 1873, this was extended by treaty to the areas administered by Abu Dhabi and Sharjah.

The British found it somewhat easy to impose the ban of the African slave trade in Oman due to Islam's stance on slavery. It is seen as a meritorious act to emancipate slaves, especially if they have been converted to Islam. Children born to slave women and fathered by the owner are to be born free, and the mother freed and married to the owner. This gives her and her children rights to inheritance in Islamic law, and though the man is not required to treat her as the mother of his children, it is expected by social pressure that he do so. The children carry his name and belong to his lineage. Slaves are to be treated with dignity set out in the religion, and it must be remembered that among the close companions of the Prophet was Bilal, a former Ethiopian slave. As such, British efforts to end slavery were met with no real hostility in Oman or the lower gulf where people actually supported the antislavery efforts.[4] Nonetheless, slavery continued in Oman and its possessions in Africa and in the lower gulf until the mid-twentieth century, but British efforts to end the trade in slaves did not generally meet with mass protests by locals. In Oman and Trucial States, many slaves were from India and Pakistan rather than from Africa, a practice that continued into the twentieth century. Nonetheless, much of Omani and Emirati culture is due to African influences in music (in particular musical instruments) and dance. For example, the tall, one-sided drum called the *mesondo* used in dances, such as the liwa, is of East African origin. Similarly, such practices as *zar* or afflictions caused by spirits/jinni were seen as "African" in origin, and in Wahhabi held territory, women who were able to interpret which spirit inhabited a person were persecuted as witches. Nonetheless, such practices continued well into the twentieth century in much of the Arabian Peninsula, as attested to by such keen observers as Ronald Codrai, the British agent in Dubai in the 1940s and 1950s.[5]

The long period of Omani occupation of East African ports and the long historic interchange between the Arabs and Africans produced the Swahili (from the Arabic word for coastal or *sawahili*) language and culture. Slaving remained an important part of the economy, both for clove production on the islands off the East African (Zanzibar and Pembe) coast and for pearling in the gulf. Slaves were used as needed labor on the pearling ships and could obtain their freedom by paying off their cost to their owners. Once free, pearling remained a major source of income to former slaves and their families. Those who converted to Islam and learned Arabic were more likely to be freed, and most decided to stay in Oman and the gulf rather than return to Africa. In most of the Arabic-speaking side of the gulf, such connections remain important parts of the social structure, with former slaves of the ruling houses becoming the backbone of the modern military forces. Slaves were (and are) considered more loyal to the ruling houses, while tribal levies were unreliable, changing loyalties as need dictated.

CONTINUED SAUDI/WAHHABI INFLUENCE IN THE TRUCIAL STATES

As the British influence grew in the gulf, conflicts became more local. Oman, as an ally of Britain, defended itself against aggression mostly from the Wahhabis from the Najd or Central Arabia, who still claimed parts of the Buraimi oasis. The conflict was further confused by some of the local *qusur* (plural of *qasr* or fortifications) who openly sided with the Wahhabis. The first Saudi incursion into Buraimi ended in 1818 as a real threat to Oman and the fall of the amir 'Abdallah to the Ottoman/Egyptian forces. In 1824, a revival of Saudi-Wahhabi power emerged with the rule of Turki bin 'Abdullah and then Faisal bin Turki. This would not be resolved until 1974 when Shaykh Zayed of Abu Dhabi and King Faisal of Saudi Arabia brought an end to the dispute. As noted, the Saudis arrived in 1800 with a force of some seven hundred cavalry, a rather large force in desert warfare. They quickly took control of several of the local forts and became allies of the Qawasim shaykhs, forcing the Na'im and Dhawahir tribes to capitulate. By 1803, most of the lower gulf was in Saudi control, and they intended to launch an invasion of Oman against the Ibadi Khawarij Al Bu Sa'idi family. They became the enemies of the Bani Yas, pushing them into some of the peripheral communities of Jimi, Qattara, Hili, and Wadi Mas'udi, while the Dhawahir held the forts of al-Ain, al-Daudi, al-Kharid, Mujairib, and Mutaird, located near the center of the oasis. The Na'im held the main oasis settlement of Buraimi. However, in 1812, Muhammad 'Ali of Egypt defeated the Saudi leader in the Najd and conquered their home oasis of Dar'iyah. The Saudis reemerged as a major power in 1830 under the leadership of Turki (ruled 1824–1834) and his son Faisal (ruled 1834–1838). In 1830, Turki retook the gulf oasis of al-Ahsa.[6] He was careful to not provoke the Ottoman and Egyptian troops stationed in the Hejaz by not insisting the Muslims declare adherence to the Wahhabi creed as was required in the past. With the gulf open again to the Saudis, the amir sent a force that returned to Buraimi after attacking Bahrain. In 1834, Turki was killed leaving a mosque after Friday prayer, and his son, Faisal succeeded him as ruler. Faisal was beset by internal intrigue among his relatives as well as a renewed Egyptian force sent to subdue him. In 1836, Egyptian troops landed in the Hejaz and marched into the Najd. They brought with them a cousin of Faisal named Khalid, who was installed as an Egyptian puppet once Faisal was removed. In 1838, Faisal was defeated, Khalid installed in his place, and Faisal was taken to Cairo; however, Faisal escaped from captivity and returned to Arabia.[7] The Egyptian forces withdrew from Arabia in 1840, leaving Khalid on his own, and in 1841, Faisal returned to challenge Khalid. Faisal retook his position as leader from his cousin and ruled until his death in 1865 as a "loyal subject" of the Ottoman sultan, paying taxes and recognizing the sultan as the legitimate ruler of Arabia. Faisal's four sons contested the right to rule in the Najd and weakened the new state until it fell in 1890 to the Shammar (a Bedouin tribe from the northern region of Ha'il), ending the second Saudi/Wahhabi state. Despite the defeat by the Egyptians in 1838, the Saudis did not give up their claim to Buraimi and had local representatives—mainly from the Na'im tribe—pressed their claim until 1974. These Saudi/Wahhabi "invasions" did not include much fighting because those residents under Qawasim protection submitted to Wahhabi domination. Wahhabi warlike ambitions were aimed at Oman rather than the small sheikdoms along the lower gulf that did not produce much in the way of income. The initial Wahhabi force of several hundred horsemen was sizeable for the Arabian Peninsula at the time and could easily intimidate local tribal groups to surrender to them. Their friendly demeanor also allied fears, and once the Qawasim leadership became allies, there was little hostility to the Saudi claim other than from the Bani Yas.

TRIBAL RIVALRIES AMONG THE EMIRATES

Generally speaking, the British were concerned that the local disputes did not include the sea and sea trade but were maintained on land. Most of the disputes changed in nature and were mainly debts local people owed in another of the numerous, small, independent states, and the local rulers did not bring them into the sea but fought them on land. Conflict was more on the level of raids between tribes, and this gave rise to the *firqah harbiyah* (literally the war groups that perform at weddings and celebrations today, with love poetry replacing that of heroes and war exploits) poetry and dance that is still popular in the lower gulf. Conflicts between the local rulers were kept on land and out of British control, though all the local leaders turned to the British to solve many of their problems. The British agent was located in Bushehr, in Iran, and had a deputy housed in Sharjah (later, the agent in Bushehr moved to Bahrain, and the agent in Sharjah moved to Dubai) until 1971.[8] They considered themselves the virtual rulers of the Trucial States and conducted themselves as such until 1939 when Sir Trenchard Craven William Fowle retired and died of lung cancer within a year.[9]

Conflicts occurred through the first half of the twentieth century between Sharjah, Dubai, and Abu Dhabi, occasionally bringing in other tribes in the area. The Bani Yas could often count on the Bedouin Awamir and Manasir in that they not only used the oasis at Liwa but also owned some of the date groves and lived part of the year in Abu Dhabi. The Manasir are today considered to be both Emirati and Saudi citizens, but the tribe has married into the ruling al-Nahyan of Abu Dhabi, who also has influence in the selection of the Bani Yas shaykh.[10]

While the Manasir are closely tied to the ruling shaykh of the Bani Yas, the Awamir are more associated with Oman and Saudi Arabia. A small section of the Awamir moved in and out of Abu Dhabi until the 1940s. The tribal leader, Salim bin Hamad bin Rakkad, moved to al-Ahsa (along the gulf coast in Saudi Arabia) in 1943. He moved back and forth between both places. Bin Rakkad lost position to Salim bin Musallam bin Ham, backed by the Bani Yas leadership, and left for Saudi Arabia, taking part of the Awamir with him. Bin Rakkad became an important player in the dispute over Buraimi, while those who remained loyal to Salim bin Ham supported the Emirati side of the dispute. The Awamir were among the tribes listed by the British as Omani as well, in that they often moved between the modern states of Oman, the Emirates, and Saudi Arabia. As such, their men enlisted in conflicts against the Qawasim and their allies.

The Qawasim, especially of Sharjah, were often in conflict in the second half of the nineteenth and first half of the twentieth centuries. The lands they claimed along the shores of the Indian Ocean were contested by the sultan of Oman and by local tribes. The Sharqiyin frequently resisted Qasimi control and often sought help from Oman. Although the Qasimi leadership tried to force them to recognize Qasimi control, eventually, in 1952, they were recognized by the British as an independent emirate. In 1879, the shaykh of the Sharqiyin, Hamad bin 'Abdullah, refused to pay taxes to Sharjah and, though not recognized by the British, he acted as his own lord. He frequently sought protection from the sultan of Oman, declaring loyalty when necessary and acting independently when convenient for him. Despite military attempts to force him to recognize Sharjah's claim to lands around Fujairah, the shaykh exerted his own will over the region, and eventually, the British recognized him as an independent ruler.

PEARLING AND THE COLLAPSE OF THE INDUSTRY

Pearls served as the major source of economic power in the Arabian Gulf, and while dates were also exported, they could not compete with the price of pearls. Bahrain became the major center for the trade, and many Hawali families were involved in dealing with European buyers. Each year, European buyers came to Bahrain to see what types of pearls were offered for sale. For the pearl divers, it was an important time, when the ship captains and admirals of pearling fleets not only sold pearls to the buyers but also paid the sailors and divers. Bahrain had a number of good harbors that made it ideal for trade.[11] It was also surrounded by smaller ports on the mainland of the peninsula, which included Uqair, Qatif, Zubara, and Bida' on the mainland of the Peninsula. Al-Qasimi notes that Bahrain's trade in pearls had a steady growth from 1790 to the 1820s. It is estimated that twenty-five hundred ships were engaged in pearling, and the income from pearls rose to 2,459,200 Maria Theresa thalers (a silver coin similar to a U.S. silver dollar) or £490,000.[12] Of this total amount, the shaykh of Bahrain taxed the sales of pearls at £10,000 (the amount for all the merchants annually as a group) for providing protection to the merchants. The harbors of Bahrain hosted *baghlah* and *bum* from Kuwait and Basrah to Bombay and Mombasa that brought in products from the Indian Ocean and the Arabian Gulf, including "rice, sugar, cloth, indigo, iron, brass, ghee, and timber from the Malabar Coast twice a year. From the Gulf ports Bahrain imported dates, sugar, ghee, cloth, gunpowder, swords, matchlocks and from the Hasa region and Qatif, goats, sheep, bullocks, cows, dates, donkeys, and horses."[13]

Ras al-Khaimah (originally called Julfar) also had extensive trade in dates and pearls. Many of the Qawasim ships were large, able to hold cargos of some three to four hundred tons.[14] The shaykh commanded a fleet of four hundred ships of different sizes, and the pearl fishing area had high-quality pearls that were located at a depth of six to seven fathoms close to the shore controlled by the Qawasim.[15] The sale was around 40,000 Tumans (an Iranian currency) or the equivalent of 10,000 dinars, equaling one Tuman. The shaykh exacted a tax of one or two Maria Theresa thalers per ship, depending on the size, and 10 percent of sales on dates. The pearls from Ras al-Khaimah/Julfar were among the very best produced in the gulf, and foreign merchants tried to establish trading missions. However, the Qawasim traded mostly with other gulf ports and fewer, but still significant amounts with foreigners (non-Arabs). Sharjah also functioned as a pearling port, but until the defeat by the British of the Qawasim fleet, it was less important. After the defeat, the Qawasim capital moved to Sharjah, and its importance grew. Other ports in the lower gulf had fleets of pearling ships. In Dubai and Abu Dhabi, even though their populations were mainly desert nomads, the people used pearling as a means to supplement pastoral income. Fleets went out for about four months a year, and crews were paid at the end, after merchants bought up the supply of pearls. Often, crews remained in debt to the ships' owners when the pearling season had low results. This kept a good portion of the crews tied to particular ships and to the specific merchants that owned them. From the period of maritime peace, the rulers of the Trucial States became interested in the income from pearling and owning ships or acting as merchants with foreign buyers.[16] New forms of taxation were devised by the rulers so that they could partake in the profits. By 1927, Sharjah was in turmoil over a dispute between rival claimants to the throne: Khalid bin Ahmad, the recently deposed ruler, and Sultan bin Saqr, the young, then-current ruler. Khalid, backed by the Bedouin, attacked the city, and Saqr sent out ships ahead of the season to gain more money from what he called a "small dive." He helped finance the dive by taking divers who were in debt to the notables of the town. He did not compensate the notables because they could send out their own ships later, in the proper season. This ensured that Saqr would have more profit and many of the notables would not because returned ships had no pearls or only a small haul. Something similar was done by the ruler of Ajman when Humaid ibn Abdulaziz sent out his ships before the season was to begin and banned men of the Bin Lutah family, a major family owning a fleet of ships, from participating either in his "small dive" or in the proper pearling season. He forbade 160 divers who worked for the Bin Lutah family to dive at all, and they all moved to Sharjah and Dubai to find work.[17]

This was altered greatly in 1928 when cultured pearls replaced natural pearls. The process of cultured pearls was invented in Japan by Mikimoto Kokichi as early as 1916. In order to produce a more perfectly shaped pearl, a piece of another oyster shell is placed inside the oyster, which causes the pearl to grow. At first, freshwater oysters were used, and then later, Baron Iwasaki (founder of the Mitsubishi Group) set up beds in the Philippines for commercial sales. Cultured pearls could be produced in two to four years on a regular basis and were superior in shape to the natural pearls from the gulf. They were also cheaper in price, as the company selling the pearls also owned the farms, cutting out much of the cost of traditional pearling. After 1930, the demand for natural pearls collapsed, as Japan became the biggest supplier of cultured pearls, and the world was recovering from the financial crisis of 1929. For about ten years, the income of the Trucial States collapsed with the loss of pearl sales to Japan before exploration for oil was able to replace it. In 1929, some sixty ships from Dubai did not go to sea for the pearling season because demand had already dropped as Japan quickly took over the market. In 1928, sales to Indian merchants on credit were not being paid because they could not dispose of their stocks in pearls in Paris. In 1930, Indian middlemen could not sell gulf pearls, forcing both merchants and fleets into bankruptcy.

Prices collapsed quickly, with sales of gulf pearls reaching an all-time low in 1930. In Kuwait, the harvest of pearls was poor, and prices were 50 percent less than those of 1929; in Bahrain, prices were even lower—only 25 percent of the previous year.[18] By 1943, due to World War II and the lack of buyers from Europe and the United States, prices were less than one-tenth the 1929 prices. The situation was made worse by the British government, which asked the Indian government to restrict the purchase of "unnecessary" items and also asked the Indian government to balance its books under conditions of war. Given that most of the buyers were Indian, this only furthered the collapse of the industry in the gulf. As a result, the British Board of Trade sought to find alternative buyers for gulf pearls in the United States and Canada, but they were greatly disappointed. The United States had its own companies that sold cultured pearls, and by 1948, cultured pearls were also produced in the Red Sea by Egypt. Although gulf merchants were successful in getting the British to ban sales of cultured sales in Bahrain, the local industry was nearly dead from more than a decade of losses. Only Bahrain, Kuwait, and Qatar were able to survive the lean years.[19]

The 1930s saw a resurgence in raiding on land as a result of the worldwide depression, and specifically in the production of pearls. Bedouins could not seek seasonal employment on the pearling ships, and the dismissal of many of the crews added to the number of homeless people seeking some way to make a living. In addition, raiding afforded a means to seek revenge in long-standing blood feuds between tribal groups. Such raids carried off household objects that Bedouins could no longer afford to buy. By as early as 1931, several incidents began to be recorded in attacks on caravans carrying goods from Fujairah to Dubai, Sharjah, or Ras al-Khaimah. Bedouin of the Awamir and allied tribes were often the perpetrators of such attacks, as were the Bani Yas and Manasir that hung around the outskirts of towns such as Dubai, Sharjah, and Ras al-Khaimah. These were often the continuation of old conflicts between the Hinawi and Ghafiri tribes.[20] Oman was also brought into these conflicts over claims to Buraimi that continued to plague relations between Saudi Arabia and the Trucial States with Oman. Minor conflicts, locally called "wars," continued through the 1930s to the 1950s between the individual emirates, with Bedouin men using them for expressions of "manliness." As some rulers, such as Shaykh Zayed in the oasis of Buraimi/al-Ain, were friendlier to Bedouins than others, Bedouins felt more comfortable there than in cities such as Sharjah. Among those branded as "brigands and robbers" was Wilfred Thesiger's travel companion, the Omani Bedouin of the al-Rashid tribe, ibn Ghabaisha, in a "war" against Sharjah where he developed a reputation as a robber.[21]

The southern or Omani Bedouins were called the Mashqas.[22] The division between the southern and northern Bedouins is overtly displayed by the type of camel saddle used, as well as in their clothes. The southern tribes were seen by northern Bedouins as lesser in "wealth," and, therefore, lower in social standing. Nonetheless, people like Wilfred Thesiger preferred the southern tribes because of

A camel race in the backcountry of Fujairah. In 2002, jockeys aged fifteen and under were banned from races, and in 2007, mechanical robot jockeys were introduced. This particular race in the backcountry of Fujairah was breaking the ban. (Courtesy of John A. Shoup)

their harsh lifestyle, which he felt made them "true Bedouin." These include the al-Rashids (his preferred travel companions) and the Bayt Kathirs (whom he considered inferior to the al-Rashid).[23] Conflict between northerners and southerners was intense, and tribes such as the Awamir were seen as more northern than southern, even though they also used grazing in Oman and the Trucial States. The Awamir were allied with the Bani Yas, and in 1895, they declared war on the Na'im, who sent a written complaint to the shaykh of the Bani Yas. The Awamir eventually split into three sections, administered by different countries issuing different passports: Saudi, Omani, and Emirati. Other tribes whose traditional lands include Oman, the Emirates, and Saudi Arabia decided on which state to move to after the discovery of oil, depending on which gave them the better deal. These include the Ajman, Manahil, and the al-Murrah, who were seen as more northern than southern tribes including switching clothing styles. The styles of the daily long shirt, called a *thawb* or dishdasha, and the headdress, called a kaffiyeh or *shemagh*, with the accompanying agal or black goat-hair ring that holds it in place are different even today between the countries of the gulf. They form what is called "national dress" and, in many of the Arab Gulf countries, it is illegal for anyone who is not a national to wear them in public.

Small wars between the emirates also caused movement from one side to another, and Thesiger notes conflicts between Abu Dhabi and Dubai and between Dubai and Sharjah, with old hostilities between tribal groups coming to the fore in selection of which side to fight for. Often, smaller tribal groups played important roles in these wars, especially the Na'im, the Bani Qitab, the Dhawahir, and the Bani Ka'ab. In addition, continued tribal conflicts over raids for camels were also important in the late 1940s, with the Dahm of Yemen frequently the "untrustworthy enemy" of many Omani Bedouin. In 1947–1948, Thesiger made his second crossing of the Rub' al-Khali with a company of al-Rashid and Sa'ar tribesmen and describes the enmity between the two divisions of Bedouins, north and south.[24] Thesiger also describes one of the raids carried out by Mashqa tribesmen, clothed in only their indigo loincloths, that left a number of dead on both sides.[25] Eventually, employment in the oil fields and the salaries offered to the Bedouins caused movement from one side of the Rub' al-Khali to another and eventual political identity for a number of tribes. Those who began to reside in the north took on the outward dress of the north, while those who remained in the south adopted the dress associated with Oman or the Trucial States.

WIND-TOWER HOUSES

Wind-tower houses, called *barajil* in Arabic from the original Persian, *badgir*, were a feature of the pre-oil architecture of the Trucial States.[26] They were originally invented in Iran and were brought to the Arab side of the gulf by the Arabic-speaking Hawali families. Such urban architecture became an important mark of the gulf in places such as Dubai and Sharjah. Today, both states are trying to preserve them and areas of Dubai that are now seen as important to cultural heritage. In Dubai, the quarter where these Arab-Persian families settled was/is called Bastakiya, after the original town of Bastak in Iran, though some families originated in Lingah. Lingah was under Qawasim control until 1889, when the Qajar shah of Iran, Nasir al-Din (ruled 1848–1896) took the city from the Arabs and stationed troops there to prevent the Qawasim from retaking it. In 1898, the Qawasim tried to retake Lingah from the shah, Muzaffar al-Din (ruled 1896–1909), but the effort failed, and the city remained in Persian hands. Lingah was one of the most important ports in the gulf and reached the height of its wealth and prestige in the late nineteenth century. Its trade remained in the hands of its Arabic-speaking Sunni merchants, who controlled trade in the gulf states and in Iran between the gulf to Shiraz and on to Yazd in the Iranian heartland. Recently, the government of Dubai restored a number of the houses, and many have been converted into upscale shops and restaurants.

The wind-tower houses were made of cut coral stone, the idea originating on the East African coast, as well as in local palm-frond huts called *barasti*. The houses were made with a tall windcatcher collecting wind from all four sides, depending on the direction. The towers opened up to all four sides and, daily, a wet cloth was placed underneath the part where all four sides met in order to cool the breeze. The cooled breeze was then funneled into the main room of the house in the smaller single-roomed *barasti* huts or into one or more of the important rooms in the more substantial houses made of cut coral rock. Dubai and nearby Sharjah became the home for a number of families that immigrated from the northern Persian side of the gulf to the southern Arab side. Dubai's shaykh made efforts to welcome these families to his territory; they were given land to build their new homes and paid low taxes. By 1870, Dubai had overtaken Abu Dhabi in size and population.[27] Some one thousand Persian families moved to Dubai, and by 1939, Dubai had become the largest settlement in the Trucial States, with a population of twenty thousand.[28]

In 1912, the shaykh of Dubai, Sa'id, "fostered immigration of merchants, traders, craftsmen, and artisans from southern Iran to contribute to the development of Dubai."[29] They helped Dubai through the loss of the pearl trade, providing other industries that continued trade. Among the first to come were the Al Awar, 'Abd al-Razaq, Kazim, and Faruq families, all originally from Bastak.[30] Of them, the Faruq were the wealthiest, with pearl customers from distant places such as Paris, whom the head of the family, 'Abd al-Karim Faruq, visited in Europe. Other important members of Bastak and Lingah origins settled in Bahrain, Qatar, and Kuwait, in addition to Dubai. Sharjah also welcomed merchants from Iran and developed a building style based on that of Iran, with cut coral rock and wind towers. Within the community from Bastak, the 'Abbassi family had the highest social status and were called khans, or the community leaders in Iran's Bastak town. In addition, other high-status families were the Mirs, or those whose mothers were from the family of the Prophet, and the Sayyids, whose fathers were from the Prophet's family. Most of the Bastaki community, wherever they settled in the southern shores of the gulf, maintained these social standings and intermarried among themselves, though it is noted that the men could and did marry outside to whomever they wanted, while fathers would not allow their daughters to marry beneath their social level. Connections remain in place between these Arabic-speaking Persian families, with relatives in southern Iran, India, and gulf countries. They were important to the Maktoum vision of Dubai's growth, and in the 1920s, 'Abbas 'Abd Allah 'Abbas began direct steamer ship service (using steam-powered ships) with India.[31]

Dubai's shaykh Sa'id did not discriminate against the Bastaki merchants. 'Abd al-Karim Faruq, 'Abd al-Razzaq 'Abd al-Rahim al-Bastaki, and 'Abd al-Qadir 'Abbas were close friends with Sa'id and his successor to the position of shaykh, Rashid. Another Bastaki family produced Muhammad Sharif, who became head of the council of religious scholars or the ulama.[32] When Dubai set up its municipal council, members of the Bastaki community were included in its membership because of the high regard the shaykh held for them. Bastakiya, the Bastak settlement, is located near the fort of Dubai, al-Fahidi Fort, and near the homes of both shaykh Sa'id and shaykh Rashid, the Grand Mosque, and the suq or market area. These were the only built-up areas of Dubai, along with Shindagha Palace of the Maktoum family, built in 1916, on the extreme north of the city.[33] The rest of the town was built of *barasti* or *'arish*, date palm fronds on a wooden frame built of split palm trunks or hardwood imported from India starting in the 1930s.[34] These also had wind towers built into them, which helped cool the houses in the summer. Some of the houses were built with deep foundations that were lined with gypsum called *saruj*, but the more expensive ones used cement imported from India starting in the 1950s.[35] While the *barasti* houses provided shade in the summer, in the winter months, they were covered with tarpaulins that made them watertight. As the population became more permanent and no longer needed summer housing, the winter houses were built with sloping roofs that allowed rain to drain off, and the sides were like fine basket weave that also helped protect the inhabitants from the wind and rain. The winter sections were called *khaymah*, literally meaning a tent, a reminder of past times when winter months were spent in goat-hair tents in the desert, away from the coast.[36] Until recently, the wind towers were seen as part of the old, pre-oil life and many were destroyed to make room for new developments. In Dubai, this trend was begun with detailed plans of all the buildings declared worthy of preservation starting in 1971, and later, Sharjah began programs to restore and even rebuild many of these structures.[37] Today, wind-tower houses are part of the national markers for Dubai.

PRE-OIL LIFE IN THE UNITED ARAB EMIRATES

Life in the pre-oil and early oil period was recorded best by two Englishmen: Wilfred Thesiger, in his book *Arabian Sands* (and it subsequent republished titles) and British agent Ronald Codrai, who published numerous books that include *Abu Dhabi* and *Dubai Arabian Collections*. Both men witnessed the period at the end of the pre-oil life and beginning of the oil period. Ronald Codrai worked for the British oil company, trying to get the local rulers and the tribal leaders to agree to oil exploration. He spent his leisure time learning to understand the ways of the Bedouin and the Bedouin leaders, as well as the end of the pearl trade. He took a large number of photographs that depicted the life of the people at that time. While Thesiger's book deals with his observations of the Bedouin and the desert environment, Codrai's photos are of the life in the urban centers. Both men had a profound effect on the future memory of this transitional period, serving as a collective memory for the country once most of that life was no longer available. When oil was discovered and the states began to develop, they began a massive race to modernize and wipe away the vestiges of the past, as in other oil-rich Arab gulf states.

The Pearl Trade

The pearl trade served as the major share in the region's wealth. The North African geographer, al-Idrisi, noted in 1154 that Julfar was a major center for the pearl trade.[38] In the early sixteenth century, European buyers became very interested in pearls found near Julfar and named for the port. The pearls were collected in certain seasons of the year (summer), and while the income provided was seasonal, it was significant for many, both Bedouin and settled villagers. It was estimated that over twelve hundred ships operated out of the ports, each with a crew of eighteen men, totaling twenty-two thousand men working on the ships. The annual value sold to mainly Indian buyers was around £1,434,399 in 1900.[39] In addition, they sold some £30,439 of mother of pearl, again mainly to Indian buyers. This lasted until the 1930s and the introduction of cultured pearls and the economic collapse of the Great Depression.

Life for divers was very hard. They rose for a light breakfast of dates and coffee an hour before dawn, and the workday lasted until an hour before sunset. They rested for prayers and a short break for coffee. The diver had a nose clip made of turtle shell, his ears were stuffed with wax, and a stone was attached to his foot to help him descend into the depths. He was connected to the ship by a rope held by his companions on board to help pull him to the surface once he filled the woven basket attached to a rope around his neck. In the evening, the major meal of fish and rice was served to all of the boat's crew.[40] The captain did not touch the oysters until the next day, and then he recorded the intake of pearls, making special note of those big enough for individual sales. The pearling fleet was visited periodically by local merchants called a *tawash* who bought the pearls either for wholesalers or for specific clients who ordered a certain type and size of pearl. The local buyer called a tawash sorted the pearls according to size using a graded sieve, a scale, and a magnifying glass. Pearls were washed in clean rainwater to get rid of the greenish tarnish that frequently formed on newly removed pearls.[41] After they were sorted for size, weight, and quality, the pearls were wrapped in red cloths.

The crew was paid after the season in shares according to the *ikhluwi* system that was organized and controlled by the *'amil* for the specific sheikdom.[42] The *shuyukh* became involved in the trade and imposed a tax on the ships and owned fleets that competed with private owners. They also changed the season and declared an early season when no private ship was allowed out of the harbor. The royal families came to dominate the trade, but the region was rich in pearls, and even with the change in the season, there was enough for small private fleets to make money and pay their crews.

Shipbuilding Craft

Shipbuilding in the gulf became specialized, with techniques passed between builders from Oman to Basrah in Iraq. The Arabs developed a number of ships usually called dhows in English (perhaps from the Hindi word *daw*).[43] These were light in draft and utilized lateen (triangular) sails that allowed them to sail closer to the wind than the square-rigged sails used by the Europeans.[44] Wooden planks were not nailed but were laced together with an oiled rope, although they sometimes used nails wrapped in an oiled rope.[45] The laced construction gave the ships greater ability to move with the ocean than European ships and allowed the ships a greater ability to haul weight. The ships were prone to water leakage, and after European influence, they began to nail the planks together.[46]

Teak wood was imported from India for the ribs of the ship, and specially grown trees with bends were used for the bent portions. Mango was also used. The gulf coast did not have enough mangos to cut, so they were imported from Somalia and Kenya on the east African coast. The Arab boatbuilding techniques were exported to the Swahili coast. Rope was imported from Zanzibar, but the sails were made in Bahrain, Kuwait, or locally from imported Indian cotton cloth.[47]

Today, the largest shipbuilding yard, once in Umm al-Quain, is in Ajman in the United Arab Emirates.[48] All the sheikdoms had their own shipbuilding yards in the past, and most now include them as tourist sites. There are a number of different sizes of ships with different names, but the main ones found in the gulf today are the *bum*, the *baghlah*, and the sambuk.[49] Most of today's ships are from Iran and Somalia for long-distance trade or are involved in local fishing.[50]

Date Production

Dates formed another source of income prior to oil wealth, and the Emirates still produce both high quality and large quantities of dates. Farms are located in the main oases of Liwa and Buraimi/al-Ain in addition to smaller oases such as Hatta. Dates have several names, depending on when they were picked and the amount of sugar in them.[51] The high amount of sugar means they can be kept with no refrigeration for a month, making it one of the most practical products for the Bedouin lifestyle. In addition, date palms need the extreme heat of the lower gulf to grow, and they thrive in the brackish water available that would mean death to other varieties, although if the water is too salty, it can cause lower production of dates or death.[52] Dates ripen between the months of May and September, some five to eight months after the tree has been pollinated.[53] There are no wild types of date, and there is a need for human intervention for a good crop. The trees need humans to help pollinate them; one male tree is planted per thirty or so female trees, and the farmer spreads the pollen by hand rather than depend on insects or the wind to do so.[54] This used to be done by the settled peoples living in the oases, but today it is done mainly by Pakistani laborers.

The date palm produces an important source of food to the settled and Bedouin population of the Arabian Peninsula as freshly picked fruit, but it also produces *'ajwah* or pressed dates for long-distance treks in the past. *'Ajwah* is used in cooking, such as in date-stuffed cookies. When stacks of dates are left for a long period of time, they produce a sweet syrup called *dibs*. The high sugar content means that even in temperatures of over 54°C (over 129° F), it does not spoil or become alcohol.[55] Often, forts had a room where stacks of dates were stored with a special place for the collection of *dibs* that dripped down from the storage bags. In the process, the dates themselves were pressed due to their own weight and thus become *'ajwah*.

Palm trees provide a great deal to the local culture, from housing to baskets and mats. Different parts of the tree were/are used for different crafts. The trunk is split and serves as the ceiling beams of houses or the lintels above the doors and windows. They are also used as troughs for livestock or are split and sealed with clay and stone for beehives. The fiber found around the base of the frond is made into rope or as padding in camel trappings. It is also used as a filter for coffee pots, as a scouring pad for cleaning, and as kindling for fires. To help the fibers come loose, they are spread across a busy road today, and this helps in making ropes. The palm fronds are split or are used as whole pieces to make items such as boat docks, drying tables for dates, baskets for fruit or fish bait, bird traps, or fumigators for clothes.[56] Other parts of the date palm are also used. The spine near the base of the frond is used as a needle for sewing and weaving. The leaves of the palm frond are used for finer baskets and are twisted into a fine twine. The fruit stems are made into brooms or into fish traps.

The palm leaves are braided into wide strips, often colored black, purple, green, or magenta by soaking them in chemical dyes.[57] They are/were woven into large mats to cover the floor, used for eating. They were woven into cone covers to protect food from flies, as well as numerous other household items.

The house called either *barasti* or *'arish* is constructed using split palm trunks for the most important pillars, and the sides are made from woven palm leaf mats or from palm fronds bound together with rope. The house could have a wind tower to help cool the structure, and the house was placed so that summer winds were collected. Winter versions were placed so as to be protected from harsh winds. The roof was gabled, allowing rain to run off to the side, and the interior had aboveground shelving to prevent bites from snakes or poisonous insects.[58] The amount of matting or of a panel made of palm-bound palm fronds called a *da'an* determined how much light appeared on the inside and how wind- and waterproof the structure was.

BEDOUIN LIFE

Bedouins formed an important part of pre-oil life in the United Arab Emirates. Bedouin tribes owned a number of date palms that were required for their harvest. They often set up homes made of *barasti* or set up tents during the four summer months. As some Bedouin moved to the United Arab Emirates year-round, they supplemented dates with work on pearling ships during the summer season. The date harvest frequently began in June, and the summer pearling season began at least one month later, so the Bedouin who were needed for date harvest could not join the pearling season. When the ships left the port, they did not return until the season was over in early November.[59] Bedouin could join only if their dates were already harvested before the ships left their ports. As time progressed, Bedouin began to count on pearling as a chance for ready cash that was needed throughout the year. As the fleet began returning in October, it prompted celebrations, as the crewmen were visited onboard the ships by their families, especially the children.[60]

Some of the Bedouin in Abu Dhabi only came for part of the year, and they frequently did not bother with tents or palm frond huts. Instead, they threw a blanket over some dry branches and made it a home. This was a common method among the southern Bedouin and was one of the main differences between northern and southern tribes.[61] The tents are made of the same woven black goat hair, but they are small, basically a single sheet of cloth, unlike the great tents of north Arabia.[62]

Travel in Bedouin territory often required outsiders to be accompanied by someone who acted as the guarantor of the travelers' good behavior. He is referred to in the north as a *rafiq* (meaning a friend or companion), and in the south as a *rabi'a* (an oath-sworn companion).[63] Thesiger noted the difficulty in finding a *rabi'a* acceptable to the Duru, a warlike Bedouin tribe that live between the United Arab Emirates and Oman. They were very hostile to Thesiger and his Bedouin companions after finding out that he was a Christian, and the imam of Nizwa wanted him to be arrested.[64] Thesiger finally obtained *rabi'a* from not only the tribes of the Duru, the Junubah, and Wahibah but also a representative of the imam, and he was able to complete his journey. Honor is the supreme vehicle of the Bedouin, and the system of companions is the tangible expression of honor of both the traveler and his *rabi'a*. Bedouin learn to respect their elders, tribal honor, and proper behavior as small children, and male children are encouraged to attend open, public meetings to understand how politics works.

They are not to say anything, but they are encouraged to attend. Girls are given instruction by their mothers, elder sisters, aunts, and grandmothers in the same customs and tribal laws.[65] Larger tents are separated into a public section, where guests are welcome, and private or family sections that are closed to outsiders. Women can join the guests or they can remain on their side, but they are allowed to speak through the tent wall that separates the sides. Thesiger noted that Bedouin women are not locked away in *purdah* (sanctuary), but their labor is needed for family survival, and they are required to go outdoors to collect firewood, draw water, or attend smaller livestock. In addition, due to the small, open construction of the tents, it is impossible to lock them up. A woman can divorce her husband by refusing to live with him and seeking the protection of her family.[66]

The Bedouins' livelihood is based on their livestock. The great Bedouin tribes are based on herds of camels, and they are called the noble or *asil* tribes. Those who raise sheep and goats are the *shawiyah* or the small tribes, and those who practice farming and have herds of sheep and goats are called *ru'a* or herders. In the south, camels were the most important animal, and they gave life to the Bedouin. Sheep and goats require water on a daily basis, while camels can live several days without water. Camels supply milk, which is drunk by the nomads and is used to water their horses. The daily water needs of sheep and goats make them hard to keep in the United Arab Emirates unless they are tied to an oasis with a constant water supply.

Bedouins are ruled by a loose kinship system and close relatives frequently camp in the same group all year long. These related camping groups are called a *khamsah* or a five-level relationship. Tribes have a number of divisions based on kinship: the largest, called a *qabilah* or a confederation of tribes; an *'ashirah* or tribe; a *batin* or set of lineages; a *fakhdh*, which are narrowly defined lineages; a *saq*, which refers to a more-refined lineage; and a *qadm* or individual household. Tribes are subject to both pressures of fraction and of fusion and are in constant social movement. Tribal leadership is subject to selection by members of the tribe and not necessarily direct succession from father to son. The person best qualified to lead is chosen to be the leader, but tribal leaders do not have much power. They are not able to make agreements with states, as they do not have the power to order their people to do anything. They serve as judges to make sure people obey the law (called *'urf* or customary law).

Tribal leaders hold daily councils called *majlis*, which are open to all. Coffee plays a central role, and agreements are made over a cup

Trucial Oman and the Discovery of Oil

An official *majlis*, or council room, that was used by Shaykh Zayed while he was governor of the Eastern Province in al-Ain. His portrait as a young man is mounted on the back wall. (Courtesy of John A. Shoup)

of coffee and a handshake. This is how the two shaykhs of Abu Dhabi and Dubai, Zayed and Rashid, agreed to form the union of the United Arab Emirates. Today, many agreements seem to disappear from public view to behind the doors of diplomacy, where leaders then decide for their people. The *majlis* of today remain one of tribal leaders or of the members of various shaykhs' families, more or less according to Bedouin traditions. Coffee serves as an important indicator for the Bedouin, and the preparation of coffee was an invitation to all in the vicinity who could hear the distinct sound of coffee beans being crushed in a wooden or brass bowl. In the United Arab Emirates, coffee remains the seal to a bargain in politics and business, as it has for centuries before.

PRE-OIL LIFE—CONFLICTS

The last minor "war" between the tribes in the Trucial States was between Abu Dhabi and Dubai in 1948–1949.[67] Early in 1948, near the oasis of Liwa, fifty-two members of the Manasir tribe were killed, and many more were wounded. This caused great apprehension among the people of Abu Dhabi, who feared further attacks. Britain became directly involved in solving the problem and forced the final agreement between all the involved parties. As a result, in 1951, the British established a ground force led by British officers called the Trucial Oman Levies.[68] In 1956, the name was changed to the Trucial Oman Scouts, and they were used to bring peace to the unruly countryside.

Not only did the new force take on the problems of tribal conflict, but it also took on the renewed trade in slaves taken from Africa and across the gulf in Baluchistan (in modern Pakistan). The slave trade had a renewed resurgence in the 1940s, with most slaves being sold to Saudi Arabia, where the main slave market was located in the town of Hamasah in the Buraimi oasis.[69] This caused Great Britain, as the local power responsible, embarrassment once this activity leaked to the world press. The Omani Levies quickly brought an end to the slave trade as well to the arms trade to Balochistani separatists who were fighting both the Omani and Persian governments. Most of the arms were from East Africa and were shipped through ports in the Trucial States, such as Dubai.

The fort of Hamasa in Omani Buraimi, which was contested by Saudi Arabia during the 1950s. The dispute was settled in 1974 by the Treaty of Jiddah between King Faisal of Saudi Arabia and Shaykh Zayed of the United Arab Emirates. Three of the villages were claimed by the sultan of Oman, and they were returned to his control. (Courtesy of John A. Shoup)

The British-led forces played a major role in ending the Buraimi crisis and forcing Saudi forces to leave the oasis. The British used the force starting in 1957 in Oman in the war between the sultan of Muscat and the imam of Nizwa. The Trucial Oman Scouts stayed until 1959 and had a distinguished military record in the conflict.[70] The scouts included one regiment of Dhufari men who had left their poverty in Oman to seek employment in the oil fields in Kuwait, Saudi Arabia, and Bahrain, where they were trained, gaining experience until locals could take over their jobs. They then migrated back to Oman and found ready employment in the new Trucial Oman Scouts. However, as a unit, they did not get along with the men from the Trucial States because they spoke a different language (South Arabian) and not the Arabic the rest of the men spoke.[71]

As employment with the oil companies grew, the scouts suffered in that they were not paid as well as the oil employees, and fewer men could be recruited. In addition, the individual states began to raise their own defense/police forces starting in Dubai in 1956, followed by Abu Dhabi in 1957.[72] During the 1960s, the various emirates organized separate militaries, often officered by the British or British-trained Arabs such as Jordanians.

OIL EXPLORATION IN THE TRUCIAL STATES

Oil exploration began in the pre-World War II period, in the late 1930s. Various, mostly British companies, tried to get permission from the shaykhs to explore for oil in their territories. It was hard, initially, for the company men to understand the borders of territorial control or how much control certain tribal leaders held over their people. In addition, there was strong competition from American companies. The Americans had an advantage over the British, with a better reputation among local Arabs through the two medical hospitals they set up early in the 1900s, one in Bahrain and another in Oman. As such, they had established a positive reputation, unlike the British, whose local agents had ruled the region harshly, causing many local leaders to want to turn away from them. Saudi Arabia set the standard by refusing British overtures for exploration, but King 'Abd al-'Aziz ibn Sa'ud allowed Standard Oil of California a concession. Some tribal leaders, such as the Duru in Oman, refused to allow oil company men in their areas, and the oasis of Buraimi refused to allow oil men to look for oil.

The reputation of the British greatly suffered as the result of actions by the resident for the Trucial States, especially after the 1910 Hyacinth incident. The incident is named for the British warship, the HMS *Hyacinth*, which landed troops in Dubai to search for illegal guns. Four of the British soldiers from the landing party were killed, and nine were injured,[73] but the Arab loss was much larger; thirty-seven men were killed.[74] The incident grew as a result, and the British in India demanded that the shaykh of Dubai, Butti bin Suhail, pay a fine, surrender the illegal arms, and submit to a British resident agent in Dubai. Butti complied with the first two conditions, but could not to the last of the conditions for fear of the reaction of his people. The British backed down, understanding that this would put Butti in danger of his position, but this incident created a fear of British interference in local affairs. Many of the local shaykhs were involved with gunrunning and slave trading and did not want British oversight of their affairs. Slave trading continued well through the 1950s, with other incidents that brought British military intervention. Several of the emirates were subjected to British naval bombardment in punishment for slave trading. In 1921, Ajman, and in 1925, Fujairah were subjected to shelling.[75] The Fujairah incident was over a young Baluchi woman held by the shaykh, Hamad bin 'Abdullah of the Sharqiyin tribe. The British resident considered shaykh Hamad's behavior and attitude as not showing proper respect for the British agent, and Colonel F.B. Prideaux, was insulted more by Hamad's refusal to turn over the slave girl than the issue of slavery. In the end, the British shelled the fort, causing Hamad to finally make his peace with Prideaux. It also was among the important acts demonstrating Fujairah's independence from Sharjah.

Until the discovery of oil and the flow of income from the wells, slavery remained among the most lucrative trades, especially once the pearl industry collapsed in 1929. Slave trade and gunrunning were outlawed by the British, but both continued, with most of the sales (of both guns and slaves) directed toward the Najd in contemporary Saudi Arabia. Slaves for domestic use were allowed in the Trucial States and Oman, but children were stolen from Balochistan in western India (today's Pakistan), as well as from East Africa and Oman, and sold as slaves. This continued through the early 1950s with the knowledge of the local rulers, though they frequently denied this to the British.

Oil in the gulf was first discovered in Bahrain in 1932. Other oil fields were quickly discovered in Saudi Arabia, Kuwait, and Qatar though World War II stopped any further development of these discoveries until the war ended. In the 1930s, several of the tribal leaders in the Trucial States gave permission to look for oil exploration, and Abu Dhabi was among the first. In 1939, Shakhbut of Abu Dhabi gave a concession to the Superior Oil Company, and in 1950, oil was discovered offshore on the continental shelf. This was contested by the company that held the concession of 1939, the Petroleum Development Trucial Coast (PDTC).[76] Shakhbut had to defend his second concession and was successfully proved in court that the continental shelf was not in the 1939 concession. In 1952, Superior sold its concession to D'Arcy Exploration, which was one-third French-owned and two-thirds owned by British Petroleum (then called Anglo-Iranian Oil Company). D'Arcy morphed into the Abu Dhabi Marine Areas Ltd, and in 1958, struck oil offshore in Abu Dhabi. In 1960, oil was found on land, and the old PDTC changed its name to the Abu Dhabi Petroleum Company.[77] In 1966, oil was discovered offshore in Dubai, but the amount was not as large as the Abu Dhabi fields. In 1973, oil was discovered in an offshore field owned by Sharjah near the island of Abu Musa. Subsequently, the other emirates have not been as lucky, with most of the wealth being found in Abu Dhabi.

THE REIGN OF SHAKHBUT OF ABU DHABI AND THE START OF THE OIL MONEY

Shakhbut had been considered among the best of the local rulers and, at first, had a good reputation among the foreigners in the country. Shakhbut came to power in 1928 after a power play in the al-Nahyan ruling family when his father, Sultan, was replaced by an uncle, Saqr, in 1922. Shakhbut and a brother, Hazza, were sent to Buraimi by their father just before he was killed and replaced by Saqr. Saqr tried to lure them back with promises of safety and gifts, but the two stayed away from Abu Dhabi and visited Sharjah and Qatar, gaining support from these leaders, and eventually went to Saudi Arabia. Meanwhile, Saqr continued to have problems with relatives, especially from his brothers Khalifa and Muhammad. Khalifa had the support of the Manasir tribe. Though he did not want to commit a murder, Khalifa helped arrange for a Baluchi slave (who belonged to Shakhbut) and men of the Manasir to kill Saqr. They accomplished this task January 1, 1928.[78] Khalifa then sent a message to Shakhbut in Sharjah to come and take the throne, which he did a few days after the murder in 1928.

Shakhbut established firm control over Abu Dhabi and between 1928 and 1966 brought more territory in the Buraimi oasis under the Bani Yas. He brought in a period of stability to Abu Dhabi, different from the time of the last shaykhs before him (the period starting with Tahnun in 1909 and ending with the death of Saqr in 1926). He successfully countered Saudi and Omani claims, ending Saudi influence of the governor of the eastern Province of Saudi Arabia, 'Abdallah ibn Jiluwi. Ibn Jiluwi, from his secure base in al-Ahsa, forced many of the tribes in Abu Dhabi and northern Oman to pay tribute in the form of zakat (a type of Islamic tax of usually 10 percent of yearly income) and interference in judicial procedures, making many of the local qadis subservient to Saudi judges. In 1930, Bertram Thomas noted that the Na'im were pro-Saudi and that the Na'im, Awamir, Duru and Bani Qitab tribes paid zakat to ibn Jiluwi as the representative of 'Abd al-'Aziz ibn Sa'ud. For the Na'im, this policy was a way to take back power from the Dhawahir, who backed the Bani Yas. Ibn Jiluwi had the support of the Na'im, and this challenge brought Shakhbut to declare war on the Na'im in 1931.[79] Shakhbut defeated the Na'im and forced ibn Jiluwi's tax men to stay north of the settlement Dhafra after several of them were beaten up and forced to retire with no animals or money collected. Nonetheless, some sections of the Manasir tribe preferred Saudi control and either decided to move to Saudi-controlled territory or continued to pay zakat to ibn Jiluwi. Shakhbut began using Buraimi, now called al-Ain, on the Trucial side of the oasis as a summer residence away from the severe humidity and heat of Abu Dhabi town. Shakhbut began a policy of returning to the older homeland of the Bani Yas, Liwa oasis and the Bedouin tribes of the interior, and he was assisted in this by his younger brother, Zayed.[80]

The policy of continuing to buy property in Buraimi/al-Ain remained until much of oasis was in Bani Yas' hands, leaving only the original settlement and two other forts in Oman. Zayed spent much of his life in al-Ain with his mother, Salamah, and in the 1930s, Shakhbut had Zayed accompany the first European expedition to look for oil. Zayed knew, and was known by, many of the interior peoples. Thus, the expedition had no problems with locals, and Zayed served his brother well. In 1946, Zayed was appointed the wali or governor of the Eastern Provinces of Abu Dhabi, where his knowledge of the Bedouin, their customs, and their traditional laws, set him in good stead for his post. He was a kind and courteous host to Wilfred Thesiger in 1948, who stayed for a month in the oasis before striking out for distant Wahiba Sands in Oman. Both Ronald Codrai and Wilfred Thesiger had good impressions of the young Zayed. Unlike his older brother, Zayed did not fear the influence foreigners and foreign ways would have on his people. and he wanted monies paid by the oil companies to be a boon, not a curse to them. He easily made friends with the oil men, allowing them to search for petroleum and encouraging them to do things such as build schools and health clinics, which the oil companies were willing to do for their employees.

In 1966, Shaykh Shakhbut ibn Sultan was deposed in favor of his brother, the highly popular Zayed. Shakhbut did not approve of too much oil money, which he felt would corrupt his people and bring too much change far too quickly. He was reluctant to release the money he was being paid and stuffed his mattress with wads of British pounds and U.S. dollars. He was rumored to distrust banks and kept his supply of gold bullion in his palace, among the few permanent buildings in Abu Dhabi town. As a result, the Trucial Scouts overthrew him with the support of the al-Nahyan ruling family and placed his brother, Zayed ibn Sultan on the throne of Abu Dhabi. Shakhbut was exiled to London but went only as far as Lebanon, where he stayed. In 1971, Zayed was made the president of the newly formed United Arab Emirates, and he allowed his brother, Shakhbut, back to Abu Dhabi. Shakhbut had two sons, both of whom died young and left only one child each. Zayed was the uncontested shaykh of Abu Dhabi and the president of the seven emirates that make up the United Arab Emirates.

NOTES

1. Heard-Bey, Frauke. *From the Trucial States to the United Arab Emirates*. Dubai: Motivate Publishing, 2004, 287.
2. Ibid., 288.
3. Ibid.
4. Ibid., 289.
5. Codrai, Ronald. *Dubai: An Arabian Album*. Dubai: Motivate Publishing, 1996, 200–205; Doumato, Eleanor Abeella. *Getting God' Ear: Woman, Islam, and Healing in Saudi Arabia and the Gulf*. New York: Columbia University Press, 2000, 182–183.
6. Al Rasheed, Madawi. *Politics in an Arabian Oasis: The Rashidis of Saudi Arabia*. New York: I.B. Tauris, 1991, 38.
7. Ibid., 39.
8. Zahlan, Rosemarie Said. *The Origins of the United Arab Emirates: A Political and Social History of the Trucial States*. London: Macmillan Publishers, 1978, 198.
9. Ibid., 179.
10. Heard-Bey, 37.
11. Al-Qasimi, Sultan bin Muhammad. *The Myth of Arab Piracy in the Gulf*. New York: Routledge, 1988, 10.
12. Ibid., 11.
13. Ibid.
14. Ibid., 13.
15. Ibid.

16. Heard-Bey, 219.
17. Ibid., 219.
18. Ibid.
19. Ibid., 222.
20. Ibid., 231.
21. Thesiger, Wilfred. *Crossing the Sands*. Dubai: Motivate Publishing, 2006, 170.
22. Thesiger, Wilfred. *Arabian Sands*. London: Longmans and Green, 1960, 187.
23. Ibid., 45.
24. Ibid., 174–190.
25. Ibid., 192–193.
26. Coles, Anne and Jackson, Peter. *Windtower*. London: Stacey International, 2007, 26.
27. Ibid., 8.
28. Zahlan, 4.
29. Coles and Jackson, 16.
30. Ibid., 13.
31. Ibid.
32. Ibid.
33. Ibid., 9.
34. Ibid., 153.
35. Ibid.
36. Ibid., 149.
37. Coles, Anne and Jackson, Peter. *A Windtower House in Dubai*. Dubai: Art and Archaeology Research Papers, June 1975, 1.
38. Hellyer, Peter, editor. *Waves of Time: The Maritime History of the United Arab Emirates*. London: Trident Press, Ltd., 1998, 114.
39. Ibid., 116.
40. Ibid., 120.
41. Ibid., 121.
42. Ibid., 122.
43. Shoup, John. "Dhows," in *Saudi Arabia and the Gulf Arab States Today: An Encyclopedia of Life in the Arab States*, edited by Sebastian Maisel and John A. Shoup. Westport, CT: Greenwood Press, 2009, 111.
44. Hellyer, 124.
45. Ibid., 129.
46. Ibid., 130.
47. Ibid., 129.
48. Ibid., 126.
49. Ibid., 133; Richardson, Neil and Dorr, Marcia. *The Craft Heritage of Oman*, vol. 2. Dubai: Motivate Publishing, 2003, 269.
50. Shoup. "Dhows," 113.
51. Shoup, John A. "Dates," in *Saudi Arabia and the Gulf Arab States Today*, 103.
52. LaBonte, Frances. *The Arabian Date Palm*. Dubai: Jerboa Books, 2006, 9.
53. Ibid., 11.
54. Ibid., 10–11.

55. Richardson, Neil and Dorr, Marcia. *The Craft Heritage of Oman*, vol. 1. Dubai: Motivate Publishing, 2003, 90.
56. Ibid., 91.
57. Ibid., 99.
58. Ibid., 107.
59. Codrai, Ronald. *Dubai: An Arabian Album*. Dubai: Motivate Publishing, 1997, 132.
60. Ibid., 85.
61. Thesiger, 167.
62. Ibid., Illustration plate 21, between 114 and 115.
63. Thesiger, 66.
64. Ibid., 162.
65. Maisel, Sebastian. "Bedouin Culture," in *Saudi Arabia and the Gulf Arab States Today* 62.
66. Thesiger, 78.
67. Heard-Bey, 302.
68. Ibid., 311.
69. Ibid.
70. Ibid., 312.
71. Ibid., 313.
72. Ibid., 314.
73. Zahlan, 2–3.
74. Morton, 100.
75. Ibid., 71.
76. Zahlan, 193.
77. Ibid.
78. Ibid., 44.
79. Ibid., 133.
80. Heard-Bey, 28.

8

Independence and the Birth of the United Arab Emirates to the Death of Shaykh Zayed (1971–2004)

The United Arab Emirates grew out of the union that made up the Trucial States (also called the Trucial Oman States) and formed an independent country on December 2, 1971. Britain made the decision to withdraw from the emirates in 1968. Britain felt it was losing considerable influence in southern Arabia, fighting in conflicts in South Yemen and in Dhufar province in Oman starting in 1967, and in South Yemen starting in 1963. In 1966, the Defense White Paper recommended, for financial reasons, to withdraw from Britain's commitments in Arabia, in particular to withdraw from Aden (South Yemen).[1] Britain felt it had to withdraw from places such as the emirates where it still had importance in order to keep the local rulers happy. Trucial Oman troops had been used in Dhufar and served both the British and the sultan of Oman well, but it was feared that troops from the Trucial states could be easily affected by anti-British sentiment in Dhufar and Yemen, but especially in Dhufar, where the British and the sultan of Oman were supposed to be fighting a Communist rebellion.

CHALLENGES TO INDEPENDENCE

The announcement came as a shock to the small states in the gulf. Originally, the withdrawal also included Qatar and Bahrain. In 1961, the shaykh of Bahrain, Shaykh Isa bin Salman al-Khalifa, became the ruler of Bahrain, and in the summer of 1971, the country declared its own independence, months before the scheduled independence of the United Arab Emirates. This prompted Qatar to announce its independence in September 1971. Both countries did not like the proposed weights in government of each emirate given that Bahrain was, at that time, well ahead of the rest of the gulf countries in infrastructure and education. Bahrain had its own problems with the shah of Iran, who claimed sovereignty over the island, but Bahrain was able to get both a United Nations referendum on independence and a new treaty with Britain to guarantee its independence. Qatar is connected to Bahrain, with both ruling houses being close cousins, the al-Khalifa of Bahrain and the al-Thani of Qatar. Bahrain was among the first of the gulf countries to benefit from oil monies, starting in 1932, when oil was discovered, and began major exploitation in 1936. This gave the British a second source of oil in addition to Iran, since petroleum was discovered in large quantities in Iran in 1908. In the nineteenth century, Bahrain served as the major exporter for pearls from the gulf and was also where the first modern hospital was built by American missionaries. It also has the oldest girls' school in the gulf; both the hospital and girls' school were built in the early decades of the twentieth century. Starting in the 1920s, rich parents from Bahrain began sending both their sons and daughters to schools in Cairo and Beirut, bringing back ideas of Arab nationalism that caused the British resident in Bahrain severe problems in the 1950s. In 1956, due to the war against Egypt's Jamal 'Abd al-Nasir by Britain, France, and Israel, Shaykh Salman had to dismiss the British resident, but he then named another Brit to the post. Nonetheless, Bahrainis saw themselves as superior to the people of Trucial Oman, feeling they were better educated and more internationally aware.

Qatar's history was one of recent recognition as an independent state and began as a result of the 1867–1868 war with Bahrain. Bahrain asked for support from Abu Dhabi in its attempt to suppress Qatar's

Independence and the Birth of the United Arab Emirates 105

rebels against Bahraini control. Abu Dhabi helped Bahrain, which resulted in the sacking of the towns of Doha and al-Wakrah, but this conflict broke the 1820 agreement with Britain for peace in the gulf. The British agent, Lewis Pelly (British resident in Iran from 1862 to 1872), forced an end to the war in 1868 and recognized Shaykh Mohammed bin Thani as ruler of Qatar, ending Bahraini claims over the area.

However, shortly after the end of the Bahraini threat, Qatar was incorporated into the Ottoman Empire in 1871. Qatar was in a militant mood under Shaykh Jassim bin Mohammed al-Thani (ruled 1878–1913). In 1882, Qatar tried to invade Abu Dhabi, but the Ottomans refused to support the attack, which eventually faltered. In 1888, the Ottomans supported another person, Muhammad ibn 'Abd al-Wahhab, as the qaimaqam (a term that means a mayor or local leader) of Qatar instead of Jassim al-Thani. As a result, in 1892, the entire province refused to pay taxes to the Ottomans. The following year, the Ottomans tried to take Qatar and force payment of back taxes, but the Ottomans were defeated by a force of both infantry and cavalry, and the Ottomans retreated to Hofuf Oasis. Qatar remained outside of the empire's control and was recognized again as independent in 1916 when Britain wanted to make sure that the local ruler would remain hostile to the Ottoman forces in Hofuf. Oil was discovered in 1939, but production did not begin until after World War II in 1949. Profits from early oil monies were invested in the improvement of living standards of the ordinary people, with the first school opening in 1952 and the first modern hospital in 1959. However, the local rulers, Shaykh 'Ali (ruled 1949–1960) and then Ahmad ibn 'Ali (1960–1972) were less interested in ruling than in spending oil monies on frivolities in foreign countries. In 1972, a nephew, Khalifa, took control of the country and ruled until a bloodless coup by his son Hamid overthrew him in 1995. As a result of historical relations with Abu Dhabi, Qatar saw itself as independent and, like Bahrain, more advanced (and richer) than the other emirates, and withdrew from the union before it even began.

Initially, the United Arab Emirates was composed of six emirates, with Ras al-Khaimah staying out of the political organization until 1972 after the failed coup in Sharjah. Although Ras al-Khaimah had a long history of independence, it was brought under Sharjah's control after the war with Great Britain in 1819–1820. The capital of the Qawasim state was moved from Ras al-Khaimah to Sharjah. In the second half of the nineteenth century, Sharjah experienced an expansionist period, confronting the Bani Yas of Abu Dhabi and Dubai;

challenging the Bedouin Sharqiyin tribe in Fujairah and the power of the sultan of Oman; and serving, on occasion, Saudi influence. Ras al-Khaimah gained its independence from Sharjah in 1869 under a separate branch of the Qasimi family under Humaid ibn Abdullah. Sharjah formally gave up claim to Ras al-Khaimah in 1921, with Britain recognizing its independence. As a result, Ras al-Khaimah's ruler, Shaykh Saqr bin Muhammed al-Qasimi (ruled 1948–2010) was reluctant to join the union, but after three months, he decided it would be best for his emirate if he did.[2]

Sharjah joined the union, but in the first few weeks, a former shaykh, Saqr ibn Sultan al-Qasimi, staged an attempted coup. Saqr became the ruler of Sharjah in 1951 after the death of his father, Sultan ibn Saqr, when his uncle, Muhammad, did not take the throne himself, but in 1965, the people of Sharjah deposed Saqr, and he left for exile in Cairo. Sharjah was ruled by one of his nephews, Khalid bin Mohammed. In 1972, shortly after the union was formed, he tried to come back and take over the government. The then-ruling shaykh of Sharjah, Khalid, was killed by forces loyal to Saqr, who was killed himself in the coup attempt by soldiers of the Trucial Oman Scouts. In February 1972, the new shaykh of Sharjah was named, Shaykh Sultan ibn Muhammad

The Blue Suq, or Central Market, in Sharjah abides by local architectural styles of the gulf and includes a wide variety of shops. Its wind towers are not functional but are decorative. (Courtesy of John A. Shoup)

Independence and the Birth of the United Arab Emirates 107

al-Qasimi, who continues to rule today.[3] Sharjah remains a strong member of the union.

Abu Dhabi and Dubai are the most powerful sheikdoms and were so prior to the unification. Both had their own oil discoveries, and Abu Dhabi shared some of the new oil wealth with the other sheikdoms that were less fortunate in their natural wealth. Abu Dhabi is the largest of the seven emirates, and the Bani Yas leadership rose to dominance in the past under Shaykh Zayed ibn Khalifah (ruled 1855–1909). He is called, even today, Zayed the Great.[4] This shaykh Zayed exercised a good deal of power, but it was lost until Shakhbut reestablished Abu Dhabi's dominance after a period of instability due to intrafamily disputes over leadership. In 1928, Shakhbut ibn Sultan took control from his uncle, Saqr ibn Zayed, and since then, Abu Dhabi has been led by strong rulers.

In 1949, Saudi Arabia reasserted its claim over a good amount of Abu Dhabi's land, including the oasis of Buraimi. This was partially prompted by exploration for oil near the oasis, but the two countries had different agreements with British and American companies for rights to oil exploitation. In 1922, all the shaykhs of the Trucial States signed a treaty with the British, giving exclusive rights to British companies, and in 1937, Shaykh Shakhbut signed a seventy-five-year agreement with a British company. In 1952, Saudi forces occupied the village of Hamasah in Buraimi oasis and were welcomed by the local leader of the Al Bu Shamis tribe, a section of the Na'im. The Na'im had been able to play a political game between sultan of Oman and the Saudi ruler during much of the nineteenth and early twentieth centuries, paying one or the other taxes when it suited Na'im ambitions. The Al Bu Shamis division of the Na'im had become somewhat independent of the main leadership of the tribe and often set its own course. At this time, Shaykh Rashid bin Hamad was the leader of the Al Bu Shamis section and had influence over the Bedouin sections of the Bani Qitab and Ka'ab, two other tribal groups who, on occasion, gave loyalty to the sultan of Oman or one of the leaders of the Trucial States. Until the dispute in the 1950s between Oman, Saudi Arabia, and Abu Dhabi, these "free" tribes were able to shift power between the states, supporting one side and then the other. However, after the dispute, they could not remain free agents but had to choose which state they would join. Most of the Na'im, Bani Qitab, and Ka'ab chose to remain in Abu Dhabi, but some chose Oman, and others Saudi Arabia.

In 1949, the Arabian American Oil Company (ARAMCO) extended their exploration into Abu Dhabi's territory, and the Saudi governor of Ra's Tanura, Turki bin Abdullah bin Utaishan, occupied the town of Hamasah, claimed by both the sultan of Oman and the imam of Nizwa. The small Saudi force set about the usual distribution of gifts of food and clothing to gain popular support by asking locals to sign statements of support to the Saudi king.

In 1946, Shaykh Zayed bin Sultan was named the wali or governor of al-Ain/Buraimi oasis under Abu Dhabi's control, and though the three villages claimed by Saudi Arabia were located in the Omani zone, Zayed played a major role in finally settling the issue.[5] It is said that Saudi Arabia offered Zayed a substantial bribe for his support, but he did not use his influence with the Bedouin sections of the Na'im and other tribes in Saudi Arabia's favor. Instead, with the advice of his longtime friend, Edward Henderson (a former British oil representative, but at that time, he had become a British government representative), he sided with Oman (and Great Britain).[6] Oman called in the Trucial Oman Scouts, supplemented by the British Air Force, but soon after arriving in Sharjah, there was a mutiny among the scouts from Dhufar in Oman. No action was taken, and the dispute was given to an international court to decide. However, by 1955, no decision could be made to untangle the complicated claims of tribal groups with loyalty to Abu Dhabi, Oman, and/or Saudi Arabia. In addition, Saudi Arabia's representative tried to bribe the court's decision, and settlement was suspended.[7] In the end, Great Britain decided to send in the Trucial Scouts to dislodge the Saudis, who had been reinforced in the meantime. The oasis was divided between Oman, given the three disputed villages, and Abu Dhabi getting the rest of the land.[8] Nonetheless, Saudi Arabia did not give up its claim to the three villages that belong to Oman, and a number of disgruntled shaykhs moved north into Saudi Arabian territory.[9] Abu Dhabi gained the most from the dispute, expanding its authority over six of the villages in the oasis, including al-Ain, which quickly became the largest town in the Abu Dhabi–held section of the oasis and became the name for the oasis on the Emirate side of the border. Buraimi, the old, historic name, became the name on the Omani side. Other tribes in northern Oman, such as the Duru also lost their power-making position and were fully on the Omani side. Today, most live around the Omani town of Ibri (in the past seen as part of Trucial Oman), which lies southwest of Buraimi.[10] Today, they form one of the largest tribes in Oman.[11] Even though the Buraimi dispute was basically over, Saudi Arabia did not give up its claims over the area.

In 1954, the British decided that the borders of the various emirates had to be determined. They hired a local historian, 'Abdallah al-Reyyes employed by Shaykh Zayed, to visit every village, town, and Bedouin encampment in order to determine the hodgepodge of claims by each of the seven emirates. He narrated that this took him a good deal of time. His method, which was to ask which shaykh the people said they followed, produced the current map of the emirates and is responsible for some of the very strange and disjointed borders of the countries. In addition, Oman used to claim the entire coast along the Indian Ocean, but in the nineteen century, the Sharqiyin tribe moved in and took much of it. At that time, the Sharqiyin were dependent on Sharjah, but the tribe's shaykh grew independent and was recognized as such by the British in 1952 as the separate territory of Fujairah.[12] Precise borders were made imperative once oil was discovered, and agreements with various shaykhs became necessary for payments to be made. As a result, conflicting claims were noted between Sharjah, Fujairah, and Oman, and joint administrations were established, and small enclaves belonging to Sharjah, Ajman, Dubai, and Fujairah within the territory of other emirates were given precise details, even though the shaykhs seem unconcerned about such matters today.[13] The tip of the Arabian Peninsula, the Musandam Peninsula, is part of Oman. It is home to the Shihuh tribe (a South Arabian-speaking people) and is important politically because the land helps form the Straits of Hormuz between Arabia and Iran. Ras al-Khaimah's shaykh includes several subsections of Shihuh as part of his emirate.

Qasr al-Hisn served as the home of the shaykhs of Abu Dhabi and the seat of government for the emirate until recently. It is now a museum of the emirate and of Shaykh Zayed. (Courtesy of John A. Shoup)

The union was worked out, mainly between Shaykh Zayed of Abu Dhabi and Shaykh Rashid al-Maktoum (ruled 1958–2015) of Dubai. They had very different personalities and different interests. Shaykh Rashid was seen as a practical man who was interested in business but not politics. The al-Maktoum family had ruled Dubai since it broke away from Abu Dhabi in 1833.[14] Very early on, even before the collapse of the pearl trade, the al-Maktoum took a keen interest in trade with Iran and India. The rulers of Dubai built a multinational society, quickly making Dubai the most populous of the emirates. Beginning with the period of Shaykh Maktoum bin Hasher (ruled 1894–1906) and his son Sa'id (ruled 1912–1958), the city grew, with migrants arriving from Iran in particular. These Arabo-Iranians had a considerable influence on Dubai's economic growth, as did merchant families from India. Dubai gained economic influence not only in the pearl trade but also in other commodities once Lingah in Iran lost its importance. Dubai inherited not only the Arabo-Iranian families but also their international connections, making Dubai among the most important ports in the gulf. Shaykh Rashid was not interested in politics but in making money, and Dubai quickly became the center for moneymaking in the gulf. Shaykh Rashid was interested in building a huge port at Jabal Ali and dredging the creek that opened up to the gulf, allowing oceangoing vessels to sail up to deliver cargo inside Dubai city. Shaykh Zayed was the president of the state and Shaykh Rashid the vice president. The two worked out an easy relationship, with both states the biggest oil producers upon which the other states were dependent. It is said that the two met and shook hands on unity.[15] When Ras al-Khaimah's shaykh, Shaykh Saqr bin Muhammed al-Qasimi (ruled 1948–2010) was approached to join the union, he was reluctant to give up what he thought was his emirate's special identity. Also, there were hopes that oil would be found that would give Ras al-Khaimah enough money to be economically independent. Suddenly, in late November 1971, Iran seized the strategic Tunb islands (as well as Abu Musa, which belonged to Sharjah) near the Straits of Hormuz. The islands belong to Ras al-Khaimah. Once the other emirates stated that the Iranian occupation would be among their primary foreign policy concerns and the treaty Britain promised to sign with all members of the United Arab Emirates, Ras al-Khaimah's objections to joining the union began to fade. The final stroke that brought Ras al-Khaimah in was when Abu Dhabi and Dubai agreed to make it more powerful within the union, granting it six places in the governing assembly, with Abu Dhabi and Dubai each having eight. This gave Ras al-Khaimah a much larger say

Independence and the Birth of the United Arab Emirates

in politics than even Sharjah. In addition, Ras al-Khaimah's shaykh was granted the position of deputy foreign minister.[16]

FIRST YEARS OF INDEPENDENCE

During the first years of independence, old disputes and border clashes continued, and in 1972, war broke out between Sharjah and Fujairah.[17] Shaykh Zayed tried to get the various shaykhs to give up their own armies and police and depend instead on a single national force. Most did not like the idea, but Abu Dhabi finally convinced the other emirates that a national force was not for Abu Dhabi's use against them. At first, the coalition was weak, but Great Britain wanted to deal with all seven together and not as separate entities. The first act of the new government was to sign a new treaty with Great Britain that cancelled all previous treaties with all of the emirates. With the new treaty of friendship, the United Arab Emirates began a new era of great prosperity.

Nonetheless, Saudi Arabia was still hurting after its loss of Buraimi due to British pressure and actions taken by Oman and the then–Trucial Oman (meaning the actions taken by Shaykh Zayed to get the Bedouin tribes to stop supporting Saudi Arabia). In 1974, it to annex the border area of Abu Dhabi with Saudi Arabia and took over a major oil field. Since the arrival of the Bani Yas in Abu Dhabi in the eighteenth century, the entire coastal region up to the border with Qatar was under the Bani Yas shaykhs, including the area called Khor al Udaid containing the Shaybah/Zarrara oil field. The Khor al Udaid was lightly settled, with a small population of fishermen and farmers, but most of the region was uninhabited. It stretched south to the Rub' al-Khali, a place equally uninhabited. Nonetheless, the region proved to have oil, and production was underway. Saudi Arabia simply annexed the border region, and Shaykh Zayed, with a very small army, decided it would not be worth fighting over. It is reported that he said, "Let them have a few oil wells. We have more than enough for our needs."[18] Saudi Arabia's king, King Faisal (ruled 1964–1975) met with Shaykh Zayed in Jeddah and agreed to sign the Jeddah Treaty that brought an end to the Buraimi Dispute. Saudi Arabia was able to keep the border area it had annexed and was also given a percentage of Abu Dhabi's oil revenue.

The same strategy was used to deal with Iran, and Sharjah's Shaykh Khalid bin Mohammed agreed to share oil revenue earned from the oil production from the Abu Musa wells. The other shaykhs considered the deal treasonous. Saqr returned to Sharjah to take back power and reject the deal with Iran, but he lost his position to the current ruler, Sultan bin Muhammad al-Qasimi.[19] Nonetheless, the deal with Iran stood.[20] Shaykh Zayed paid off the two much larger countries but also backed his own side with recognition in the Arab League (within days of independence in 1971) and the United Nations (also within days of independence). In addition, he could count on Great Britain's treaty of friendship signed at the same time as independence. Afterward, the United States and the United Arab Emirates signed security protocols allowing U.S. Navy ships to dock in United Arab Emirate ports. In fact, the United Arab Emirates hosts more American naval vessels than any other port worldwide. For the United Arab Emirates, the presence of American naval vessels in the Gulf is seen as protection against possible Iranian aggression since Iran's seizure of the two Tunb islands has not been solved.

UNITED ARAB EMIRATES GOVERNMENT

The first draft of the constitution for the United Arab Emirates was at the initiative of Qatar. As the wealthiest of the small Arab states, it hired an Egyptian legal expert, Dr. 'Abd al-Razaq al-Sanhuri, to draft the constitution under the assumption that the two leading states would be Qatar and Bahrain.[21] When they withdrew from the union, Abu Dhabi and Dubai were the main powers. The two were not the same, but Abu Dhabi was the richer of the two. Initially, Shaykh Rashid wanted to go it alone and declare Dubai's independence based on the model of Hong Kong, but his sons were against the move. They saw the dangers in such a move, highlighted by the 1961 attempt by Iraq to "recover" Kuwait that had been saved by seven thousand British troops from Bahrain.[22] They did not want the same to happen to them, and they were also caught between Saudi Arabia and Iran. The new constitution was written by another legal expert, Adi Bitar, whose constitution served as the basis for the 1971 union and was made permanent in 1996, when all points were agreed upon by all seven of the emirates. Only Ras al-Khaimah suggested that the seven form a republic, but this was rejected by all the other leaders.[23]

The organization of the government of the United Arab Emirates is federal (in that all seven of the emirates keep internal affairs to themselves, like the states in the United States), presidential (in that the shaykh of Abu Dhabi is the president of the country), and a constitutional monarchy, but each state is ruled as an absolute monarchy in its own territory. Nonetheless, there is an overall federal constitution

Independence and the Birth of the United Arab Emirates 113

whose jurisdiction over certain matters, as in all federal states, overrides the laws of individual member states. The constitution states that the ruler of Abu Dhabi is the president and head of state, but the ruler of Dubai is the vice president and head of government as the prime minister. The other rulers form the Federal Supreme Council that meets to enact federal laws and policies. The Supreme Council is supported by a twenty-two–member Council of Ministers or a cabinet headed by the shaykh of Dubai as prime minister. The Council of Ministers is under the control of the president (the shaykh of Abu Dhabi) and the Supreme Council.

In addition, there is a forty-member Federal National Council, composed of twenty members appointed by the rulers of the seven emirates and twenty members (in advisory positions only) that are elected from an electoral college of 6,689 names from all of the seven emirates. They must be at least twenty-five years old and literate. Their numbers in the National Council are based on the population of each of the emirates, with Dubai having the most; it was to be a *shurah* or advisory council.[24] As a legislative body, they review proposed laws but do not have the power to veto them. They can question ministers and call into question a ministry's performance. They are, according to the constitution, to see if new laws fit within the Islamic basis of the nation's legal system, the sharia. They do not have the right to inspect a separate emirate's laws—only those seen as within the federal system.

The capital was temporarily placed in Abu Dhabi for the first seven years while a new city, al-Karamah, was to be built on the border between Dubai and Abu Dhabi. The new city was never built, and in 1996, with the adoption of all the parts of the 1971 Constitution, Abu Dhabi became the official capital of the United Arab Emirates. The plan for the new capital never went beyond the drawing board due to the difficulties that arose between Rashid and Zayed.

In 1973, the problem of what currency to use was solved with the issuing of the official United Arab Emirate dirham. The economic boom began in the early 1970s and continued through the 1980s, with the two main leaders, Zayed and Rashid, taking different paths. Zayed, in his Bedouin manner of doing things, often preferred arbitration, while Rashid, in his very businessman manner, took a harsher stance. The two men continued to rule the country, but there were some difficult times. Both men set off a race to see which emirate would modernize the fastest, often with Abu Dhabi running to catch up with Dubai. Given the freedom that each emirate was able to exercise, tensions were kept to a minimum, with Dubai and Ras al-Khaimah often at odds with the other five.²⁵ The two differed greatly about their oil wealth, with Zayed opting to share his with the other, poorer emirates, and not demanding full control but a 40 to 60 percent share with the oil companies. Rashid, on the other hand, did not share Dubai's wealth and wanted full control over the wells in his territory.²⁶

Despite the issues between Shaykh Zayed and Shaykh Rashid and the fact that several banks collapsed during the first decade of the United Arab Emirates' independence, much of the country enjoyed the rapid growth in wealth. The small population and the general low literacy rate among the citizens meant there was a need to bring in people to help run the nation. The country quickly became dependent on professional people from the United States, Great Britain, and Australia, as well as from India and Pakistan, Syria, Jordan, and Egypt. Like the other gulf states, laws were enacted to protect high positions for "nationals," meaning citizens of the United Arab Emirates. Kuwait, Saudi Arabia, and Bahrain had already gone through this stage, and all decided on a process of localization of positions. By the 1980s, foreigners outnumbered nationals in nearly all jobs. Pakistanis, Indians, and Afghanis served as the main workforce in hard, manual labor, such as building the new cities that emerged from the temporary *barasti* homes. Shaykh Zayed had new housing districts built in all seven emirates, though Dubai would go its own way. Being the desert Bedouin shaykh to the end, Zayed felt that his people should enjoy the oil wealth in whatever ways were available. He built infrastructure even before the oil money was available, building the first school in al-Ain in 1959 with his own personal money. His son, Prince Khalifa bin Zayed, as well as sons of others in his court, attended the school.²⁷ This was the first of a number of primary schools founded and funded by Shaykh Zayed that are called al-Nahyan Niyyah Model Schools (al-Nahyan being the family name of the shaykh).

In addition to schools, he also instituted roads and airports, as well as housing projects for his people. Housing projects need to conform to local culture, and most villas (for single-family dwellings) also include an additional guest house (as in Saudi Arabia) as a separate structure that allows the women of the house to appear or not, depending on how close the visitors are to the family. Apartments are also built with local culture in mind with two entrances—one main entrance for the man of the house and guests to use and another separate entrance that allows women the chance to come and go without guests seeing them.

Public health was also a concern of Shaykh Zayed, and a number of hospitals and clinics were built in all seven emirates. They were staffed

Independence and the Birth of the United Arab Emirates 115

by doctors and nurses from other countries, in particular Great Britain, but the need for Arabic-speaking personnel made it imperative to hire Egyptians, Jordanians, Palestinians, and Syrians who could deal with the local patients. All of this was underwritten by Abu Dhabi, which took on the responsibility of the federal budget in 1977. Three of the smaller emirates each paid only 2 percent of the budgetary needs, with Dubai and two others initially refusing to pay anything at all.[28] Several of the shaykhs, including Rashid of Dubai and Saqr of Ras al-Khaimah, were suspicious of the motives of Shaykh Zayed. However, Saqr understood that Zayed's efforts were to maintain the unity. While Saqr did not like Zayed's methods, he was, nonetheless, unable to resist the gifts of money Zayed offered. In 1976, Zayed was "reelected" (elected by the other emirates' shaykhs) as president of the country, and Rashid as vice president for another term.[29]

The two main emirates kept separate development agendas, with Dubai unwilling to share in the burden of payment. Abu Dhabi sustained the United Arab Emirates and funded development in the smaller member states that were less endowed with oil, yet many of the shaykhs remained skeptical about the reasons for this generosity. Shaykh Zayed resigned (or threatened to resign) twice. The first time was in 1978 over Zayed appointing his son Sultan as commander of the federal armed forces. The second time was in 1979, when Zayed pushed a ten-point plan to strengthen the union, which was opposed by Dubai and Ras al-Khaimah but approved by the other emirates.[30] The dispute was resolved through mediation by Kuwait. Both problems showed that old loyalties and old suspicions remained, despite Zayed's attempt to build a sense of being an Emirati. Many political scientists in Jordan, Syria, Iraq, and Egypt predicted that the country would collapse into tribal regions again; however, they were proved wrong, and Zayed's struggle to unify the country worked. Dubai's ruler, Shaykh Rashid, remained skeptical until his end, but he felt he needed to remain in the union no matter his personal feelings about the United Arab Emirates, Abu Dhabi, and Shaykh Zayed.

THE 1980S AND FOREIGN POLICY CONCERNS

From the Nixon presidency (1969–1974) onward, the Americans came up with a defensive strategy to deal with the British withdrawal from the gulf. It was furthered by what President Jimmy Carter (1977–1981) called the "two pillars": Saudi Arabia and Iran. Saudi Arabia was too concerned with its internal issues to assume a protective role in the gulf, and as a result, Iran assumed the mantel of protector, especially after the Soviet invasion of Afghanistan in 1979. However, the shah fell in the same year, and Iraq invaded Iran in 1980. Saudi Arabia was not in a position to become the protector of the gulf, and it was suspected by other gulf states of pursuing its own agenda rather than having the affairs of other gulf states in mind. Concern over the Iran-Iraq War led to the formation of the Gulf Cooperation Council in 1981.[31] The Iran-Iraq War caused problems in the United Arab Emirates, with Abu Dhabi (and reluctantly Dubai) siding with Iraq. Ras al-Khaimah and Sharjah, with large Persian and Arab-Persian communities, wanted to stay neutral, but the sentiment of most of their people was with Iran.

The United States needed Saudi Arabia to step into Iran's place as protector of the gulf states; however, Saudi Arabia was experiencing the rise of homegrown Islamic fundamentalism, which threatened Saudi rule. In 1979, the main mosque in Makkah was attacked by a group of gunmen. On the morning of November 20, 1979, as the imam began preparations to lead prayers for the fifty thousand worshipers gathered in the mosque, the group attacked. They were well armed and well prepared for the attack, calling for the end of the Saudi regime and declaring Mohammed Abdullah al-Qahtani as the Mahdi who would restore the Muslim world before the arrival of the last days. The number of the group was estimated to be around five hundred men, led by a former member of the Saudi National Guard, Juhayman al-'Utaybi. Both al-Qahtani and al-'Utaybi belonged to important families of the Saudi Ikhwan, the organization founded in 1910 by 'Abd al-'Aziz ibn Sa'ud that conquered the kingdom for the Saudi family.[32] Al-'Utaybi was a follower of the fiery Saudi cleric Shaykh 'Abd al-'Aziz ibn Baz (one of the main voices of Salafism in the kingdom). The group was well organized and able to hold out for weeks before the Saudi king ordered an attack that finally forced its surrender to Saudi, Pakistani, and French special forces.[33]

The royal family executed sixty-three of the sixty-seven survivors of the siege in strategic cities across the kingdom. This attack was the start of al-Qaida, with members from all over the Muslim world actively participating in the attack. It also served as a start for Osama bin Laden who was living in Jeddah, only an hour away from Makkah by car. The Saudi royal family turned much of the anti-Western sentiment in the kingdom against the Russians in Afghanistan. Many of the demands made by Saudi clerics to retrench Salafi ideas were instituted in Saudi Arabia by the royal family, which put back development in the kingdom by at least a generation. They funded Salafi madrassas,

Independence and the Birth of the United Arab Emirates 117

fired female announcers on television, and promoted the ultraconservative 'Abd al-'Aziz ibn Baz to the chief position in the kingdom by making him the mufti of the state. The result was the rise of Salafi institutions (and anti-Western sentiment), funded by the Saudi government throughout the world. Unknowingly, the Saudis helped train future recruits for al-Qaida.

Almost at the same time, the American embassy was taken over by an angry crowd in Tehran because the Saudis tried to blame the new Iranian government for the mosque attack. Ayatollah Khomeini retaliated by saying the attack was a Zionist-American plot and not connected to Iran. In anger, a crowd of Iranians took over the American embassy in Tehran, taking a number of the Americans hostage. The American press focused on the events in Iran with the American embassy hostage crisis and not on the mosque attack, thus not recognizing the rise of global Jihadism.[34] Other attacks on U.S. embassies happened throughout the Muslim world, including in the United Arab Emirates. An attack in Pakistan was much worse than the one in Tehran. The entire building was burned to the ground, and several embassy employees were killed. Saudi Arabia and Iran became enemies, with neither being able to serve as protector of the gulf.

In 1980, the war between Iran and Iraq broke out, and most of the Arab world, being Sunni, supporting Iraq. As noted before, Abu Dhabi and Dubai supported Iraq, although other emirates wanted to stay neutral, as large portions of their population were Shi'ite and of Iranian origin. Iraq was driven back into Iraqi territory, and the United States and Saudi Arabia feared that if Iran won, it would mean a second Shi'ite state that could threaten the gulf as well as the world supply of oil. Iraq's leader, Saddam Hussein, turned to the West for aid, and it came from the United States as well as from Britain and France, traditional allies of the Arab gulf states. In addition, the gulf states gave Iraq millions of U.S. dollars in aid to prevent an Iranian victory.[35] Iraq saw itself as the logical heir to the British as the protector of the Arab gulf states, in that the ruling family in Iraq was also Sunni. He also felt that the Arabs needed no outsider to guarantee the freedom of Arab states and began to pursue a policy line to advocate his role. However, Saddam Hussein, though a Sunni Arab, belonged to the secular Ba'ath Socialist Party and was not very religious. This made many of the gulf Arab states suspicious of him, and they felt they needed to band together to prevent this.

In 1981, the Gulf Cooperation Council (GCC) was formed by the Arab gulf states (Bahrain, Kuwait, Oman, Qatar, Saudi Arabia, and the United Arab Emirates). Among the first topics discussed, after the initial meeting in Riyadh, Saudi Arabia, on May 25, 1981, was mutual defense. The defense ministers met soon after the founding meeting to establish a joint, integrated military against any outside threat (from Iraq or Iran); however, they soon discovered that they were handicapped by buying equipment from different sources (the United States, Great Britain, France and Russia), which were not easily integrated.[36] In 1984, the Gulf Cooperation Council began to establish an integrated military unit composed of two brigades of five thousand men from all six nations. The force was stationed in Saudi Arabia under the command of Saudi officers.[37] It was to be a rapid response force that could go wherever a threat loomed, and it began military exercises with forces from the United States and Great Britain under the name Peninsula Shield.

In 1987, Sharjah had an attempted coup while the shaykh, Shaykh Sultan, was out of the country. His brother, 'Abd al-'Aziz, staged a take-over and announced that Sultan had abdicated due to financial mismanagement. This came as a total surprise to Sultan, and the two main powers of the United Arab Emirates, Zayed of Abu Dhabi and Rashid of Dubai, argued over what to do. In the end, they agreed that Sultan should be brought back to Sharjah as the head of state but that 'Abd al-'Aziz should be named as the crown prince of Sharjah. Sultan was not happy with the state of affairs, but there was nothing he could do. He agreed to name his brother as crown prince, but after giving it some time, Sultan eventually dismissed him. 'Abd al-'Aziz went into exile and has not bothered Sharjah again. Sharjah continued as before, with Sultan making efforts to promote Sharjah as the center of culture in the gulf.

Despite support for Iraq, deep suspicions remained for many of the rulers of the Arab gulf states about what Saddam Hussein would expect from them. Saddam Hussein told the U.A.E. leadership that he would return the occupied Tunb Islands to United Arab Emirates control if they joined him in his war against Iran. However, the offer was rejected.[38] The GCC could not agree about U.S. presence in the gulf, with some countries (such as Oman) seeing nothing wrong with the American presence and others (such as Saudi Arabia) very much against it. The American presence was due to the threat both sides in the war gave to the free flow of oil and the need of oil to Western economies. The Iran-Iraq War ended in 1988 in a negotiated peace that left both countries economically shattered. Iraq turned to the Arab gulf states to make up for the economic losses the country suffered.

Independence and the Birth of the United Arab Emirates 119

Suddenly, in August 1990, Saddam Hussein invaded Kuwait and quickly defeated the Kuwaiti military.

THE GULF WAR

With Kuwaiti independence in 1961, Iraq invaded and pressed its historical claim, stating that the British had forced Kuwait's separate identity while it was part of the Ottoman province of Basrah in Iraq. Kuwait successfully countered this verbal attack, and Iraq's government agreed to exchange ambassadors in 1963, although it did not formally accept Kuwait's independence. In 1990, Iraq brought its claim back and added the "fact" that Kuwait had "stolen oil" from Iraqi wells during the war with Iran. Saddam Hussein invaded his much weaker neighbor and quickly occupied the entire country. As a member of the GCC, Kuwait expected the other members to come to its aid, and. suddenly, any objections to American troops in the Peninsula vanished. In order to supply the allied effort, Abu Dhabi nearly doubled its oil output to over one million barrels of oil a day, a feat accomplished in only three weeks. The United Arab Emirates also opened its ports to U.S. naval ships and its airbases to U.S. Air Force.[39]

The defense forces of the United Arab Emirates numbered over forty thousand men, and in addition, the seven emirates called for volunteers to fight Iraq. There was an overwhelming answer to the call, but only a few actually qualified both by age and physical fitness. The United Arab Emirates participated in the fighting at Khafji and helped drive out the Iraqi army, suffering casualties. Many saw the war as a defense of their own lands, believing that Saddam Hussein meant to punish all the Arab gulf states for his loss against Iran. However, hosting American troops on gulf soil was among the accusations by Islamists against the leaders of the gulf states that helped give rise to such organizations as al-Qaida. Most American soldiers were/are not Muslim, and the Saudi regime in particular was castigated by Osama bin Laden, among others, for allowing them into the kingdom. Osama bin Laden had his own plan, using only Arab troops to dislodge the Iraqis—an army composed of veteran fighters from the war in Afghanistan—but the Saudi royal family and their generals did not believe it would work and did not give it a second thought. Bin Laden continued to verbally attack the Saudi royal family, and they deported him in 1992 and revoked his citizenship in 1994.

In the United Arab Emirates, Shaykh Rashid died in 1990 and was succeeded by his son Maktoum (ruled 1990–2006). Rashid's policy of economic diversification paid off, with Dubai becoming a major international emporium. During Rashid's time, Dubai had hit oil, but oil would not be the mainstay of economic growth. He had the creek that connected Dubai with the gulf dredged to allow oceangoing vessels to unload inside the town and spent oil money to build a large port just outside of Dubai town at Jabal Ali.[40] Dubai was/is connected to the other emirates by a highway system, making it the destination for shipping goods to any of the emirates. Maktoum inherited his father's position as not only shaykh but also as vice president and prime minister of the United Arab Emirates.

In 1991, there was a major financial scandal revolving around the Bank of Credit and Commerce International (BCCI). Its management personnel were staffed by a number of "shady" characters, and it was rumored that they were involved in laundering the drug money of such people as General Manuel Noriega of Panama. In July 1991, the Bank of England closed the BCCI down after receiving numerous reports of fraud, seizing some £13 billion in assets. Abu Dhabi owned 77 percent of the bank shares.[41] The BCCI was a private bank, founded in Abu Dhabi in 1972 by a Pakistani businessman named Agha Hassan Abedi. It quickly became the seventh-largest private bank in the world, but in the 1980s, its link to drug money became a well-known rumor. In that the state of Abu Dhabi supported it, it was often used by migrant workers from Pakistan and India. When the Bank of England closed it down, the worst hit were the thousands of migrant workers who lost their savings. As a result, Shaykh Zayed declared that Abu Dhabi would cover the monies lost and began massive money payouts to those who had lost everything with the bank's closure. Although Abu Dhabi lost massive amounts of money—£2 billion—Zayed set aside £50 million to cover the small account losses.[42] A number of the bank officials were arrested and in 1994, twelve were convicted of fraud and were jailed in the United Arab Emirates. The BCCI affair did not tarnish the reputation of Shaykh Zayed but enhanced it by his making good the losses from numerous small accounts held by migrants and local people.

In 2004, a meeting of the GCC was to be held in Abu Dhabi, and the city began the preparations. Streets were cleaned and painted, and a new hotel to house the delegates was built. However, the meeting was moved without explanation, and the people understood the Zayed was beginning to fade. He died in that year and was succeeded by his eldest son, Khalifa, both to the head of Abu Dhabi and as president of the United Arab Emirates.

Independence and the Birth of the United Arab Emirates

NOTES

1. Morton, Michael Quentin. *Keepers of the Golden Shore: A History of the United Arab Emirates.* London: Reaktion Books, 2016, 179.
2. Heard-Bey, Frauke. *From Trucial States to United Arab Emirates.* Dubai: Motivate Press, 2004, 84.
3. Ibid., 85.
4. Ibid., 69.
5. Hellyer, Peter and Buckton, Rosalind. *Al Ain: Oasis City.* Dubai: Motivate Press, 1998, 23.
6. Ibid.
7. Morton, 160.
8. Zahlan, Rosemarie Said. *The Origins of the United Arab Emirates: A Political and Social History of the Trucial States.* London: Macmillan Publishers, 1978, 192.
9. Morton, 160.
10. Carter, J. R. L. *Tribes in Oman.* London: Peninsular Publishing, 1982, 10, 29.
11. Ibid., 29.
12. "The Rise of the Gulf," 'Abdallah al-Reyyes. Accessed May 8, 2019. https://www.youtube.com/watch?v=y22p-F1PIO4; Heard-Bey. 90.
13. "The Rise of the Gulf."
14. Zahlan, 12.
15. Morton, 185.
16. Heard-Bey, 370.
17. Morton, 195.
18. "The Rise of the Gulf."
19. Zahlan, 196.
20. Morton, 195.
21. Ibid., 179.
22. Ibid., 182.
23. Ibid., 186.
24. Ibid., 195.
25. Ibid., 197.
26. Ibid., 196.
27. Hellyer and Buckton, 23.
28. Morton, 197.
29. Ibid.
30. Ibid.
31. Lansford, Tom. "Gulf Cooperation Council," in *Saudi Arabia and the Gulf Arab States*, edited by Sebastian Maisel and John A. Shoup. Westport, CT: Greenwood Press, 2009, 179.
32. Maisel, Sebastian. "Islamic Fundamentalism—*Salafiyah*," in *Saudi Arabia and the Gulf Arab States Today*, 228.
33. Trofimov, Yaroslav. "The Siege of Mecca," Muslim Americans on C-Span—Unofficial, video, 56:59. Accessed May 18, 2019. https://www.youtube.com/watch?v=1hNjJY1OXmM.
34. Ibid.

35. Sater, James. "Iran-Iraq War," in *Saudi Arabia and the Gulf Arab States Today*, 223.
36. Lansford, 179.
37. Ibid.
38. Morton, 201.
39. Ibid.
40. Heard-Bey, 15.
41. Morton, 202.
42. Ibid., 204.

9

The United Arab Emirates in the Modern International Arena (2004–2020)

The death of Shaykh Zayed was a sad time for the inhabitants of the United Arab Emirates. More than anyone else, Shaykh Zayed embodied the character of the country. He used his own money to open schools and set the government policy of providing free housing, medical services, and education for all citizens of the United Arab Emirates. Toward the end of his life, he began to have doubts about the consequences of providing such services for free and not encouraging competition from within the society. Nonetheless, as a responsible Bedouin leader, he felt it was his duty to provide for his people and pay the cost so they all could benefit from the oil wealth of the nation. He remained a beloved leader throughout his entire life, and even the scandal of the Bank of Credit and Commerce International's collapse in 1991 did not touch him. He made good on the lost savings of the numerous small holders, which actually increased his personal standing among his people and among the many Afghani,

Pakistani, and Indian small account holders. He was greatly mourned, but his successor, Shaykh Khalifa, was equally regarded by his people. Shaykh Zayed forged an Emirati identity that is stronger than that of a single tribal group, and it has been noted by those who know the Emirates well that Emiratis responded to the question of what tribe do they belong to with the answer "Emirati" rather than "Bani Yas" or "Qasimi" or any other single tribal group.

Shaykh Khalifa had long been known as the crown prince and became popular while serving as the deputy supreme commander of the armed forces of the United Arab Emirates. Still the president of the United Arab Emirates today, Shaykh Khalifa does not like the limelight and, for health reasons, remains behind the scenes, unlike the leaders of Dubai. Because Shaykh Zayed had nine wives, the family coalesced around certain groups of sons. Two main factions arose: one around Khalifa and another one called the Bani Fatima around the sons of one of Zayed's most influential wives named Fatima bint Mubarak al-Ketbi. She was a young teenager when she met Zayed in the late 1950s/early 1960s and had her first child, a son, when she was sixteen years old. She was from al-Ain and of the Qitab tribe. Her eldest son, Muhammad, was made crown prince in 2004, beating out a half-brother named Sultan who was the choice of the Khalifa group.

Fatimah was thought of as Shaykh Zayed's favorite wife and took on the rights of Emirati women as her responsibility. She campaigned for education and employment for girls. She is greatly responsible for women being on the list of nominees for the Federal National Council when it was created in 2006.[1] She worked hard to ensure that women were on the Electoral College and that women were included in government ministries starting in 2004. She followed the example of other influential *shaykhah*s, such as her mother-in-law, Salamah bint Buti, or the *shaykhah* of Dubai. This was part of the traditions of the Arab gulf states, and women's contributions to social issues such as education, employment, and health has been key to their husbands' or sons' success. Saudi Arabia had its own set of influential women, with *Shaykhah* Hussa bint Ahmed al-Sudairi, the mother of the Saudi princes known as the Sudairi Seven, including King Fahd. Also, the wife of the Saudi monarch Faisal, Iffat al-Thunayan, opened schools for girls in the kingdom and found them jobs after graduation.[2] Royal women were often in the best place to advance women's rights and frequently did so. They were able to influence their husbands and sons to make decisions that were unpopular with the societies' men or to place sons and daughters in positions of importance. *Shaykhah* Fatimah saw that her sons had positions such as minister of foreign affairs and minister of information, in addition to governors of different provinces of Abu Dhabi.[3]

The al-Nahyan domination of the United Arab Emirates continues with Abu Dhabi's wealth, as they are able to control most events, and the crown prince, Muhammad, has good relations with the vice president and ruler of Dubai, also named Muhammad. In 2006, Muhammad bin Rashid al-Maktoum succeeded his brother Maktoum bin Rashid and expanded the economic development of Dubai, basing much of the new wealth on foreign investments and massive building projects with muscle supplied by Indian, Pakistani, Afghani, and Philippine labor. Older generations of leaders began to die and leave a legacy to their sons, starting in 1981 when Shaykh Rashid bin Humaid al-Nuaimi of Ajman died and was replaced by his son Humaid. Also in 1981, Shaykh Ahmad II bin Rashid al-Mualla of Umm al-Quwain died and was succeeded by his son Rashid, who subsequently died in 2009 and was replaced by his brother Sa'ud.[4] Most of these transitions to new rulers were smooth and peaceful, with only succession inside the al-Qasimi family open to dispute.

Both Sharjah and Ras al-Khaimah have had dynastic disputes. The issue in Sharjah was noted before, with the attempt to remove Shaykh Sultan during a trip abroad in 1987. The attempt by 'Abd al-'Aziz was not supported by either Abu Dhabi or Dubai, and with Sultan's return, the coup failed. However, both Abu Dhabi and Dubai's rulers agreed among themselves that 'Abd al-'Aziz should be nominated as the crown prince of Sharjah in order to reestablish order in the emirate.[5] Sultan accepted the humiliation as the price he had to pay to remain the ruler; however, he forced 'Abd al-'Aziz to step down and replaced him with his eldest son, Muhammad bin Sultan al-Qasimi. However, in 1999, Muhammad bin Sultan died of a drug overdose at the family's estate in England, and Sultan named another relative, Sultan bin Muhammad al-Qasimi, as the new crown prince. As a result of his son's overdose, the government of Sharjah passed strict laws against possession of and use of illicit drugs and alcohol—among the strictest of the gulf states. The strict laws are also due to the strong Wahhabi influence that has long been part of the emirate's history. Sharjah took on the demeanor of being a "family friendly" emirate and has become a "sleeper" community for people who work in Dubai, though urban planning keeps the two emirates separate, with only a few roads connecting them. Sharjah's ruler wants his emirate to be a cultural capital, as opposed to Dubai's business orientation. Dubai's reputation is for being a place where risky enterprises are rewarded, while Sharjah's more "learned" orientation is seen as in opposition.

Ras al-Khaimah also had dynastic disputes, and the current ruler, Shaykh Sa'ud became the ruler in 2010. In 2003, the then-ruler of Ras al-Khaimah, Shaykh Saqr bin Muhammad al-Qasimi, replaced the then–crown prince, Shaykh Khalid with a younger son, Shaykh Sa'ud, for unknown reasons. Among the proposed reasons for his loss of position was Khalid's participation in anti-American protests in which an American flag was burned in 2003, as well as his demand for greater political rights for women. Khalid went into exile after his father supported sending U.A.E. troops to support American troops in Iraq. Khalid tried to regain his position a number of times, but when his father died in 2010, succession went to younger brother Sa'ud and another younger member of the family became the new crown prince, Shaykh Muhammad bin Sa'ud bin Saqr al-Qasimi (one of the sons of Sa'ud); it was noted that succession had moved to the next generation, leaving Khalid out of the picture.[6] It is thought that the dynastic dispute in Ras al-Khaimah was the basis for the film *Syriana* (released in 2005), in which the plot focused on the disputes over the monarchy in a small, but rich Arab gulf state. The film was partially shot in Dubai (and Morocco), and social conditions of the working class were highlighted with the story of a young Pakistani who joins an Islamist group that, in the end, attacks and blows up an American oil tanker in the harbor.

BUILDING AND DEVELOPMENT

Dubai set the pace for development in the United Arab Emirates, and often, visitors are unaware of the rest of the country. Major construction projects such as Burj al-Arab Hotel (finished in 1999) and Burj Khalifa (formerly called Burj Dubai and renamed after the Shaykh of Abu Dhabi, finished in 2010) are what people know of the emirates. Emirate Airlines, founded in 1985, is based in Dubai, and it was not until 2003 that a new airline option was offered, Etihad, based in Abu Dhabi. It has since become a major competitor for Emirate Airline. Dubai also became the home for a number of foreign nationals because of the generous tax laws that encouraged multinational companies to locate their headquarters there. Specialized neighborhoods were and are being built, such as the palm trees in the gulf waters. These neighborhoods were/ are constructed in the form of palm trees or, one of them, like a map of the globe, but prices are too high for many people to buy or rent. Also, due to the laws around extradition, executives and former members of now-ousted governments have bought property in these exclusive neighborhoods. It was said that Tariq Aziz, Saddam Hussein's propaganda minister, was living in Dubai prior to his death in 2015. It is also a preferred place for multinational companies, such as Halliburton, to build their headquarters. Due to Dubai's extradition laws, CEOs are exempt from trials outside of the emirates.

Sharjah has concentrated on universities and reconstructing the coral rock–built section of the city. The process of preservation, restoration, and rebuilding of the houses began in early 1990s with a restoration of the old suq.[7] Careful planning and precise restoration methods were employed to ensure the buildings were restored to their original form using the techniques and architectural types of the originals. At around the same time, the streets and shops of suq al-'Arsah received the same precise treatment. The project is to be completed by 2025 and is already open to the public, with vendors selling numerous handmade crafts of the emirates, as well as traditional clothes, foods, and other objects and crafts. It is the best place in the emirates to reminisce about the 1950s and have a good taste of the pre-oil days. Nearby are several newly restored buildings that had been reduced to the outline of their wall lines. Using collections of old photos, the buildings have been rebuilt to their original size and use. This includes several mosques that had been reduced to rubble through lack of upkeep.

Burj Khalifa stands 829 meters (2,722 feet) tall and is the tallest building in the world. It was completed in 2010 and cost $1.5 billion. It is a vanity project of Shaykh Muhammad al-Maktoum and was built by the Chicago company of Skidmore, Owing, and Merrill. (Courtesy of John A. Shoup)

Laws in Sharjah were made to ensure the historic buildings were preserved, unlike in Dubai, where the law stated that all buildings thirty years old (and older) were to be torn down. Cultural heritage in Dubai came later than it did to Sharjah, and by the time the decision was made to preserve the old, much of it had already been torn down and replaced with cement and glass buildings.

While Sharjah embarked on preservation of the old, a major pull for tourism, Dubai set off to create the world's largest collection of postmodern architecture. Only a small part of Dubai's heritage was preserved at al-Bastakiya and around the Shaykh's palace, al-Fahidi Fort, the palace located at Shindaghah (a narrow spit of sand that separates Dubai from the gulf and the section of town called Deira), and old Gold Suq. Most of Dubai concentrated on building skyscrapers to rival cities such as New York and Chicago. Dubai has begun a serious operation for the safeguarding of its cultural heritage and has built a "Heritage Village" in Shindaghah to represent pre-oil life. Following

Downtown Sharjah showing the rebuilt fort that used to be the residence of the shaykh. The fort was torn down, and only the tower remained standing, but it was rebuilt in the efforts by Sharjah to reclaim historic buildings. (Courtesy of John A. Shoup)

Dubai, Abu Dhabi also has a "Heritage Village" that invited craftsmen to demonstrate traditional crafts in workshops in the villages. Both villages have given older women a chance to market their crafts, especially weaving and making food. Various artisans have been brought in to ply their trade in the village and give both locals and foreign visitors a taste of what life was like in the 1940s and 1950s. Items that they make, such as silver jewelry or copper items such as trays and coffee pots, are for sale. Other shops in al-Bastakiya offer antiques or newly made items that are popular with foreign residents and tourists. Dubai recently built a hotel in the nearby desert that offers five-star luxury accommodations in a tent setting. Called al-Maha (opened in 1999), it offers guests accommodations more akin to the *Arabian Nights* than to a Bedouin encampment. It fits in well with Dubai's over-the-top style of development, especially with the current Shaykh, Shaykh Muhammad bin Rashid, and was used in final scenes of the film *Syriana*.

Dubai's current ruler led the drive to build the tallest structures in the gulf with both the hotel Burj al-Arab and the skyscraper Burj Khalifa. Both Kuwait and Saudi Arabia have plans to build taller structures than the world's current tallest building, Burj Khalifa, which stands at 163 floors or 2,717 feet (828 meters) tall. Dubai has several tall buildings, such as Dubai Tower One, and currently boasts having four of the tallest towers on Earth. Shaykh Muhammad bin Rashid was the driving force behind Burj Khalifa. It fell well within his grand vision for the future of his country, beyond the time of oil, when economics would be driven by investments and banking. His vision for the economic development of Dubai is built on foreign tourism, with Dubai's airlines Emirates ready to carry most of the foreign tourists to the United Arab Emirates. With Saudi Arabia's current anti-tourist policies (this was changed in late 2019 and early 2020 with Saudi Arabia's crown prince allowing tourist visas to be issued), the emirates became among the most affordable holiday places for western tourists to the region. Only Qatar and Oman were open to tourists (Bahrain is also open, but neither it nor Kuwait have done major tourism campaigns and suffer from issues with their political stability). Shaykh Maktoum had a number of hotels built, as well as apartment buildings that rent places to tourists. The Shaykh concentrated on expensive, luxury-class hotels, making Dubai difficult to afford for those other than the business traveler, despite the fact that he has made obtaining a visitor's visa easier for Europeans and North Americans.

In addition, Shaykh Muhammad began hosting a number of festivals that promoted tourism to Dubai. These included his Shopping Festival held in the month of February, and the United Arab Emirates hosts more than four million tourists a year.[8] First held in 1996, the festival was expanded in 2003 when a summer version was launched to allow the inclusion of children while they are on their summer break to take advantage of the sales. The Maktoum family's interest in horses (Arabian horses as well as thoroughbred racehorses) was also converted into a yearly festival with the Dubai Cup race for thoroughbreds worth $1 million in prize money. Since 1998, they have competed in and sponsored the 200-kilometer (125-mile) endurance race for Arabian horses called The World's Most Preferred Endurance Ride. While visiting Dubai, tourists can enjoy the al-Hajar Mountains along the Gulf of Oman, the beaches in Abu Dhabi, and the desert around al-Ain. Sharjah hosts the jewelry exhibition, as well as an annual World Book Fair (emphasizing its role as cultural and education center).

AL-AIN

Al-Ain was originally called Tu'am and was seen to be a favored place for the Azd tribe to settle in the pre-Islamic era. In the second Azdite period, just before and after the introduction of Islam, it became the preferred place for Dhawahir to settle, and it came to be called al-'Ain al-Dhawahir after the Dhawahir tribe. It became more popularly called Buraimi, named after the locally important tribal groups, and was composed of a number of independent settlements.[9] It was officially the property of the sultan of Oman, but he lost his control in the early nineteenth century to the Saudi and Bani Yas leadership. With the dominance of the Bani Yas in the oasis, one of the settlements became al-Ain and began the growth of today.[10] The other, smaller settlements included an additional five on the Emirati side and three on the Omani side of the oasis: Hili, Qattara, Jimi, Muwaiji (or Mawaiqi) and Mu'tiridh in the United Arab Emirates, and Buraimi, Hamasah, and Saara on the Omani side.[11]

Al-Ain has become the third major city in the United Arab Emirates and has developed into an important tourist destination as well. It became the third-largest city in the United Arab Emirates after Dubai (as the largest) and Abu Dhabi (the second) by the 1990s. It has an international airport that services several international airlines, many of them based in the gulf and the Middle East. It has also developed a strong tourism industry focused on the two main tourism loci, the desert and the al-Hajar Mountains. It also shares the oasis with Oman, and until recently, visitors to al-Ain could easily cross from the United Arab Emirates to the Omani side to shop in the Buraimi suq. Al-Ain was the home region for Shaykh Zayed when he was governor, from 1946 until he took control of the emirates in 1966. Zayed was well acquainted with the oasis, having lived there with his mother from 1928 onward. *Shaykhah* Salamah extracted a promise that her children would not murder each other over who would rule in 1928; fratricide had been a common practice among the ruling elite of the emirates.[12] Zayed was the youngest son of Shaykh Sultan, who ruled until 1926. When Shaykh Sultan was succeeded by a nephew, Zayed felt he was no longer in the line of succession. However, in 1928, his brother Shakhbut took control of the emirate. Zayed's period as governor of the Eastern Province of Abu Dhabi was considered among the best of times by his people. He ruled as a good Bedouin shaykh does, with his interests being second to those of his people. His mother's interest in his education saw to it that he got the best available, and she also reminded her sons of the 1928 vow not to kill each other. When Zayed was forced to oust his brother due to economic turmoil in the country, it was done in such a way that it caused no unrest in Abu Dhabi. Three years later, he allowed Shakhbut to return and live out the rest of his life in al-Ain. Originally named 'Ain Dhawahir (for the Dhawahir tribe), it was taken by the Shaykh of Dubai in association with the Shaykh of Abu Dhabi in 1891. The Dhawahir had rebelled against the control of Abu Dhabi, and as a result, Shaykh Zayed bin Khalifa took several Dhawahir leaders as hostage to ensure the tribes' loyalty.[13]

Al-Ain became a favored place in Abu Dhabi, with schools, clinics, and hospitals in addition to the first of the universities in the United Arab Emirates. Opened in 1977, the United Arab Emirates University a large student body, of which 90 percent are nationals (U.A.E. citizens), and over half are women.[14] This is the influence of the two most important women in Zayed's life, his mother, *Shaykhah* Salamah, and his wife *Shaykhah* Fatimah, who actively campaigned for women's admissions to the university to be higher than for those for men. Both women championed women's rights in education and politics. Two military academies were established at al-Ain, the Shaykh Zayed Military Academy and the Shaykh Khalifa Military Academy; the first one trains army officers, and the second trains air force officers. The expressed purpose of these academies is to produce officers of the same caliber as other such academies worldwide, which would then allow their graduates to study in places such as West Point (U.S. military academy) or Sandhurst (British military academy).

In addition, al-Ain became an important place of research into the country's past, with an excellent museum that was developed in 1971 by the ruler of the province, Shaykh Tahnoun bin Mohammed al-Nahyan. The museum was placed in one of the many forts in the oasis, the fort of Sultan bin Zayed, dating from the early twentieth century (built in 1910). Items on display include materials found in and around al-Ain that date back more than five thousand years to recent ethnographic pieces that are still available in the nearby suqs of Buraimi. Due to the interest shown in archeological finds, several of the oasis's sites have been opened to the public. In particular is the large stone tomb at Hili. Known as the Hili Tower, the tomb dates to 2250 BCE and was excavated during the season of 1964–1965.[15] A number of the forts have been restored and are now open to the public, including Jahili and Muwaijah forts. Several have become museums to local and ethnographic material culture. Many of the forts that were built for protection against raids still stand, surrounded by groves of date palms that were once the wealth of the oasis. In Buraimi (Oman) stands a restored fort that was rebuilt and used by the Al Bu Shams division of the Na'im tribe and is also open to visitors. In recent years, access to Buraimi has been closed off to residents of al-Ain without a proper visa, and a consulate opened in al-Ain where people can apply for a visitor's visa to Oman.

Other places in the emirates have developed facilities for communications and transportation. Ras al-Khaimah, Sharjah, and Fujairah have international airports that service mainly Asian countries, and Sharjah's airport is for international connections to Europe and Asia. As of yet, they do not rival the big three, Dubai, Abu Dhabi and al-Ain. Nonetheless, they do provide independent connections directly to other centers, both inside and out of the emirates. They have also built port facilities that allow much of the shipping to avoid the congestion around Dubai and Abu Dhabi. Dubai and Sharjah are serviced by ships along their "creeks," which have been dredged to allow ships easy access into older harbors, and Dubai has constructed a new harbor at Jabal Ali. Jabal Ali is located some thirty-five kilometers (twenty-two miles) south along the gulf coast outside of the city of Dubai and is connected to the other emirates by a well-paved road that avoids the city of Dubai. The new harbor opened in 1980 but has steadily grown, and in 2002, over one million people lived near the port.[16] Sharjah also has a creek or *khawr* that can receive deep-water vessels, and on the coast of the Gulf of Oman, it also has fishing ports at Khor Fakkan and Khor Kalba.[17] Fujairah has been able to make good use of its geographical location on the Gulf of Oman, and ships eager to avoid the dangers of the Arabian/Persian Gulf have helped the emirate found a new free trade and industrial zone since 1983, when the port was enlarged to take cargo ships.[18]

CONFLICTS WITH NEIGHBORING COUNTRIES

Since 2015, the United Arab Emirates has been embroiled in conflicts in the Arabian Peninsula supporting Prince Mohammed bin Salman of Saudi Arabia in the Saudi-led coalition in Yemen (starting in 2015) and the Saudi boycott against Qatar (starting in 2017). Since 2019, it has also joined the Saudi-led forces against Iran. Saudi Arabian Crown Prince Mohammed bin Salman came to power since his father, Salman bin 'Abd al-'Aziz, came to the throne in 2015. Mohammed became the official crown prince in 2017 and quickly dominated Saudi politics, both domestically and internationally. With the loss of the United Arab Emirates's first leader, Shaykh Zayed, in 2004, relations with the peninsula's largest neighbor have been fraught with issues. The first was over a pipeline that ran partially through the contested Khor al Udaid, which the United Arab Emirates gave up as part of the Treaty of Jiddah that ended the Buraimi dispute. Because Saudi Arabia wants to isolate Qatar, this became an issue with the United Arab Emirates, which depended on the pipeline to supply both Abu Dhabi and Dubai with natural gas from offshore fields that belong to Qatar.[19] The problem, though not settled, disappeared behind the closed doors used by many of the Arabian gulf states. The issue between Qatar and its larger neighbor is not new and predates both the conflict over the pipeline and Salman becoming the king of Saudi Arabia.

Salman was the governor of Riyadh before he became king and served as the governor from 1955 to 2011. He became crown prince under King 'Abdallah from 2012 to 2015. As governor of Riyadh (the Saudi capital), he was known for his strong support for the Saudi National Guard, composed of mainly Bedouin recruits. Qatar's independent stance was seen as an opposition to Saudi control of the GCC and a potential threat to Saudi Arabia's opposition to Iran. Qatar has only one border with another country, and after the United Arab Emirates allowed Saudi control over Khor al Udaid, its one border is with Saudi Arabia. The population along the border belongs to the al-Murrah Bedouin tribe, which mostly live in Saudi Arabia. Other tribes, such as the Awamir, are split between Saudi Arabia, Oman, and the United Arab Emirates and, though they have been historically important, they are now numerically small in both Oman and the United Arab Emirates. The al-Murrah is a large and powerful tribe in Saudi Arabia. During the 1995 coup in Qatar, the al-Murrah organized a countercoup in support of the old amir that failed. Many of the tribe suffered from this action, with people being arrested, stripped of citizenship, and deported to Saudi Arabia.[20] The al-Murrah forms an important part of the National Guard in Saudi Arabia and is actively anti-Qatar.

As part of the Saudi anti-Iran and anti-Shi'ite policies, Saudi Arabia was able to convince its partners in the gulf to invade Yemen when the then-president of Yemen, 'Abd al-Rabbuh Mansur Hadi replaced Ali Abdallah Salih due to the Arab Spring uprisings, and conflict erupted between the government of Yemen and the Houthi rebels. The Houthi is a large, powerful tribe from the north of Yemen that belongs to the Fiver Shi'ites or Zayedis (named for the fifth imam, Zayed). Saudi Arabia joined in on the side of the Yemeni government in order to block the rise of a Shi'ite state in Yemen and accused Iran of backing the rebels (it feared it was being surrounded by possible hostile Shi'ite states in Iraq, Syria, and now Yemen). The United States provided both equipment and intelligence to the Saudis, as did the United Kingdom. Both Western countries see the Saudi-backed government of Yemen as the best to deal with the local branches of both al-Qaida and ISIL or Da'ish (the Islamic State in Iraq and Sham, an Arabic name for Syria).

The Houthis also see these two Sunni organizations as anti-Shi'ite and as a danger to their religion and community. The Houthi tribe supported the Shi'ite Mutawakkil kingdom of Yemen based in Sana'a that had historic conflicts with the Saudis in the 1930s and republican rebels backed by Egypt in the 1960s when Saudi Arabia supported the fellow king against republican Egypt. Houthi protests against the government of Ali Abdallah Salih began in 2004 and intensified in 2009. In 2012, the Houthi boycotted the elections and did not support the candidate 'Abd al-Rabbuh Mansur Hadi. In the Arab Spring in Yemen, the Houthi leaders called for the resignation of President Hadi. By 2014, the struggle over power descended into battle, with the Houthis winning most of the country, including the capital city and the presidential compound. Saudi Arabia joined the fight, initially providing air support for the Yemeni army. The Houthis have been joined by military forces once loyal to former president Ali Abdallah Salih. Initially, accusations of Iranian involvement in the conflict were denied by both Iran and the Houthis (and in a statement by the U.S. State Department) in that they are not part of Twelver Shi'ism but belong to another form of Shi'ism that has a very different approach to religion. The U.S. administration of Donald Trump took the Israeli approach of blaming Iran for supporting the Houthi side of the conflict. There is still little firm proof of Iranian interference in the Yemen conflict, but the Iranians will not stand by as a Shi'ite force is defeated by Sunni Saudi Arabia. It is generally assumed the Iranians are now helping arm the Houthis.

Saudi Arabia and most of the other Arab Gulf states consider Iran to be the biggest threat to their continued rule, and as such, in 2012, the United Arab Emirates was brought into the conflict on the Saudi side. The United Arab Emirates provided the Saudi forces with air support as well as ground forces and occupied the port of Aden in the south. Recently, the United Arab Emirates withdrew some of its military support for Saudi Arabia in response to the major Western powers' withdrawal of arms deals worth millions in U.S. dollars. Nonetheless, the U.A.E. leadership has voiced support for Saudi Arabia and has said that they will not leave a vacuum due to their withdrawals form parts of the battlefield.[21] Recently, the United Arab Emirates has militarily supported a group in Aden against the Houthis for the re-creation of a separate South Yemen.

As tensions rise in the gulf due to the animosity of the American administration vis-à-vis Iran, the United Arab Emirates is drawn even tighter into the Saudi (anti-Iranian) side. The American administration of Donald Trump supported the Saudi crown prince, Mohammed bin Salman. However, the American Congress is horrified by the killing of innocent people in Yemen and with the murder of the Saudi activist/journalist Adnan Khashoggi in the Saudi embassy in Istanbul, Turkey, which seems to have been carried out with the knowledge of the crown prince. While U.S. president Donald Trump stated his disbelief that the crown prince was responsible, the U.S. Congress is less forgiving.

In 2019, several tankers carrying crude oil from the peninsula were attacked off the United Arab Emirates in the Gulf of Oman. While no one has taken credit for the attacks, the Saudis are eager for it to be blamed on Iran. Early news reports quoted Saudi sources that were sure the attacks were carried out by Iran, but Iran continues to deny the accusations. U.S. president Donald Trump became involved with trading insults with Iran's leaders, especially after the loss of an American drone over Iranian airspace. This caused many airlines and oil tankers to become leery of the contested zone around the Straits of

Hormuz. The United Arab Emirates profited from this with an oil line that connects to the port in Fujairah that bypasses much of the disputed zone. The port was built during the war between Iran and Iraq and allowed oil tankers to avoid the conflict zone in the gulf. However, the recent attacks on at least two of the tankers were in the Gulf of Oman, a usually safe area outside the Straits of Hormuz. Both Saudi Arabia and the United States were quick to blame Iran and continue the verbal attacks.

The United Arab Emirates still has claims on Abu Musa and the Tunb islands. While the first island is claimed jointly by Sharjah and Iran, the Tunb islands are claimed by Ras al-Khaimah but are occupied by Iran. Ras al-Khaimah did not join the United Arab Emirates at first, but the other states agreed to press its claim to the islands, which became of greater importance once the shah of Iran fell and the new Islamic Republic of Iran was established. Iran denied the U.A.E. claim to them and has pushed out the small number of Arab residents and colonized the islands with troops loyal to Tehran. This pushed the United Arab Emirates closer to Saudi Arabia and the United States. The dispute over the islands remains unsolved today, though Sharjah reached an understanding with Iran over Abu Musa, 1971, both signed a British brokered memorandum of understanding, and the two share it and the profits of its oil field. Iranian claims over the islands are historic and note that in the seventeenth century, the Qasimi shaykhs were subjects of the shah, and their subsequent recognition by the British does not include the islands, while the Emiratis claim that the British recognized the Qasimi as independent, as they did the al-Khalifa rulers of Bahrain. Iran did recognize Bahrain as independent (until 1971), so, subsequently, Iran should also recognize Emirati independence and sovereignty over the disputed islands. This has become more urgent in today's conflict between Iran and its Arab neighbors (and the United States).[22]

The United Arab Emirates also became involved in the dispute between Saudi Arabia and its Arab neighbor Qatar. The dispute is over accusations by Saudi Arabia that Qatar is supporting "the wrong" Islamist rebels in Syria. Saudi Arabia and its allies are also supporting other Islamist rebels in Syria, and the two countries, Qatar and Saudi Arabia, are facing off against each other over this matter. Qatar is backed by Iran and Turkey, while Saudi Arabia has allies such as the United Arab Emirates, Bahrain, Kuwait, and Egypt, as well as other, mainly Sunni, Arab and African states. Although the conflict over support for Islamists in Syria is the main reason for the current dispute, tension between the two states dates back to 2002, with the television station, Al Jazeera, based in Qatar (and owned by the ruler of the country) and its coverage of Saudi Arabian politics. The permanent closure of Al Jazeera is one of the demands by Saudi Arabia to end the current dispute.

THE ARAB SPRING

The conflict was minimized by 2008 with the Qatari government promising to limit Al Jazeera's coverage of its neighbor's politics. Saudi Arabia relaxed the tensions at that time and seemed to forget the problems between the two countries, or they were moved behind the closed doors of gulf diplomacy. However, they both took different approaches to the Arab Spring. Saudi Arabia first took the side of Hosni Mubarak of Egypt, and then of Abdel Fattah al-Sisi after the overthrow of President Muhammad Mursi. Qatar took the side of the protesters and the Muslim Brotherhood's candidate, Muhammad Mursi, in Egypt. Saudi Arabia preferred to side with the status quo and not support revolutions (popular uprisings) in Egypt, Tunisia, Yemen, and Bahrain, sending troops to quell the uprising in Bahrain (seen to be a populist Shi'ite movement against the Sunni ruling elite). It also did not like the coverage of its interference in Bahrain by Al Jazeera. In Syria, Saudi Arabia backed Islamists (perceived as Sunni and anti-Shi'ite), who may have included the pro–al-Qaida Nusra Front. In Syria, Saudi Arabia came into conflict with other international players such as Turkey and Iran, as well as Qatar. Unable to intimidate both Turkey and Iran, Saudi Arabia chose to force Qatar to buckle under its control and gathered around it many of the other GCC countries in addition to Egypt, Sudan, Senegal, and one part of the government in Libya (the other side chose to stand with Qatar). Many outside observers have noted that Saudi Arabia was used to the clientship it had with Qatar and was unwilling to allow the small, but very rich state's attempt at total independence. It reasoned that if Qatar was able to exercise independence, what would prevent other members of the GCC from doing the same?

The United Arab Emirates, seen as a "good friend and neighbor" to Saudi Arabia was among the first to join the boycott. Bahrain, with its own issues with Qatar, also quickly joined the Saudi-led boycott. Bahrain has a history of hostility toward Qatar, between the two ruling houses (al-Khalifa of Bahrain and the al-Thani of Qatar), as well as over the Hawar Islands in the Arabian Gulf. The dispute was settled in 2001 by the International Court at The Hague at the request of both countries. The islands were of international interest due to an oil field found off their coasts, and there was a need to decide who owned what. The emirates kept good relations with both but, in 2017, was among the first countries to withdraw its ambassador from Qatar. It was joined by Bahrain, Jordan, and Egypt, the Hadi Yemeni government, and the Tobruk Libyan government, in addition to a number of African countries, such as Senegal, Djbouti, the Comoros, Mauritania, and the Maldives. The emirates recalled the words of Shaykh Zayed who said conflict over a patch of ground (meaning Khor al Udaid) was not worth the life of one of his people, and the United Arab Emirates had enough oil and doesn't need to make war over one such field.

The Qatar side was supported by Turkey and Iran, with both governments supplying drinking water and food to the population. Iran designated three of its gulf harbors as conduits for basic supplies to Qatar. Both governments also supported the Muslim Brotherhood's president in Egypt, Muhammad Mursi, and Qatar backed certain Islamists in Syria as well. Iran backed the government of Bashar al-Assad, while Turkey hosted several of the less prominent Islamist groups, as well as the combined Arab and Turkmen fighters from northern Syria. The United States also has a military base and uses a naval port for its fleet in Qatar but, due to the conflict, used naval ports in the United Arab Emirates and Bahrain already in operation before the conflict. The United States air base at al Udaid is the largest in the peninsula, and the Qatar government has been careful to walk the fine line between the United States and Saudi Arabia. In addition to withdrawing their diplomats from Qatar, the boycott imposed travel bans on flights going and coming from Qatar over the airspace of Saudi Arabia, Bahrain, and the United Arab Emirates. Qatar's airlines, al-Qatariyyah or Qatar Airways, is also not allowed to carry passengers to Qatar via any of the Arab countries allied with Saudi Arabia. In 2018, it expanded flights to or via Iran to make up for the loss of flyover rights by Arab states. To date, the boycott has not had much of an impact on Qatar, and the small state refuses to bend to Saudi threats. In 2018, the usual meeting of the GCC went ahead in Riyadh, and Qatar attended as a member state. However, the representative was not at the level of the head of state as other GCC states. Instead, Qatar was represented by its minister for foreign affairs. The shaykh of Qatar had been invited by Crown Prince Mohammed bin Salman, but the Qatari ruler declined to attend. The next GCC meeting in 2019 was scheduled to be held in the United Arab Emirates in Dubai, though nothing was decided at the 2018 meeting about Qatar.

A GOOD NEIGHBOR

The United Arab Emirates has weathered these local crises, and its population has continued to benefit from its leadership. As of now, there is no Arab Spring movement in the country, and its leadership has been successful in promoting a local brand of Islam, free of the influences of fundamentalism. This is perhaps due to the legacy of the first ruler, Shaykh Zayed, whose tolerance of others makes the United Arab Emirates a preferred place for non-Muslims and Muslims to live and work. Wages in the United Arab Emirates are among the best (also the highest salaries) in the region, with excellent quality medical care and educational opportunities. The United Arab Emirates provides high-quality services that hire qualified providers from the United States, the United Kingdom, Australia, and India. No one feels left out of the system, and all citizens can access all the services either for free or at a low cost.

The United Arab Emirates has historically been a good neighbor, and even today, the dispute with Qatar is more between Saudi Arabia and Qatar than between the United Arab Emirates and Qatar. Once the current dispute is settled, the United Arab Emirates will have no problem returning to the pre-2017 levels of conflict. Friendship between the two nations includes family members who reside on different sides of the border, and this also goes back to Shaykh Zayed who made the decision to give up a bit of land, even with a proven oil field, rather than descending into war. The deal made between King Faisal of Saudi Arabia and Shaykh Zayed was peaceful and serves as the basis for the current relationship between the two nations.

Shaykh Zayed also set the standard for Emirati nationalism. It is a strong feeling among the younger generations, but it is not fanatical. The Emiratis feel they can get along with all their neighbors, including the Iranians, as long as the others respect the Emiratis. The United Arab Emirates remains a peaceful land in the troubled waters of the Arab gulf states. Its economy is flourishing, its people are well provided for, and even those from non-oil producing emirates feel no jealousy of those from richer states. The population as a whole can move about the country, and even those from countries such as Oman can easily access jobs and services in the United Arab Emirates. The people who live in the Musandam part of Oman are separated from the rest of

Oman by the United Arab Emirates, and its people have long accessed Ras al-Khaimah for jobs, shopping, and medical treatment, as well as schools. The United Arab Emirates has risen from being among the most illiterate population in the Arab world (in the 1970s) to among the most literate (in the 1990s), and this too was thanks to the efforts made by Shaykh Zayed. Although he died in 2004, his legacy is still strong among his successors; his son Shaykh Khalifa is the ruler of Abu Dhabi and president of the United Arab Emirates.

On August 13, 2020, the United Arab Emirates and Israel signed a peace deal that was for the defense of the United Arab Emirates against its longtime foe Iran. Defense against assumed Iranian hostilities was, and is, foremost for the United Arab Emirates, and the deal was sweetened with the offer of advanced jet fighters. Until now, only Israel was allowed to buy such equipment from the United States. Perhaps for the first time, Israel did not complain or protest the U.S. sale to another country.

The United Arab Emirates is one of the small Arab gulf states that is interested in the Donald Trump/Jared Kushner peace deal, called the Deal of the Century by Donald Trump. The basic concept was announced in January 2020 by both President Trump and the Israeli prime minister Benjamin Netanyahu during an official visit to the United States. Israel is allowed to annex it settlements in the West Bank and the Jordan River Valley. The plan has been heavily criticized by both the Arab and Israeli press, with the Israeli newspaper *Haaretz* calling the annexation of the Arab lands "the joke of the century." The Palestinians are offered a $50 billion aid package in compensation for the loss of lands, and Israel is offered normalization of diplomatic ties with the Arab countries, as well as U.S. recognition of Israel's right to annex large portions of the West Bank and the Jordan River—in essence cutting the Palestinians off from water that is used for drinking and irrigation.

The idea of the plan was first announced during a U.S.-sponsored meeting of Arab states held in Bahrain in June 2019. Very few Arab countries agreed to attend, but those that did were mainly the oil-rich gulf states. Bahrain, Qatar, the United Arab Emirates, and Oman, all with major U.S. military bases in their territories and closely monitored by Saudi Arabia, have shown subsequent interest in the idea. There are other conditions to the agreement, including land swaps with Arab villages inside Israel and creating a border region in Sinai with Egypt under Palestinian control. The Palestinians have rejected the deal from the start, and Mahmoud 'Abbas called it "the slap of the century."

The United Arab Emirates decided to take advantage of the deal because they had already been in touch with Israel in the past and sees the Palestinians as "bothersome," asking for political and economic rights. Bahrain or Oman may be the next to announce a peace deal with Israel, as they also have economic interests that coincide with Israel, and Bahrain feels that the protection offered by Saudi Arabia is not enough to deter Iran. The United Arab Emirates main interest is to secure help against a possible Iranian attack rather than a more long-term interest in protecting Palestinian rights. Egypt and Jordan each have signed a separate peace deal with Israel. Perhaps the U.A.E. leadership sees this as an eventuality and are creating a place for their country in the future of the region.

NOTES

1. Morton, Michael Quentin. *Keepers of the Golden Shore: A History of the United Arab Emirates*. London: Reaktion Books, 2017, 205.
2. "'Iffat Al-Thunayan, An Arabian Queen." Middle East Institute, October 15, 2015, video, 49:03. Accessed June 3, 2019. https://www.youtube.com/watch?v=OfQnfpLX7aU.
3. Morton, 205.
4. "UAE—7 Emirates 7 Rulers 7 Prince." Dubai Help, November 10, 2017, video, 5:23. Accessed June 9, 2019. https://www.youtube.com/watch?v=vV0abkIIrak.
5. Heard-Bey, Frauke. *From Trucial States to United Arab Emirates*. Motivate Publishing, 2004, 411.
6. Morton, 206.
7. Alsammarae, Rima. "A Look Inside Sharjah's Newly Restored Bait Al Naboodah Museum," Middle East Architect, May 8, 2018. Accessed June 11, 2019. https://www.middleeastarchitect.com/portfolio/a-look-inside-sharjahs-bait-al-naboodah-museum.
8. Maisel, Sebastian. "Tourism," in *Saudi Arabia and the Gulf Arab States Today: An Encyclopedia of Life in the Arab States*, edited by Sebastian Maisel and John A. Shoup. Westport, CT: Greenwood Press, 2009, 431.
9. Heard-Bey, 47.
10. Heard-Bey, 48.
11. Morton, 99; Heard-Bey, 46.
12. Morton, 172.
13. Heard-Bey, 51.
14. Hellyer, Peter and Buckton, Rosalind. *Al-Ain: Oasis City*. Dubai: Motivate Press, 1998, 50.
15. Morton, 16.
16. Heard-Bey, 15.
17. Ibid., 17.

18. Ibid.
19. Morton, 209.
20. Maisel, Sebastian. "Al Murrah," in *Saudi Arabia and the Gulf Arab States Today*, 306.
21. El Yaakoubi, Aziz and Barrington, Lisa. "Exclusive: UAE Scales Down Military Presence in Yemen as Gulf Tensions Flare," Reuters: Emerging Markets, June 28, 2019. Accessed July 2, 2019. https://www.reuters.com/article/us-yemen-security-exclusive/exclusive-uae-scales-down-military-presence-in-yemen-as-gulf-tensions-flare-idUSKCN1TT14B.
22. Zwaagstra, D. "Unresolved Territorial Disputes: The Tunbs and Abu Musa in the Gulf." *Peace Palace Library*, October 4, 2013. Accessed July 2, 2019. https://www.peacepalacelibrary.nl/2013/10/unresolved-territorial-disputes-the-tunbs-and-abu-musa-in-the-gulf/.

Modern Shaykhs of the United Arab Emirates

Abu Dhabi

Ruler	Dates Ruled
Shaykh Sultan bin Zayed al-Nahyan	1922–1926
Shaykh Saqr bin Zayed al-Nahyan	1926–1928
Shaykh Shakhbut bin Sultan al-Nahyan	1928–1966
Shaykh Zayed bin Sultan al-Nahyan	1966–1971
His Royal Highness Shaykh Khalifa bin Zayed al-Nahyan (also current president of the U.A.E.)	2004–present
Muhammad bin Zayed al-Nahyan	Next in line as president of the U.A.E.

Dubai

Ruler	Dates Ruled
Shaykh Sa'id bin Maktoum ibn Hashir al-Maktoum	1912–1958
Shaykh Rashid bin Sa'id al-Maktoum	1958–1990
Shaykh Maktoum bin Rashid al-Maktoum	1990–2006
His Royal Highness Shaykh Muhammad bin Rashid al-Maktoum (also current vice president and prime minister of the U.A.E.)	2006–present
Hamdan bin Mohammed al-Maktoum	Next in line as vice president and prime minister of the U.A.E.

Sharjah

Ruler	Dates Ruled
Shaykh Khalid bin Ahmad	1914–1924
Shaykh Sultan bin Saqr al-Qasimi	1924–1951
Shaykh Saqr bin Sultan al-Qasimi	1951–1965
Shaykh Khalid bin Mohammed al-Qasimi	1965–1972
His Royal Highness Shaykh Doctor Sultan bin Muhammad bin Saqr al-Qasimi	1972–present

Ajman

Ruler	Dates Ruled
Shaykh Humaid bin 'Abd al-'Aziz al-Nuaimi	1910–1928
Shaykh Rashid bin Humaid al-Nuaimi	1928–1981
His Royal Highness Shaykh Humaid bin Rashid al-Nuaimi	1981–present
Ammar bin Humaid al-Nuaimi	Next in line as Shaykh of 'Ajman

Umm al-Quwain

Ruler	Dates Ruled
Shaykh Rashid ibn Muhammad	1904–1922
Shaykh 'Abdallah ibn Rashid al-Mualla	1922–1923
Shaykh Hamad ibn Ibrahim al-Mualla	1923–1929
Shaykh Ahmad ibn Rashid al-Mualla	1929–1981
Shaykh Rashid ibn Ahmad al-Mualla	1981–2009
His Royal Highness Shaykh Sa'ud ibn Rashid al-Mualla	2009–present
Rashid ibn Sa'ud ibn Rashid al-Mualla	Next in line as shaykh of Umm al-Quwain

Ras al-Khaimah

Ruler	Dates Ruled
Shaykh Khalid bin Ahmad	1914–1921
Shaykh Sultan bin Salim al-Qasimi	1921–1948
Shaykh Saqr bin Muhammad al-Qasimi	1948–2010
His Royal Highness Shaykh Sa'ud bin Saqr al-Qasimi	2010–present
Muhammad bin Sa'ud bin Saqr al-Qasimi	Next in line as shaykh of Ras al-Khaimah

Fujairah

Ruler	Dates Ruled
Shaykh Saif bin Hamad al Sharqi	1936–1938
Shaykh Mohammed bin Hamad al-Sharqi	1938–1974
His Royal Highness Shaykh Hamad bin Mohammed al-Sharqi	1975–present
Mohammed bin Hamad ibn Mohammed al-Sharqi	Next in line as shaykh of Fujairah

Notable People in the History of the United Arab Emirates

Codrai, Ronald. A longtime resident of the Arab world. After serving in the British Royal Air Force during World War II, he lived in Cairo until he was employed in 1946 by the British government in Oman. From Oman, he made the move to the then Trucial Oman Coast and was employed by British Petroleum Concessions Limited, which held the rights to search for oil from the local shaykhs in the Trucial Coast. Codrai traveled throughout the Trucial Coast for his job and was an avid photographer, taking photos that today form one of the best records of life just before the oil wealth transformed the local society beyond recognition. Eventually, his photos were published by Motivate Publishing into a number of albums under the general title of *An Arabian Album* (*Abu Dhabi, Dubai,* and *the Northern Emirates*), and a further collection of photos was published as *One Second in the Arab World: Fifty Years of Photographic Memory*, also by Motivate Publishing. His contribution was recognized by the government of the United Arab Emirates in 1993 when he was awarded the Sultan Al Owais Award from the United Arab Emirates's Cultural and Scientific Association. He and his wife retired to London, and he died in 2000.

His two sons, Christian and Justin, are still active in publishing collections of their father's photos of the gulf.

Fatimah bint Mubarak al-Qitbi. She was a young woman of about sixteen years of age or younger when she first met Shaykh Zayed at a wedding in al-Ain. He was, at the time, the governor of the region. Fatimah is of Bedouin origin and, like many other Bedouin of her age, was illiterate. She is the daughter of an important man of the Bani Qitab tribe (one of the small tribes that inhabits the area around Buraimi) and, for years, was among the strong supporters of the Al Bu Falah claims to Buraimi oasis. Zayed was taken by her beauty and her vivacious personality and married her soon afterward. She quickly became his "favorite" wife and the mother of several important males in the al-Nahyan family. She had her eldest son, Mohammed, named the crown prince of Abu Dhabi by Shaykh Khalifa bin Zayed and other sons were named to important positions in the government, such as Hamdan, first as minister of foreign affairs, and then as governor of the Western Province, and Hazza who serves on the Abu Dhabi Executive Council. Her sons and daughters form one of the most powerful blocs within the al-Nahyan family.

She is a strong advocate of women's rights and, in 2006, pushed for women to be on the Federal National Council. She has been a major supporter of women's employment and education. Her role is public knowledge, and she is called "Mother of the Nation." It is due to her influence that there are women on the council of ministers. Her work for women's rights has won her awards from such organizations as the United Nations UNESCO and a national award from Tunisia.

Maktoum bin Rashid al-Maktoum. Shaykh of Dubai and vice president and prime minister of the United Arab Emirates from 1990 until his death in 2006 and the older brother of the current shaykh of Dubai, Muhammad bin Rashid. Shaykh Maktoum followed in the footsteps of his father, Rashid, and Dubai was set on its course to have an alternative to oil wealth, based instead on international trade. Major development began on numerous large housing projects, making Dubai the international "capital" of postmodern architecture. In addition, tourism was increased by holding various festivals including the Dubai Shopping Festival, starting in 1996. The Shopping Festival concentrates on deals for electronic goods, bringing in shoppers from Asia and Russia. Dubai's attraction for tourists was included in the development plans for the city under Maktoum and was an extension of the development for Jabal Ali's business infrastructure, including massive shopping malls built throughout the city. In addition, housing projects included the fake islands constructed in the gulf in the shape of a palm tree. Dubai also constructed luxury-class hotels that have become tourist attractions themselves, such as the Burj al-Arab, made to look like a ship's sail. Visitors enter the building after going through an underwater tunnel that opened in 1999. It is located in Jumeirah, one of the sites for luxury apartment blocks. Dubai became a center for popular music concerts, while its cultural heritage was put on display at the Heritage Village in Shindaghah, the sand spit that protects the *khawr* from the gulf, and at Fahidi Fort. Before his death in 2006, Maktoum made his younger brother Muhammad the crown prince and minister of defense. It seems that much of Dubai's development was the vision of Muhammad rather than Maktoum.

Muhammad bin Rashid al-Maktoum. Shaykh of Dubai from 2006 to the present and vice president and prime minister of the United Arab Emirates. He had been the minister of defense until he became the shaykh of Dubai. Muhammad is a much more controversial person than his brother Maktoum, and his vision is to make Dubai the most innovative city on earth by 2021. Despite the success of his vision with the completion of Burj Khalifa in 2010, his personal life is now more open due to one of his junior wives, Princess Haya bint Hussein, who departed to London and petitioned for divorce in England in 2019. Her flight from Dubai with her children brought forth information about other Dubai royal women who have fled the court, but the others (Latifa and Shamsa, both daughters of Muhammad and an Algerian mother) have been returned, and both subsequently died or were killed by their father (according to internet sites). The court case has made headline news in the United Kingdom as both parties have strong support from different members of the English Royals and both have their own fortunes to use. Both parties have sued the other in English courts. The case is made more complicated by the differences between British and Emirati law about divorce and child custody. It is further complicated by the fact the Haya is a half-sister of the Jordanian king, 'Abdallah II. She is/was Shaykh Muhammad's sixth wife. His other wives include his senior wife, Hind bint Maktoum, the mother of Hamdan, the crown prince of Dubai. The law case could easily damage Dubai's reputation for being the easiest city to live in and visit in the Middle East because of the application of strict Islamic law by Dubai's court system in family matters.

Muhammad continues Dubai's push to be able to exist without oil and to emphasize the emirate's dependence on international trade. It has become a media center, with Dubai Media City hosting television channels MBC, Showtime Arabia, and al-'Arabiyyah, as well as local branches of such print media as McGraw and Hill and Associated Press. They are part of the duty-free zones, first established in 1985, in Jabal Ali. Dubai remains the "capital" of postmodern architecture, with architects given no limits as to what they can produce.

Muhammad is also an avid sportsman and competed in endurance races on horseback while he was crown prince. His son, the current crown prince, Hamdan, does the same. Since 1998, he has sponsored, competed in, and won the 125-mile (200-kilometer) World's Most Preferred Endurance Ride held in Dubai. He is also an avid breeder of Arabian horses (endurance races worldwide are dominated by Arabians), among the first of the leaders of the emirates to do so. His stable has among the finest Arabian horses imported from stud farms across the world. He is also interested in horse racing and, during the many festivals held in Dubai, the world's most-expensive horse race, the Dubai World Cup, is held, often in conjunction with the Shopping Festival in order to have a larger audience. The prize money for the Cup is over $1 million. He breeds not only Arabian horses but also English thoroughbreds, and his stable competes in English horse races and is frequently seen at the premier English races such as Ascot.

Rashid bin Sa'id al-Maktoum. Shaykh of Dubai from 1958 to 1990 and, along with Shaykh Zayed of Abu Dhabi, established the key unity of the United Arab Emirates in December 1971. Dubai did not have a major oil strike until 1969 but had developed as a trading center since the late nineteenth century. The population of the emirate was well mixed, with Arab, Persian, Baluchi, and Indian residents. It served as a base for gulf trade and was severely hit by the loss of the pearl trade, but it had been successful in replacing Persian ports along the northern gulf shore. It attracted a large number of Arab-Persian families to move from Iranian towns such as Bastak to Dubai under Sa'id, Rashid's father.

Rashid inherited a poor country that had to set up a system of privatization of public services in the 1930s. Despite its poverty, Dubai was the largest settlement on the Trucial Coast and had been competed very well with older ports such as Sharjah and Ras al-Khaimah. The state lacked funds to pay for services and turned to private enterprise to fill in the gap. Public funds were lacking because the state exempted many merchants from taxation, and this brought more residents to Dubai. The British supported the ruling shaykh, and in 1958, under Rashid, a municipal council was organized as was a local police force. Improvements in the *khawr* helped ease of access to the port, and revenue began to flow in from taxation on larger ships. Dubai began to invest in schools as early as 1953, and a branch of a Kuwaiti-British school (Chuwaifat) opened in the 1960s. Schools for both boys and girls opened with an emphasis on learning technical skills. Transportation was improved by building a bridge over the *khawr* linking Bur Dubai with Deira (the major two sections of Dubai City), and in the 1960s, an airport was built. In 1965, Dubai was chosen by the British as the headquarters of the British-sponsored Development Office of the Trucial States. All these changes were in step with Shaykh Rashid's own plans for developing his country based on international trade. When oil was discovered and wealth began to flow into the country, he continued to plan for life without oil. He used the funds to expand seaport facilities south of the city at Jebel Ali. The vision set by Rashid has continued even today by his sons, Maktoum and now Muhammad.

When asked by Zayed of Abu Dhabi to form a union of the small emirates, Rashid was skeptical but, nonetheless, agreed. Zayed's enthusiasm for the union swung most of the leaders to his side, with only Ras al-Khaimah holding out over Iranian occupation of islands that belong to Ras al-Khaimah until a few months later, joining in February 1972. With the three most powerful of the emirates agreeing to unity (Abu Dhabi, Dubai, and Sharjah), the others agreed to the union in December 1971. With the imminent withdrawal of British forces from Arabia, the small emirates had little choice. Rashid remained one of the more skeptical about the union, but with the shaykh of Dubai being granted the position of vice president of the union, Dubai's plans for non-oil development was not threatened, and Zayed promised to use Abu Dhabi's wealth for all seven emirates. Rashid died in 1999, and succession proved to go smoothly.

Salamah bint Buti. Salamah was the daughter of Buti ibn Khadim of the Qubaisat, a branch of the Bani Yas, and related to the ruling Al Bu Falah of Abu Dhabi. She was one of the important women of the United Arab Emirates and became a wife of Shaykh Sultan of Abu Dhabi and mother of Zayed, the "father of the nation." She made her sons agree to not become involved in the murderous practices of gulf politics; both her husband and his successor, Saqr, were murdered. Saqr was murdered by his brother, Shaykh Khalifa. However, her sons stayed true to their oath to her, and Zayed, when he removed his brother Shakhbut, did not spill any blood and allowed Shakhbut to return and live out his life in al-Ain. She took her son Zayed to al-Ain after the death of her husband and returned to Abu Dhabi in 1955 with the help of her sons. She died in 1970 with her sons firmly established as the rulers of Abu Dhabi.

Saqr bin Muhammad al-Qasimi. Ruler of Ras al-Khaimah from 1948 to 2010. Saqr ascended the throne in 1948 from his very unpopular uncle Sultan. Sultan had secretly signed a treaty with the British for oil exploration and had not shared the money with his people. He neglected them and their needs, while his nephew took over with the popular support of the people. Ras al-Khaimah does not have oil and remains dependent on fish, dates, traditional crafts, and the generosity of Abu Dhabi.

Saqr joined the United Arab Emirates months after the union had been formalized by all the other shaykhs due to his suspicion about the union and the other leaders' lack of interest in the islands in the gulf that had been recently occupied by Iran. Iran's shah, Mohammad Reza, took advantage of the withdrawal of British forces and, though recognized as belonging to Ras al-Khaimah, occupied the Tunb islands. Iran also took over Abu Musa Island that belongs to Sharjah, but the shaykh of Sharjah worked out a deal of joint administration and shared the oil wealth with Iran. The two Qasimi leaders were suspicious of each other (Ras al-Khaimah had fallen under Sharjah's authority several times since the 1820 war with Britain), but eventually, Ras al-Khaimah decided to join the union in February 1972 when the other leaders promised to keep the occupied islands foremost in foreign affairs of the new United Arab Emirates. Saqr died in 2010 after a long and generally peaceful rule.

Sa'ud ibn Saqr al-Qasimi. Current ruler of Ras al-Khaimah, succeeded upon his father's death in 2010 and has been uncontested since his half-brother, Khalid, was deposed as crown prince in 2003. It was said that Khalid did not support the United States invasion of Iraq and had burned a U.S. flag during a public protest. This did not go over well with the other leaders of the United Arab Emirates, who steered the country into opposition of Iraq. Sa'ud was a younger brother of Khalid and maneuvered himself into the crown prince's position. Khalid attempted to retake the crown prince's position, but he had no or very little support from the public. When Shaykh Saqr died in

2010, the succession was peaceful. Sa'ud rules the country, having taking over duties from his father before his father's death. Sa'ud helped establish a number of alternatives for Ras al-Khaimah's economy, including building a massive convention center in addition to six universities. He has ensured that the Shihuh tribesmen of Oman's Musandam Peninsula have access to markets in Ras al-Khaimah. Today, his rule is peaceful as he guides his emirate to a future without dependence on oil.

Shakhbut ibn Sultan al-Nayhan. He was the Shaykh of Abu Dhabi from 1928 to 1966 and was seen by the British as an astute politician and a good, trustworthy ally. He took over in a bloody coup from his uncle, Saqr ibn Zayed in revenge for the murder of his father, Sultan. Such violent disputes had become normal among the ruling class in the emirates. Sultan, Shakhbut's father, was shot and killed by his younger brother in 1926 after inviting him to dinner.

Saqr lost important support of Bedouin tribes by making an alliance with the Wahhabis in Saudi Arabia. He tried to kidnap two of Sultan's sons, which not only failed but also resulted in his being reprimanded by the British resident. Saqr then became convinced that his life was in danger at the hands of Khalifa, one of Sultan's popular sons. Khalifa began to plot, and eventually, Saqr was wounded by one of Khalifa's servants. In the end, Saqr was killed by Bedouin of the Manasir tribe and the position of Shaykh was open. Shakhbut's mother then made her sons swear an oath to her to not kill each other over the position of shaykh. Shakhbut was popular with the people of his emirate and was well supported by the British.

Shakhbut was an able ruler, though illiterate. He agreed to treaties only after they were read to him and fully explained. He allowed oil exploration by the British once they agreed to look for water, the most pressing problem for Abu Dhabi. As time went on, many of the local leaders became less and less awed by the oil companies and more and more aware of agreements made by other gulf leaders, such as the shaykh of Kuwait, with the companies. Oil concessions insisted on knowing and recording whose authority specific lands were under rather than the vague notions sovereignty according to local Bedouin. In addition, relations between the leaders in the Trucial States were tense and came to blows in the 1940s. When Shakhbut eventually signed a long-term lease to an oil company, it was with British Iraq Petroleum Company and not SoCal, which had concessions in Saudi Arabia. Throughout, Shakhbut was advised by his uncle Khalifa, who remained a major supporter until his death in 1945 at age 108. Khalifa's son Muhammad took over from his father, as did Shakhbut's in-laws.

In 1945, war broke out between Abu Dhabi and Dubai over an area claimed by both. Dubai moved troops, breaking the treaty with England and had to pay a sizeable fine to the British. The war dragged on until 1948 when the Bedouin tribes involved, the Awamir and Manasir of Abu Dhabi and the Bani Qitab of Dubai, reached an agreement. The issue was complicated by an oil company's desire to explore the disputed region, which included Jabal Ali. The decision was for Dubai, but this left Shakhbut feeling bitter and abandoned by the British.

In 1946, Shakhbut's brother Zayed became the governor of the Eastern Province, which included the oasis of Buraimi, and their mother, Salamah, moved there with Zayed. Zayed began a policy of paying for development projects with his own funds because Shakhbut became increasingly secretive about the financing of such with public money. Abu Dhabi made great advancement in education and health as a result of Zayed's assistance. Shakhbut never forgave the British for their involvement in the war with Dubai and the loss of territory and became deeply suspicious of the British oil companies. In the 1950s, the dispute with Saudi Arabia over Buraimi intensified. Shakhbut, though recognized as a good ruler, was removed by his brother Zayed and other family members for mismanagement of finances in 1966. It was said that Shakhbut kept the large sums paid to him by the oil companies in a trunk under his bed. He initially moved to London, but Zayed allowed him back in the United Arab Emirates in 1969. Shakhbut lived out the rest of his life in al-Ain and was involved in official ceremonies. He died in 1989.

Sultan bin Muhammad al-Qasimi. Ruler of Sharjah from 1972 until the present through a very strong period of political unrest. He became the shaykh of Sharjah after the ruler, Khalid, was shot and killed in an attempted coup by the exiled leader, Saqr. Saqr had been deposed by Khalid and sent to Cairo in 1965, but he returned in an attempt to retake the throne in 1972. The coup was unsuccessful, though Shaykh Khalid was killed. Saqr had little support, and he was put under house arrest by his cousin, the new shaykh, Shaykh Sultan bin Muhammad al-Qasimi.

The new shaykh remained steady on the policies of Khalid in trying to make Sharjah the cultural center of the gulf and pushed education rather than embark on what he saw as Dubai's "mad rush" into business and private enterprise. Being better educated himself, he wants his emirate to be a better example of what oil money can do. Sharjah has little oil wealth of its own, but does have some and, therefore, does not need to depend on Abu Dhabi's wealth. The emirate has taken its own path toward development, and though it does have major housing projects similar to Dubai's, they are more carefully planned than in Dubai. The emirate is used as a sleeper community by many of those who work in Dubai, even though the road system of the two emirates mostly do not connect. Sharjah is seen as a more religious place than Dubai, and this is partially due to the efforts of the shaykh who promotes Sharjah's commitment to family values. In addition, Sharjah has embarked on a project to restore and rebuild much of old Sharjah using the most advanced methods. This began with the restoration of the old suq called Suq al-Arsah. In addition, the Blue Market was built in Persian style using "traditional" blue tiles and wind towers. It uses a different approach to the concept of a shopping mall.

Sultan went on to earn a PhD in history and published his research as the book *Myth of Arab Piracy in the Gulf*, which explains the Arab point of view in the war between the Qawasim and the British East India Company. During his absence in the United Kingdom, his throne was under threat by his brother, 'Abd al-'Aziz. 'Abd al-'Aziz announced the abdication of Sultan due to mismanagement of funds. However, Sultan appealed this to the shaykhs of Abu Dhabi and Dubai. They decided on a compromise by reappointing Sultan as the shaykh and 'Abd al-'Aziz as the crown prince. Sultan was not pleased by the decision, and he eventually removed 'Abd al-'Aziz. His sons had been appointed the crown prince—first Muhammad, who died of a drug overdose in 1999, and then his younger son, Khalid, who died in 2019.

Thesiger, Wilfred. He was among the last of the British explorers of Arabia, and his crossings of the Empty Quarter were among his greatest accomplishments. Born in Addis Ababa, Ethiopia, in 1910, he witnessed the changes in Arabia from a desert dominated by the Bedouin to the modern oil states they became. Thesiger hated the changes and wanted the Bedouin to remain as he first knew them in the 1940s.

He was sent to school in England and returned in 1930 for the coronation of Haile Selassie. He was as the guest of the new emperor out of respect Haile Selassie felt for Thesiger's father, Wilfred Gilbert Thesiger, who had served as an official representative of the United Kingdom in the early decades of the twentieth century. In 1933, Thesiger traveled into the realm of the anti-foreign sultan of Afar with the blessings of the emperor of Ethiopia. He served in the British colonial government in Sudan and made his first crossing of the desert there, from his colonial office in Darfur to a French post in Chad, with a small party of local men.

During World War II, he served in Sudan, Ethiopia, Egypt's Western Desert, and Syria. While serving in Syria, he acted as a liaison with the Bedouin against Vichy French forces. He formed his very strong opinions about the Bedouin being the best examples of humanity at that time, which influenced his later life. Following the war, he took a job with the Middle East Anti-Locust Unit and was stationed in Oman. He took full advantage of being there to mount two expeditions to cross the Empty Quarter between 1945 and 1950. He had no European companion and instead surrounded himself with Bedouin guides. He chose his men from the Rashid tribe that lives on the southern borders of the great sand sea rather than another tribe, though related to the Rashid, the Bayt Kathir, used by another Englishman who crossed the Empty Quarter, Bertram Thomas in 1930/1931. Thesiger decided that the Rashid were "true Bedouin," while the Bayt Kathir had been "contaminated" with civilization. It was suggested that his motive was more that his main rival, Bertram Thomas, used Bayt Kathir guides. His book *Arabian Sands* is so full of ethnographic detail of Bedouin life that it remains today among the best accounts of pre-oil life.

Thesiger has been honored by the United Arab Emirates for his record. His book, in Arabic translation and in original English, was published several times by Motivate Publishing in Dubai. He was honored for his literary contributions by the government of Oman and the United Arab Emirates and remained, until his death in 2003, honored in southern Arabia.

Zayed bin Khalifa al-Nahyan, called Zayed the Great. He ruled Abu Dhabi from 1855 to 1909 and was responsible for its expansion over a large area. He also won the friendship and support of large numbers of Bedouin tribes. During his long reign, he dealt with a war with nearby Dubai and conflict over Buraimi with the second Saudi state.

Zayed is called "the Great" due to his ability to expand Abu Dhabi and effectively deal with the Bedouin and with the other leaders of the Trucial States. During his long period of rule, he gained control over much of Buraimi oasis by purchasing gardens, as well as through diplomacy and war. By 1897, several of the villages in the oasis belonged to Zayed, his sons, or allies of the Bani Yas. In 1887, he had gone to war with the Dhawahir and defeated them, subsequently becoming the ruler of the Dhawahir villages. He came into conflict with the Saudi claims to part of the oasis. These two villages were inhabited by the Na'im, but due to their constant internal squabbles, they were forced to deal with Zayed and/or his local representative, Ahmad ibn Hilal, the *tamim* or shaykh Dhawahir.

Zayed became the main advocate with other shaykhs in Bedouin affairs, and in 1905, he stood up for the rights of the Na'im in a dispute over control of Masfout, which was returned to them. He also represented the sultan of Oman with both the nomadic and settled section of the Dhawahir, even into undisputed Omani territory. By the time of his death in 1909, he maintained unquestioned leverage, if not out-and-out control over numerous Bedouin tribes of the interior. Much of this was lost during the period of 1909–1926 when the al-Nahyan leadership was fought over between Zayed's sons until Shakhbut came to power in 1926, and his younger brother, Zayed, reestablished al-Nahyan influence.

Zayed bin Sultan al-Nahyan (1918–2004). Zayed bin Sultan served first as the governor of the Eastern Province at al-Ain (1946–1966), then as the shaykh of Abu Dhabi (1966–2004), and then as president of the United Arab Emirates (1971–2004). He earned the respect and love of the people in Abu Dhabi, and later of the entire country as leader of the emirates, because he listened to the requests and needs of all his people. Also, while governor at al-Ain, he paid for the opening of schools out of his own money. He replaced his brother Shakhbut only after scandals about the budget proved that Shakhbut was unwilling or unable to handle the vast wealth that poured into the country after the discovery of oil. He is seen as a true Bedouin leader by displaying in his actions those of both a traditional leader (who keeps the needs of his people at the foremost of his actions) and a modern democrat, seeing that he deals with the issues of his constituents. In 1981, he helped establish the Gulf Cooperation Council and was willing to give in to Saudi Arabia ending the Buraimi conflict, stating that an oil field was not worth the loss of life and that Abu Dhabi could afford the loss of one oil field because it was not that vital. He lost the oil field in Khor Udaid but kept the larger share of Buraimi oasis.

Although he was personally a very conservative (religious) man, he felt that Islam was a religion of tolerance and acceptance of other faiths. He was deeply concerned about preserving the culture and customs of the gulf and gave it a high priority. He supported archeological excavations and museums in the country to display the finds, despite the fact that they exhibit pre-Islamic objects. The museums, though, also display more-recent items.

He used some of the vast oil wealth to finance education for all people of the United Arab Emirates and opened schools and universities for women. As a result, some of the most educated young women in the Arabian Peninsula are in the United Arab Emirates. He also pushed them to find jobs once they graduated, both in public and private firms. He shared Abu Dhabi's oil wealth with all the emirates; thus, he saw himself as responsible for the entire country. When a major private bank collapsed, he ensured that most of the small account holders recovered some of their money by using his personal funds—for both Emirati nationals and foreigners. He remains, for nearly everyone in the United Arab Emirates, the founder of the country and the most beloved leader.

Glossary

Abba or *Bisht*. The large outer cloak worn by men. It can be made of wool or camel hair or with very thin, sheer cloth for the hot summer months.

'Abrah (plural *'Abrat*). A small, local craft used for ferrying passengers short distances between the shores of small inlets along the coast, such as in Dubai.

Amir (plural *Umara'*). Prince or military commander.

'Aqal. The head rope, often made from twisted and braided goat, hair that holds a head cloth in place. The word originally meant hobbles for camels or horses and was used as portable hobbles that also was used to hold the head cloth in place.

'Ardhah. The ceremonial war dance used by tribes to demonstrate their bravery. Today it is used in wedding celebrations and is performed by a group of men singers called a Harbiyyah. A Harbiyyah

means warlike and refers to the subject of war and the heroes of songs they used to sing.

Badwi (plural *Bedw*). The word "Bedouin" comes from the grammatically declined Arabic plural and was borrowed into English. It means an inhabitant of the Badiyyah or the livable desert, unlike the Sahra' (Sahara), which is a true desert that is not for year-round living by man.

Barasti or *'Arish*. A dwelling made from palm fronds. Most of the housing in the United Arab Emirates was made of date palm fronds until the 1970s.

Barjil (plural *Barajil*). This is a Persian word in origin (originally *bargil*) and refers to the wind towers that serve as air conditioners in traditional architecture in much of the gulf.

Burj (plural *Abraj*). A watch tower to help repel a raid.

Burqa. The woman's face veil or mask. In the United Arab Emirates, it is made of stiffened cloth that exposes her mouth and chin but covers her face from the nose up but with eye openings.

Dallah. Coffee pot, usually made of brass. Those made in the United Arab Emirates and Oman have flat tops, while those made in Syria have rounded tops.

Dhow. Not an Arabic term but is perhaps of Hindi or Persian origin. It is the collective name for Arab sailing vessels with lateen (triangular) sails.

Falaj (plural *Aflaj*). A system of underground irrigation canals. It was invented in Iran but spread to the gulf with Iranian administration in pre-Islamic times.

Haj. An honorific title for someone who has made the pilgrimage to Mecca once in a lifetime. While it is easier today, in the past, the journey was very hard and could take many months or even years to accomplish by walking, camel, or sea voyage.

'Id (plural A'yad). Holiday. There are two religious holidays in Islam, 'Id al-Fitr at the end of Ramadan (the month of fasting) and 'Id al-Adha at the end of the Haj. Other holidays include the Prophet's birthday and national celebrations for the independence of the country.

Imarah (plural *Imarat*). A princedom.

Jirz. A walking stick with a small ax head on one end. It seems to have originated among the Shihuh of the Musandam Peninsula in ancient times and today is often decorated with silver mountings on the handle and an inlaid ax head.

Khalij. The Arabic word for gulf. The name of the Persian Gulf (al-Khalij al-Farisi) is often the Arabian Gulf (al-Khalij al-'Arabi) in countries such as the United Arab Emirates or simply the Gulf.

Khawr. A small inlet from the gulf, often translated as a creek.

Kufiyyah or *Ghutrah*. The name for the head cloth worn by Arab men. It is made of cotton, and the better ones include silk. The better ones are often made in Syria, but they are also made in India. It is called a *Shumagh* when it is mostly made of silk.

Majlis (plural *Majalis*). A council of elders or decision-makers.

Nawkhudah. A Persian word for a captain of a boat. It is used in the gulf to denote the chief of a fleet of pearling ships.

Qabilah (plural *Qaba'il*). A group of closely related lineages; a tribe.

Qahwa or *Gahwa*. The Arabic word for coffee.

Qarqur. A large wire trap used to catch fish.

Rub' al-Khali or al-Ramlah. A large sand desert located in the southeast of Saudi Arabia, extending into Oman and the United Arab Emirates. It is 620 miles (1,000 kms) long and 310 miles (500 kms) wide. The Bedouin who live near it call it al-Ramlah, which means the Sands.

Sabkhah. A salt flat. The United Arab Emirates is separated from Qatar and Saudi Arabia by a large salt flat. They are often nearly impossible to cross even though the top layer dries. The underlying layers for a gluey, blue mass that is nearly impossible to extract a sunken camel or motorized vehicle from.

Sahil. The word for coast.

Shaykh or *Tamimah* (plural *Shuyukh* or *Tama'im*). A tribal leader or a member of his family.

Suq (plural *Aswaq*). Market or a marketplace.

Tamr. The word for dates. There are words for different types and qualities of dates, but this is also generic word for the fruit.

Thawb or *Dishdasha*. A long shirt worn by Arab men. It is the generic name for cloth in some Arabic dialects, but in the United Arab Emirates, it means a very long ready-to-wear shirt.

Wadi. A valley or a dry stream that occasionally has water.

Wasm. A tribal brand that designates ownership of camels or sheep but is rarely used on horses. It also marks ownership of a well.

Wazir (plural *Wuzara'*). A Persian word that was borrowed into Arabic that means a minister of state.

Bibliographic Essay

Bibliographic information on the United Arab Emirates in English is limited in distribution, but in the United Arab Emirates, it is very present. There is a local publishing house, a branch of the British company Macmillian House, called Motivate Publishing, that publishes nearly everything in print on the county. It includes titles originally published by numerous publishers located in the United Kingdom and the United States, such as Stacey International and Longman, both presses that have a long history of publishing on Arabia. I.B. Tauris also publishes several titles on Arabia, including on the gulf states. This work is greatly indebted to Motivate Publishing in that many of the works owned by and consulted by the author are from the company's long list of published works. Motivate Publishing includes a number of works that cover the time period before oil was found and transformed the society into wealth, such as the works by Ronald Codrai and Wilfred Thesiger. These are extremely valuable for those interested in the quick transformation. They contain important social observations that are not present today, such as holding what Codrai called a *murid* or a Sufi *dhikr* or *hadrah* for curing illnesses. Codrai also presents photographic record of cauterization—a medical treatment using a hot iron on the skin or wound. This was a popular treatment among the Bedouin, who used it to "strengthen" their arm muscles in order to hold guns steady.

Interest in early life in the United Arab Emirates was given official sanction by the ruler of Abu Dhabi, Shaykh Shakhbut, and his brother Shaykh Zayed in the 1940s. Exploration for oil began to find and investigate ancient sites, and this interest was furthered by excavations of sites in Bahrain. A Danish team of archeologists was invited to excavate both the tombs on Umm al-Nar near Abu Dhabi and Jabal Hafit near al-Ain in the 1950s. Local interest in ancient sites has continued, and museums were established to display the finds. Also, the Department of Antiquities and Tourism was born out of the local interest and as a means to capitalize on possible tourism. Research continues, and publications, especially by Motivate Publishing, have been made available to the public in English and Arabic. Books such as *Waves of Time: The Marine Heritage of the United Arab Emirates*, edited by Peter Hellyer, discuss the maritime heritage and importance to the economy of the United Arab Emirates from the earliest times. Published by Trident Press, it covers the importance of the Persian/Arab Gulf through history and its importance to local culture. It emphasizes the sea as opposed to the desert, the other major influence on life in the United Arab Emirates.

Other publications that deal with early regional history include Michael Quentin Morton's *Keepers of the Golden Shore: A History of the United Arab Emirates* published by Reaktion Books. This book not only covers the importance of the sea but equally covers the desert and the third major influence, the al-Hajar Mountains. The mountains were one of the sources for copper needed by other states in Iran, Pakistan, and Iraq—thus the start of the history of sea trade. Richard Bulliet's *The Camel and the Wheel* published by Columbia University Press traces caravan trade from south Arabia north by land and the domestication of the camel beginning around 3000 BCE in Yemen. The development of the different saddles used and their diffusion became an important aspect of the history of the United Arab Emirates and of the Bedouin Arabs. It also played a major role in the spread of Islam.

Sayed Hamid Hurreiz's book *Folklore and Folklife in the United Arab Emirates* published by Routledge deals with many of the Bedouin aspects of life in the United Arab Emirates that the country is trying to prevent from being lost, as the people today have little in common with the past generation. The book deals with some of the history of the country and its geography, although its main purpose was to provide a record of the folktales and customs of the majority of the Emiratis who

Bibliographic Essay

are of Bedouin or oasis-farming origins. This is also true of the book *Fabled Cities Princes and Jinn from Arab Myths and Legends* by Khairat al-Saleh that deals with many of Arabia's ancient stories of vanished cities and towns. Some of these ancient tales have been partially substantiated by modern exploration, such as that for the "lost" city of Ubar/Wabar by Ranulph Finnes documented in his book *Atlantis of the Sands*, which forms a chapter in the book *Travelling the Sands: Sagas of Exploration in the Arabian Peninsula* by Andrew Taylor. Taylor's book covers generations of Europeans who traveled through distant locations in the peninsula, including the British couple, Wilfrid and Lady Anne Blunt; Charles Doughty; Bertram Thomas; and Wilfred Thesiger. The book includes chapters on each of the travelers, though few were interested in what became the United Arab Emirates.

A more substantial book is the history of the Arabs written by the eminent Lebanese scholar, Philip Hitti, *History of the Arabs*. Although the book is now out-of-date and does not cover events after 1967, it is a "classic" covering in great detail the development of events from pre-Islamic times through the end of the Ottoman Empire (1923). It covers the Roman attempt to conquer Yemen in 24 BCE under the command of Aelius Gallus. It is also an excellent source for the Medieval period that includes the Umayyad, Abbasid, Buyid, and Seljuq periods, for which documentation for the region of the United Arab Emirates is hard to find. It does note that, generally speaking, the region now called the United Arab Emirates fell under Persian control for much of the Medieval period. A more contemporary history of the Arab people is Eugene Rogan's *The Arabs: A History* published by Basic Books in 2009, with an updated version in 2011. It covers the period after the Tanzimat Reforms of the Ottoman Empire and the growth of Arab nationalism to, more or less, contemporary times. Rogan's books are excellent sources on the Arab world and its complex politics beginning with the end of the Ottoman period until the current times. *The Arabs* was updated in 2011 to include the Arab Spring.

One the best sources on the United Arab Emirates is *From Trucial States to United Arab Emirates* by Frauke Heard-Bey and published by Motivate Publishing in Dubai and Acre House in London. Heard-Bey is one of the authorities on the emirates, and her book covers nearly every aspect of social, economic, and political history. It is one of the most complete coverage of the United Arab Emirates, but it begins relatively late and does not contain information about the more ancient histories of the region. This is a common problem with other histories, such as that of Rosemarie Said Zahlan's *The Origins of the United Arab*

Emirates: A Political and Social History of the Trucial States published by Macmillan Press in 1978. It is also an excellent source on intertribal wars and the influence of both the British in India and Saudi Arabia in Emirati affairs.

An important source for the late eighteenth and early nineteenth centuries is the book by Sultan bin Muhammad al-Qasimi (shaykh of Sharjah) *Power Struggle and Trade in the Gulf 1620–1820* published in 1999 by Forest Row. The book presents a different historical perspective to that of Britain and emphasizes Britain's threat to Qasimi control of trade with India. Instead of presenting the Qasimi as pirates, they are seen as reacting to the British East India Company's takeover of trade, and this legitimizes their reaction. It gives a local view of the war between the Qasimi *shuyukh* and the British as a power struggle that ended, unfortunately, with the Qasimi defeat. The text uses numerous letters of correspondence to support the arguments and gives a very different perspective than the generally accepted one of legitimizing the British and criminalizing the Qasimi response. The book grew from the shaykh's PhD dissertation and his family's interest in U.A.E. history.

Emirati affairs have long been influenced by the outside, especially by Iran, one of the major powers in the gulf. The Portuguese and the British have been among the important European powers to influence local affairs, but Saudi Arabia's various Wahhabi states have been and remain among the most important. Originally used by local rulers as a foil against the Europeans, the Saudis became deeply involved in local politics to spread their Wahhabi doctrine as opposed mainly to the religious doctrine of the Ibadi Khawarij from Oman. Buraimi (which still belongs to Oman today) became the most important place in the struggle, and the Buraimi dispute is well covered in *Buraimi: The Struggle for Power, Influence and Oil in Arabia* by Michael Quentin Morton. This book covers the various aspects of the struggle and the settlement of it (perhaps not, as the current crown prince of Saudi Arabia may challenge the treaty signed by both King Faisal and Shaykh Zayed) that began at the start of the nineteenth century and the first Saudi state. Saudi Arabia was named such in 1932 by King 'Abd al-'Aziz ibn Sa'ud, the first king of the third Sa'udi state. A comprehensive study of Saudi Arabia is found in the books *A History of Saudi Arabia* and *Politics in an Arabian Oasis: The Rashidis of Saudi Arabia*, both by the female Saudi historian Madawi Al Rasheed, published by Cambridge University Press and I.B. Tauris. Although they are not directly concerned with the United Arab Emirates, they do cover the rise of three Saudi states, and the second, *Politics of an Arabian Oasis*, covers the author's family's challenges to the Saudi family, which did not end until the Saudi conquest of Ha'il in 1921. It gives excellent insight into the conflicts in Arabia before the establishment of the Kingdom of Saudi Arabia. This is also true of the book *The Arab of the Desert: A Glimpse into Badawin Life in Kuwait and Sau'di Arabia* by H. R. P. Dickson published by Allen and Unwin, third edition in 1989 (first edition dated 1949). Dickson served as the British resident in Kuwait from 1929 to 1936 and again from 1941 until his death in 1959; he was well aware of the region of the northern gulf. His source serves those with an interest in the southern gulf in matters such as social organization, the influence of sea trade, and Bedouin life.

Among the most important records of life in the United Arab Emirates are the books by Wilfred Thesiger and Ronald Codrai, both British who lived and worked in the region just before the oil wealth transformed it from poverty to extreme wealth. Their records are invaluable today for researchers who want to understand the rapid growth due to oil. Thesiger's interest was in the Bedouin tribes that lived along the south of the Rub' al-Khali, the huge expanse of sand dunes that covers much of the south of Saudi Arabia and the north of Oman. He became a recognized authority on the Bedouin, and his book *Arabian Sands* published by Longmans in 1960 has become a classic. It has been reprinted in full or in an abridged edition numerous times, including both a full English and Arabic version by Motivate Publishing as *Wilfred Thesiger: Crossing the Sands* in 1999, with further reprints in 2002, 2004, and 2006. The Arabic title reflects that of his original work, *al-Ramlah al-'Arabiyyah* (or *Arabian Sands*). The book covers his travels (also covered in a chapter in *Travelling the Sands* mentioned above) across the Rub' al-Khali in an attempt to surpass his compatriot Bertram Thomas.

Another book that discusses the tribes in Oman (including some in the United Arab Emirates) is *Tribes in Oman* by J. R. L. Carter published by Peninsular Publications in 1982. The book gives a good account of the issues between the Ghafiri (north Arabian) and Hinawi (Yemeni or south Arabian) tribes and how the conflict started. It gives a very detailed account of individual tribal groups and includes population numbers, as well as particular things they are known for. It divides tribes into two main categories, settled farmers and nomadic Bedouin.

Thesiger's book documents Bedouin life in Oman in the 1940s, while Ronald Codrai's photos serve as an important insight into life in the United Arab Emirates just before and during the discovery of oil.

His photos have been published as books in a series called *An Arabian Album* by Motivate Publishing, one for each of the major emirates: Abu Dhabi, Dubai, Sharjah, and one for the Northern Emirates, as well as a book of photos from the all the individual albums called *The Emirates: An Arabian Album*. These books have been deemed important to local heritage by the Emirati Ministry of Culture because the photos depict aspects of local culture, much of which have subsequently been abandoned by the current generation. They depict the cities such as Abu Dhabi and Dubai composed mainly of *barasti* huts (made of palm fronds) and very few permanent buildings other than the rulers' forts. The transformation was so quick that much of the local culture has been lost. In addition, many nonnationals live and work in the countries of the gulf—about one in five people are nationals, and the rest are foreign workers, mainly from India, Pakistan, and Afghanistan. This foreign mix is well represented in the 2005 Hollywood film *Syriana* set in a mythical gulf state, but parts were filmed in Dubai. Abu Dhabi served as a film set for the 2007 Hollywood film *The Kingdom*, supposedly set in Saudi Arabia. Both films are Hollywood attempts at explaining the complicated politics of the Middle East, but *Syriana* does a much better job of explaining the oil companies' attempts to control local politics for their own purposes.

Michael Quentin Morton's book *Keepers of the Golden Shore: A History of the United Arab Emirates* is among the best source on the modern period of U.A.E. history. Published by Reaktion Books in 2017, it covers more of the modern developments and does not concentrate on the impact of oil only. Many other sources tend to concentrate on the importance of oil when discussing the gulf states, even though oil is not the beginning and end of all things in the region. Perhaps because Morton was born and raised in the gulf, he includes other factors that are important to local people.

Anne Coles and Peter Jackson's book *Windtower* deals with the traditional wind tower or *barjil* that serves as air conditioning in houses built of stone coral, as well as in palm frond structures. The wind towers were brought to the United Arab Emirates by Iranian migrants that belong to Sunni Arab families and come from the Hawali, named for the fact that they frequently shifted shores of the gulf and form a strong merchant class. The book is a study of the district called al-Bastakiya of Dubai (named for the town of origin in Iran, Bastak), when Dubai became interested in preserving aspects of pre-oil life. The book is published by Stacey International after an earlier study was published by the Dubai City Council (by the same authors) about a decade before

Bibliographic Essay 169

this major study. Similarly, the book *The Bazaar: Markets and Merchants of the Islamic World* by Walter Weiss and Kurt-Michael Westermann published by Thames and Hudson in 1998 covers the traditional markets in Dubai. In reality, Dubai's markets pale in comparison to those in Sharjah. Dubai has developed a reputation for maintaining its traditional suqs despite the fact that Sharjah's market district has been and continues to be rebuilt. Dubai is also known for its gold trade, and finished items (or ones custom ordered to taste) are found in its suqs. Dubai alone consumes over five hundred tons of gold a year, more than any other place in the world, and spends over thirty times as much on gold as anywhere else in the world.

Another important source on the gulf states and Saudi Arabia in the two-volume encyclopedia published by Greenwood Press in 2009, *Saudi Arabia and the Gulf Arab States Today: An Encyclopedia of Life in the Arab States*, edited by Sebastian Maisel and John Shoup. It covers nearly everything from dates and Arabian horses to economics and politics. In addition, there is a two-volume book on the crafts of Oman (including the United Arab Emirates) published by Motivate Publishing in 2003, *The Craft Heritage of Oman* by Neil Richardson and Marcia Dorr. It deals with Oman's material culture province by province—and much of the material culture is shared with the United Arab Emirates. Two other sources deal more with Saudi Arabia than the United Arab Emirates but are important to note: Heather Ross's book *Bedouin Jewellery of Saudi Arabia* published by Stacey International in 1981 and John Topham's *Traditional Crafts of Saudi Arabia* also published by Stacey International in 2003. Both books deal mainly with Saudi Bedouin groups, but due to the constant contact between the United Arab Emirates and Saudi Arabia, much of the information provided is relevant to the United Arab Emirates as well. The same can be said of the two books by Dionisius Agius on the dhow or traditional sailing vehicle of the Arabs, *In the Wake of the Dhow: The Arabian Gulf and Oman* published by Garnet Publishing in 2002 and *Seafaring in the Arabian Gulf and Oman: The People of the Dhow* published by Kegan Paul in 2005.

Index

Note: Page numbers followed by a t indicate a table; page numbers in *italic* type indicate an image.

'Abbas, Mahmoud, 140
'Abbas I, 45, 51, 65
Abbasid dynasty, 41–43
'Abbassi family, 85
'Abd al-'Aziz, 118, 125
'Abd al-'Aziz ibn Baz, Shaykh, 116, 117
'Abd al-'Aziz ibn Sa'ud, 63, 95, 116
'Abd al-Karim Faruq, 85, 86
'Abd al-Muttalib, 38
'Abd al-Qadir 'Abbas, 86
'Abd al-Rabbuh Mansur Hadi, 134
'Abd al-Razaq al-Sanhuri, 112
'Abd al-Razaq family, 85
'Abd al-Razzaq 'Abd al-Rahim al-Bastaki, 86
'Abdallah, 65, 76–78, 133
'Abdallah al-Reyyes, 108–109
'Abdallah ibn Ibad al-Tamimi, 41, 42
'Abdallah ibn Jiluwi, 98
Abdel Fattah al-Sisi, 137
Abdisho, 35
Abiel, 32
Abraha, 35, 38
Abraham, 42
Abu Bakr, 39
Abu Dhabi: building and development, 126, 129, 130; challenges to independence, 104–111; conflicts, 78, 93–94; economy, 20–21; government and human rights, 19, 112–113; Gulf War, 119, 120; modern shaykhs, 143*t*; oil exploration, 96–97; overview, 2–4, *3*; people of, 14–15, 17

Abu Dhabi-Dubai war, 93–95
Abu Musa, 136
Abu Talib, 38
Adi Bitar, 112
Aflaj system, 28–29
African slave trade, 74–76
Agha Hassan Abedi, 120
Ahmad al-Buwayh, 42–43
Ahmad al-Tayeb, 4
Ahmad ibn Ibrahim al-Ghazi Gran, 50–51
Ahmad ibn Sa'id, 53
Ahmad II bin Rashid al-Mualla, Shaykh, 125
Ahmad Shah (ship), 69
Ahriman, 34
Ahura Mazda, 34
Ajman, 8, 144*t*
'Ajwah, 89–90
Al-Akhtal al-Taghlibi, 40
Al Awar family, 85
Al Bu Falah, 15, 59, 60
Al Bu Shamis tribe, 107
Al Jazeera, 137
Al-Ain, 130–133
al-Budyah Mosque, 44
Albuquerque, Afonso de, 44
Albuquerque, Pero de, 44
Alexander the Great, 28, 32
Al-Hajar Mountains, 2, 3
'Ali, Imam, 16
'Ali, Shaykh, 105
Ali Abdallah Salih, 134
Al-Idrisi, 87
'Ali ibn Abi Talib, 40–41
Al-Mansur, 42
Al-Murrah Bedouin tribe, 133–134
Al-Mustakfi, 42–43
Al-Mu'tadid, 41
Al-Qaida, 116, 117, 119
Al-Qasimi. *See* Qawasim
Al-Rahman, 42

Al-Tahir, 42
American embassy hostage crisis (Iran), 117
'Amr ibn al-'As, 39
Arab Spring, 137–139
Arab tribes, 31–32
Ardashir, 33
Ashurbanipal, King, 27
Assistance (ship), 66
Assyrians, 26–27
Augustus Caesar, 33
Awamir, 78–79
Azd, 32
Aziz, Tariq, 127

Badr al-Din, 45
Baghlah, 55
Bahrain, 45, 104–5
Bahria, 38
Baluchis, 15–16
Bani Yas, 14–15, 53, 59–61
Bank of Credit and Commerce International (BCCI), 120
Barasti, 85, 86
Batil, 55
Bedouin tribes, 11–12, 82–84, 91–93
Beglerbeg (ship), 66
Bey, Ali, 45
Bilal, 75
Bin Lutah family, 81
Black Stone (of the Ka'abah), 42
Blue Suq, 7
Bronze Age, 24–26
Bum, 55
Buraimi, 76–78
Burj Khalifa, 126, *127*, *128*, 129
Butti bin Suhail, 96
Buyids, 42–43

Cairati, Giovanni Battista, 46
Cambyses, 28
Camels, 27–28, *83*

Index

Carter, Jimmy, 115
Christianity, 34
Clothing styles, 83–84
Codrai, Ronald, 76, 87, 98, 147–148
Coffee, 92–93
Coins, 32
Constitution, 112–113
Covilha, Pero de, 43
Cyril of Alexandria, 34
Cyrus, 28

Darius I, 28
Date production, 89–90
Daws ibn al-Tha'laban, 35
Desert, 11–12
Dhiyab bin Isa al-Nahyan, 59–60
Dhows, *68*
Dhu Nuwas, 34, 35
Dibba, 39–40, 43
Dilmun, 24–25
Dubai: building and development, 126–130; business in, 125; challenges to independence, 110; economy, 20–21; government and human rights, 19–20, 112–115; Gulf War, 120; modern sheikhs, 144*t*; overview, 4–6; people of, 16–17; transportation, 132; wind-tower houses, 84–87
Dutch East India Company, 52

Emirates. *See* Abu Dhabi; Ajman; Dubai; Fujairah; Ras al-Khaimah; Sharjah; Umm al-Quwain
Ethiopia, 34, 50–51

Fahd, King, 124
Faisal, King, 65, 76, 111, 124, 139
Faisal bin Turki, 76, 77

Falah, 59
Faruq family, 85
Fatimah bint Mubarak al-Ketbi, 124–125, 131, 148
Faymiyun, 34, 35
Fiennes, Ranulph, 34
Fowle, Trenchard Craven William, 78
Francis, Pope, 5
Fujairah: British military intervention, 96; challenges to independence, 109; house in, *10*; modern sheikhs, 145*t*; overview, 10–11; people of, 15
Fury (ship), 67

Gabriel (angel), 38
Gaifar, 39
Gallus, Aelius, 33
Gama, Cristovoa da, 51
Gama, Vasco da, 43
Great Britain, 65–71
Gulf Cooperation Council (GCC), 117–118
Gulf War, 119–120

Hadr, 14
Hamad bin 'Abdullah, 10, 79, 96
Hamdan Qarmat, 42
Hamasa, fort of, *94*
Hamerton, Atkins, 2
Hamid, 105
Hasan, 68, 69–71
Hasan ibn Muhammad ibn Ghayth, 69
Hasan ibn Rahma, 73
Haya, Princess, 20
Hazza, 60, 97
Henderson, Edward, 108
Hinawi Azd, 31
Hormuz, 43–46, 51
Hormuzd IV, Shah, 36

Houthi tribe, 134–135
Humaid ibn Abdulaziz, 81
Humaid ibn Abdullah, 106
Human rights, 19–20
Husayn ibn Ali, 73
Hussa bint Ahmed al-Sudairi, Shaykhah, 124
Hussein, Imam, 16
Hussein, Saddam, 117, 118–119, 127
Hyacinth incident (1910), 95–96

Ibn Ghabaisha, 82
Ibn Hanbal, 63
Ibn Sa'ud, 61
Ibn Taymiyyah, 63–64
Ibrahim, 64, 68
Ibrahim Pasha, 61
Iffat al-Thunayan, 124
Iran, 135–136. *See also* Iran-Iraq War
Iran-Iraq War, 116, 117–118
Iraq. *See* Gulf War; Iran-Iraq War
Iron Age, 26–29
Isa bin Salman al-Khalifa, Shaykh, 104–105
Isma'il I, Shah, 44
Israel, 140–141
Iwasaki, Baron, 81

Jalal al-Din Murad Mahmud, 45
Jamal 'Abd al-Nasir, 104
Jassim bin Mohammed al-Thani, Shaykh, 104, 105
Juhayman al-'Utaybi, 116
Julandah family, 39, 40, 41
Julfar, 43
Justin I, 35

Karbala, 16
Kazim family, 85
Khalid bin Ahmad, 80–81
Khalid bin Mohammed, Shaykh, 7, 77, 106, 126, 111–112

Khalid ibn al-Walid, 39, 40
Khalifa, 61, 97, 105, 120
Khalifa, Shaykh, 124, 140
Khalifa bin Zayed, Prince, 114
Khashoggi, Adnan, 135
Khawarij, 41
Khawja 'Ata, 44, 45
Khojah, 16
Khomeini, Ayatollah, 117
Khosrow Anushirvan, 36
Kokichi, Mikimoto, 81. *See also* Baron Iwasaki
Kufa, 16
Kushner, Jared, 140
Kuwait, 119

Laqit (prophet), 39, 40
Lingah, 84–85
Lively (ship), 67

Magan, 24–26
Majlis, 92–93, *93*
Makkah mosque attack, 116
Makkans, 38–39
Maktoum bin Buti, 61
Maktoum bin Hasher, Shaykh, 110
Maktoum bin Rashid al-Maktoum, 119–120, 125, 129, 148–149
Manasir, 78
Mansoor, Ahmed, 20
Maritime Treaty (1820), 73–74
Melukha, 24–26
Minerva (ship), 68, 69
Mirs family, 85
Mohammed Abdullah al-Qahtani, 116
Mohammed bin Salman, Crown Prince, 133, 135, 138
Mohammed bin Thani, Shaykh, 105
Mohammed bin Zayed, 4

Index

Mountains, 13
Mu'awiyyah ibn Abi Sufyan, 41
Mubarak, Hosni, 137
Muhammad, 97
Muhammad, Crown Prince, 124, 125
Muhammad (Dubai vice president), 125
Muhammad (son of Shakhbut), 61
Muhammad al Sa'ud, 61, 64
Muhammad 'Ali, 61, 64, 65, 77
Muhammad bin Nasir, 52
Muhammad bin Rashid al-Maktoum, 5, 125, 129, 130, 149–150
Muhammad bin Sa'ud bin Saqr al-Qasimi, Shaykh, 125, 126
Muhammad ibn 'Abdallah (prophet of Islam), 38–39
Muhammad ibn 'Abd al-Wahhab, 63, 64, 105
Muhammad ibn Hazza, 73
Muhammad ibn Isa, 53
Muhammad ibn Nur, 41, 42
Muhammad Sharif, 86
Muzaffar al-Din, 84
Muqrin ibn Adjwad ibn Zamil, 45
Mursi, Muhammad, 137
Musaylimah, 39

Nadir, Shah, 53
Nahyan, al- family, 19
Na'im, 63, 65, 98, 107
Napoleon, 67
Nasir al-Din, 84
Nasir ibn Murshid, 52
Nasir ibn Qahtan, 53
National Council, 19
Nearchus, 28, 32
Neptune (ship), 67
Nereide (ship), 67
Nestorian Church, 35, 40

Nestorius, 34
Netanyahu, Benjamin, 140
Nixon, Richard, 115
Noriega, Manuel, 120

Oases, 12
Oil exploration, 95–97
Oman (region of lower gulf), 37, 39, 40–41, 46, 49–50, 51–53, 107–109
Omanis, 66–67, 70–71
Osama bin Laden, 116, 119
Ottomans, 45, 49–51, 105

Pade, King of, 27
Palm trees, 90
Pearling industry, 79–82, 87–88
Pelly, Lewis, 105
Philby, Harry (St John), 11
Piri Reis, 45
Pliny the Elder, 31, 32, 33
Polo, Marco, 43
Portuguese, 43–46, 49–50, 51–52
Prideaux, F. B., 96
Ptolemy, Claudius, 32, 34

Qadib ibn Ahmad, 73
Qaramitah movement, 42
Qasr al-Hisn, *109*
Qatar, 104–105, 133–134, 136–139
Qawasim, 8–9, 15, 53–54, 62–63, 65–71, 79
Quraysh tribe, 38–39

Rahma bin Matar, 62
Ra'is Sharaf, 45
Ras al-Khaimah: British in, 65, 69–71; challenges to independence, 105–106, 110–111; dynastic disputes, 125, 126; modern sheikhs, 145t; overview, 8–10; pearling industry, 80; Tunb islands, 136

Rashid, Shaykh, 86, 93, 112, 113–115, 118, 119–120
Rashid al-Maktoum, Shaykh, 5, 110
Rashid bin Ahmad Al Mualla II, 125
Rashid bin Hamad, Shaykh, 107
Rashid bin Humaid, Shaykh, 125
Rashid bin Sa'id al-Maktoum, 150–151
Riddah, wars of, 38
Rub' al-Khali, 11–12

Sa'ad ibn Maktoum, 4–5
Safavids, 43–46
Sa'id, 85, 110
Sa'id al-Hasan al-Jannabi, 42
Sa'id bin Sultan, 62
Sa'id Shaykh, 86
Saif II bin Sultan, 52–53
Sajah, 39
Salafism, 116–117
Salamah, 98
Salamah, Shaykh, 131
Salamah bint Buti, 124, 151–152
Salim bin Hamad bin Rakkad, 78
Salim bin Musallam bin Ham, 78–79
Salman, 39
Salman, Shaykh, 104
Salman bin 'Abd al-'Aziz, 133
Sambuk, 55–56
Sanjar, 43
Saqr, 97, 111–112, 115
Saqr bin Muhammed al-Qasimi, Shaykh, 106, 110, 126, 152
Saqr bin Rashid al-Qasimi, 66
Saqr ibn Isa, 53
Saqr ibn Zayed, 107
Sassanid period, 33–36
Sa'ud, Shaykh, 126
Sa'ud bin Rashid Al Mualla, 125

Saudi Arabia, 76–78, 107–108, 115–118, 133–137, 139
Sa'ud ibn Saqr al-Qasimi, 152–153
Sayf ibn dhi Yazan, 36
Sayyid family, 85
Sayyid Sa'id, 69
Sayyid Sultan bin Ahmad, 66
Sea, 12–13
Shakhbut, Shaykh, 60, 61, 71, 96–99, 107, 131, 153–154
Shakhbut bin Dhiyab, 73
Shannon (ship), 67
Sharjah: attempted coup in, 118; Britain in, 70; building and development, *127*, 127–128; challenges to independence, 105–107, 109; disputes, 125–126, 136; education, 18; modern sheikhs, 144*t*; overview, 6–8; pearling industry, 80, 82; people of, 16–17; shipbuilding, 54; transportation, 132; tribal rivalries in, 78–79
Sharqiyin tribe, 15, 59, 79
Shi'ites, 16
Shindagha Fort (Dubai), *62*
Ships and shipbuilding, 25–26, 54–56, 88–89
Shu'ai, 55–56
Slave trade, 74–76
Sokollu Mehmed, Wazir, 50
Strabo, 32
Success (ship), 66
Sudairi Seven, 124
Sultan, 61, 97, 115, 124
Sultan, Shaykh, 118, 125, 131
Sultan bin Muhammad al-Qasimi, 18, 67, 106–107, 112, 125, 154–155

Index

Sultan bin Saif I, 46, 52
Sultan bin Saqr, 69, 80–81, 106
Sultan II bin Saif, 52
Sultan III bin Muhammad, 7
Sylph (ship), 67

Tahnoun bin Mohammed al-Nahyan, Shaykh, 61, 73, 132
Talhah, 39
Taylor, Mrs. Robert, 68
Theophrastus, 32
Thesiger, Wilfred, 12, 28, 55, 82, 84, 87, 91–92, 98, 155–156
Thomas, Bertram, 11, 98
Trimmer (ship), 67
Trucial Oman Levies, 94–95
Trucial States, 73–78, 93–97
Trump, Donald, 135, 140
Tunb islands, 136
Turki bin 'Abdullah, 65, 76, 77
Turki bin 'Abdullah bin Utaishan, 108
Tusun, 64

Ubar, 33–34
Umayyad dynasty, 41–43
Umm al-Nar, 25, 26
Umm al-Quwain, 8, 15, 16, 145*t*
United Arab Emirates (UAE): Abbasid dynasty, 41–43; Abu Dhabi/Dubai war, 93–95; Ajman, 8; Al-Ain, 130–133; Arab Spring, 137–139; Arab tribes and Persian rule, 31–36; Bani Yas, 59–61; Bedouin life, 91–93; boundaries, *xxxii–xxxiii*; Britain's withdrawal from, 103–104; Bronze Age, 24–26; building and development, 126–130; challenges to independence, 104–111; conflicts with neighboring countries, 133–137; constitution, 112–113; date production, 89–90; early antiquity, 23–29; economy, 20–21; education, 17–18; emirates, 2–11; Ethiopians, 50–51; first years of independence, 111–112; foreign policy concerns in 1980s, 115–119; geography, 1–2, 11–13; government, 112–115; government and human rights, 18–20; Great Britain in lower Gulf, 65–71; Gulf War, 119–120; Iron Age, 26–29; life of prophet Muhammad and wars of Riddah, 38–41; maps, *xxxi–xxxiii*; modern sheikhs, 143–145*t*; notable people, 147–158; oil exploration in Trucial States, 95–97; Oman (region of lower gulf), 49–50, 51–53; Ottomans, 49–51; pearling industry, 79–82, 87–88; people, 13–17; Portuguese, 49–50, 51–52; Qawasim Empire, 62–63; reign of Shakhbut, 97–99; rise of Arab sheikdoms in lower Gulf, 53–54; Safavids and Portuguese, 43–46; Sassanid period, 33–36; shipbuilding, 54–56, 88–89; tribal rivalries, 78–79; Trucial States, 73–78, 93–95; Umayyad dynasty, 41–43; viewed as good neighbor, 139–141; Wahhabis, 63–65; wind-tower houses, 84–87

Viper (ship), 66

Wahhabis, 66, 76–77
Wind-tower houses, 84–87

Ya'rubah, 51–52
Yemen, 134–135

Zayed, 118, 120
Zayed, Shaykh, 3, 17–18, 76, 82, 93, 98–99, 109, 110, 111–112, 113–115; legacy, 123–124, 139–140
Zayed bin Khalifa al-Nahyan, 107, 131, 156–157
Zayed bin Sultan (the Great), Shaykh, 99, 108
Zoroastrianism, 34

About the Author

JOHN A. SHOUP is professor of anthropology at Al Akhawayn University in Morocco. He is author of numerous ABC-CLIO and Greenwood books, including *Culture and Customs of Syria*, *The History of Syria*, and *The Nile: An Encyclopedia of Geography, History, and Culture*. He has conducted field work in Lesotho, Jordan, Syria, Egypt, Tunisia, Morocco, and, most recently, in Mauritania on topics related to pastoralism, the impact of tourism on local communities, traditional land use systems, and popular culture.

Titles in the Greenwood Histories of the Modern Nations
Frank W. Thackeray and John E. Findling, Series Editors

The History of Argentina
Daniel K. Lewis

The History of Australia
Frank G. Clarke

The History of the Baltic States,
Second Edition
Kevin C. O'Connor

The History of Brazil
Robert M. Levine

The History of Bulgaria
Frederick B. Chary

The History of Cambodia
Justin Corfield

The History of Canada
Scott W. See

The History of Central America
Thomas Pearcy

The History of the Central Asian
Republics
Peter L. Roudik

The History of Chile, Second
Edition
John L. Rector

The History of China, Third
Edition
David Curtis Wright

The History of Congo
Didier Gondola

The History of Costa Rica
Monica A. Rankin

The History of Croatia and Slovenia
Christopher Deliso

The History of Cuba, Second
Edition
Clifford L. Staten

The History of the Czech Republic
and Slovakia
William M. Mahoney

The History of Ecuador
George Lauderbaugh

The History of Egypt, Second
Edition
Glenn E. Perry

The History of El Salvador
Christopher M. White

The History of Ethiopia
Saheed Adejumobi

The History of Finland
Jason Lavery

The History of France, Second
Edition
W. Scott Haine

The History of Germany
Eleanor L. Turk

The History of Ghana
Roger S. Gocking

The History of Great Britain,
Second Edition
Anne B. Rodrick

The History of Greece
Elaine Thomopoulos

The History of Haiti
Steeve Coupeau

The History of Holland
Mark T. Hooker

The History of Honduras
Thomas M. Leonard

The History of Iceland
Guðni Thorlacius Jóhannesson

The History of India, Second Edition
John McLeod

The History of Indonesia
Steven Drakeley

The History of Iran, Second Edition
Elton L. Daniel

The History of Iraq
Courtney Hunt

The History of Ireland
Daniel Webster Hollis III

The History of Israel
Arnold Blumberg

The History of Italy
Charles L. Killinger

The History of Japan, Second Edition
Louis G. Perez

The History of Korea, Second Edition
Djun Kil Kim

The History of Kuwait
Michael S. Casey

The History of Libya
Bukola A. Oyeniyi

The History of Mexico, Second Edition
Burton Kirkwood

The History of Myanmar
William J. Topich and Keith A. Leitich

The History of New Zealand
Tom Brooking

The History of Nicaragua
Clifford L. Staten

The History of Nigeria
Toyin Falola

The History of Pakistan
Iftikhar H. Malik

The History of Panama
Robert C. Harding

The History of Peru
Daniel Masterson

The History of the Philippines, Second Edition
Kathleen Nadeau

The History of Poland, Second Edition
M.B.B. Biskupski

The History of Portugal
James M. Anderson

The History of Puerto Rico
Lisa Pierce Flores

The History of Russia, Second Edition
Charles E. Ziegler

The History of Serbia
John K. Cox

The History of Singapore
Jean E. Abshire

The History of Somalia
Raphael Chijioke Njoku

The History of South Africa, Second Edition
Roger B. Beck

The History of Spain, Second Edition
Peter Pierson

The History of Sri Lanka
Patrick Peebles

The History of Sweden
Byron J. Nordstrom

The History of Syria
John A. Shoup

The History of Taiwan
Xiaobing Li

The History of Thailand
Patit Paban Mishra

The History of Turkey, Second Edition
Douglas A. Howard

The History of Ukraine
Paul Kubicek

The History of Venezuela, Second Edition
H. Micheal Tarver

The History of Vietnam
Justin Corfield